INSTRUCTOR'S MANUAL

MANAGEMENT ACCOUNTING

DON R. HANSEN
Oklahoma State University

MARYANNE M. MOWEN
Oklahoma State University

Prepared by
MARVIN BOUILLON
Iowa State University

PHILIP G. COTTELL, JR.
Miami University

BARBARA J. MILLIS
University of Maryland, University College

SOUTH-WESTERN College Publishing

An International Thomson Publishing Company

Accounting Team Director: Mary H. Draper
Sponsoring Editor: Elizabeth A. Bowers
Developmental Editor: Leslie Kauffman
Production Editor: Jason M. Fisher
Marketing Manager: Steve Hazelwood
Cover Design: Fusion Design/Kellie Schroeder

ISBN: 0-538-86558-X
1 2 3 4 5 6 7 PN 2 1 0 9 8 7 6
Printed in the United States of America

TO THE INSTRUCTOR:

This instructor's manual provides a good overview of the material presented in <u>Management Accounting</u>, Fourth Edition, by Don R. Hansen and Maryanne Mowen. There are about 135 teaching transparency masters included in the manual. These transparency masters, along with the PowerPoint transparencies available for this text, should provide you with an excellent library of teaching materials.

The organization of this manual corresponds with each chapter in <u>Management Accounting</u>. The learning objectives and the key topics are discussed first. Each key topic is then used as a major heading of the sections in the chapter. The last section in each chapter is entitled, "Information about Warm-up Exercises, Exercises, Problems, and Cases." Here you will find warm-up exercise/exercise/problem/case number, topical content, learning objective(s) being covered, and the level of difficulty of each problem.

Below you will find a road map between the Hansen/Mowen (4th ed.), Hansen/Mowen (3rd ed.), Garrison/Noreen (7th ed.), and Hilton (2nd ed.) textbooks. This should help you when adopting the Hansen/Mowen book assuming you are currently using Garrison/Noreen or Hilton.

ROAD MAP

TOPICS	4TH ED. HANSEN/ MOWEN	3RD ED. HANSEN/ MOWEN	GARRISON/ NOREEN	HILTON
Management and financial accounting	Ch. 1	Ch. 1	Ch. 1	Ch. 1
Ethical behavior	Ch. 1	Ch. 1	Ch. 1	Ch. 1
Certification	Ch. 1	Ch. 1	Ch. 1	Ch. 1
Basic cost concepts	Ch. 2	Ch. 2	Ch. 2	Ch. 2
Statement of COGM	Ch. 2	Ch. 2	Ch. 2	Ch. 2
Functional classification of costs Ch. 2	Ch. 2	Ch. 2	Ch. 2	
Functional income statement-mfg firm	Ch. 2	Ch. 2	Ch. 2	Ch. 2
Functional income statement-service firm	Ch. 2	Ch. 2	---	Ch. 2
Cost behavior	Ch. 2	Ch. 2	Ch. 2	Ch. 2
Variable-costing income statement	Ch. 14	Ch. 2	Ch. 6	Ch. 7
Activity drivers	Ch. 2, 4	Ch. 6	Ch. 5	Ch. 2
Unit costs	Ch. 4	Ch. 3	Ch. 3	Ch. 3
Job-order costing	Ch. 5	Ch. 3	Ch. 3	Ch. 3
Overhead application	Ch. 4	Ch. 3	Ch. 3	Ch. 3
Accounting for product costs	Ch. 4	Ch. 3	Ch. 3	Ch. 3
Process costing - weighted-average	Ch. 6	Ch. 4	Ch. 4	Ch. 4
Process costing - FIFO	Ch. 6 app.	Ch. 4 app.	App. B	Ch. 4
Support cost allocation - direct	Ch. 7	Ch. 5	Ch. 16	Ch. 17
Support cost allocation - sequential	Ch. 7	Ch. 5	Ch. 16	Ch. 17
Support cost allocation - reciprocal	Ch. 7	Ch. 5 app.	Ch. 16	Ch. 17, app.
Activity based costing	Ch. 4	Ch. 6, 13	Ch. 5	Chs. 3, 5
JIT manufacturing	Ch. 4	Ch. 6, 13	Ch. 5	Ch. 5
High-low method	Ch. 3	Ch. 7	Ch. 6	Ch. 6
Scatterplot method	Ch. 3	Ch. 7	Ch. 6	Ch. 6

TOPICS		4TH ED. HANSEN/ MOWEN	3RD ED. HANSEN/ MOWEN	GARRISON/ NOREEN	HILTON
Method of least squares	Ch. 3	Ch. 7	App. D	Ch. 6, app.	
Reliability of cost formulas		Ch. 3	Ch. 7	App. D	Ch. 6, app.
Multiple regression		Ch. 3	Ch. 7	App. D	Ch. 6, app.
CVP analysis		Ch. 15	Ch. 8	Ch. 7	Ch. 7
Impact of ABC on CVP analysis		Ch. 15	---	---	---
Variable versus absorption costing		Ch. 14	Ch. 9	Ch. 8	Ch. 11
Tactical decisions making		Ch. 16	Ch. 10	Ch. 13	Ch. 13
Linear programming		Ch. 16 app.	App. G	Ch. 13, app.	
Present/future value concepts		Ch. 17	Ch. 12	Apps. H, J	Ch. 15, app.
Capital budgeting models		Ch. 17	Ch. 12	Ch. 14	Ch. 15
Capital budgeting with taxes		Ch. 17	Ch. 12	Ch. 15	Ch. 16
Capital investment in an advanced manufacturing environment		Ch. 17	Ch. 12	---	---
EOQ model		Ch. 18	Ch. 13	App. E	Ch. 8 app.
Theory of constraints		Ch. 18	---	---	Ch. 9
Segmented reports		Ch. 14	Ch. 13	Ch. 12	Ch. 11
Master budgets	Ch. 8	Ch. 14	Ch. 9	Ch. 8	
Zero-based budgeting		Ch. 8 app.	Ch. 14 app.	Ch. 9	Ch. 8
Standard costing		Ch. 9	Ch. 15	Ch. 10	Ch. 9
Variance analysis: materials		Ch. 9	Ch. 15	Ch. 10	Ch. 9
Variance analysis: labor		Ch. 9	Ch. 15	Ch. 10	Ch. 9
Variance analysis: variable overhead		Ch. 9	Ch. 15	Ch. 11	Ch. 10
Variance analysis: fixed overhead		Ch. 9	Ch. 15	Ch. 11	Ch. 10
Accounting for variances		Ch. 9 app.	Ch. 15 app.	App. F	Ch. 9
Activity-based management		Ch. 10	Ch. 16	---	Ch. 9
Process value analysis		Ch. 10	---	Ch. 5	Ch. 9
Life-cycle cost management		Ch. 10	Ch. 16	Ch. 12	Ch. 8
Financial/nonfinancial measures of activity performance	Ch. 10	---	---	Ch. 9	
Flexible budgeting		Ch. 10	Ch. 16	Ch. 11	Ch. 10
Quality costs		Ch. 11	Ch. 17	App. K	Ch. 9
Productivity measurement		Ch. 11	---	---	Ch. 9
Decentralization		Chs. 12, 13	Chs. 18, 19	Ch. 12	Ch. 12
ROI and RI		Ch. 12	Ch. 18	Ch. 12	Ch. 12
Transfer pricing	Ch. 12, 13		Chs. 18, 19	Ch. 12	Ch. 12
International environment		Ch. 13	Ch. 19	---	---
Foreign currency exchange		Ch. 13	Ch. 19	---	---
Measuring performance in MNC	Ch. 13	Ch. 19	---	---	

NOTE: Hansen/Mowen does not present material on financial statement analysis and the statement of cash flows. If you need these topics, supplements are available from the publisher upon request.

Every effort has been made to achieve a high level of quality control in the production of this instructor's manual. Wherever practical, the vocabulary of the text has been used.

No endeavor is successfully completed without the assistance of others. I would like to acknowledge my wife, Vicki Bouillon, for her professional assistance in preparing the teaching transparencies. In addition, special thanks to the authors of the text, Don R. Hansen and Maryanne Mowen; my editor Leslie Kauffman; and my production editor Jason Fisher; for their timely responses when I needed them.

A completely error-free instructor's manual has been my goal in preparing this text supplement. I want to know about any errors, omissions, or corrections that you may note. Please contact me at the address given below.

July 1996

Marvin L. Bouillon
390 Carver Hall
Iowa State University
Ames, Iowa 50011
(515) 294-9276

TABLE OF CONTENTS

INSTRUCTOR'S MANUAL

prepared by Marvin Bouillon

COOPERATIVE LEARNING TECHNIQUES

prepared by Philip G. Cottell, Jr. and Barbara J. Millis

CHAPTER 1

INTRODUCTION: THE ROLE, HISTORY, AND DIRECTION OF MANAGEMENT ACCOUNTING

Chapter 1 can be covered on the first day of class. Students should understand what management accounting is and how it is changing over time. This chapter is also a good place to introduce a discussion on ethical behavior. The Institute of Management Accountants' (IMA) code of ethics is presented on pages 17 and 18 of Hansen and Mowen. There are several good problems on ethics at the end of the chapter.

LEARNING OBJECTIVES

After studying Chapter 1, students should be able to:

1. Explain the need for management accounting information.

2. Explain the differences between management accounting and financial accounting.

3. Provide a brief historical description of management accounting.

4. Identify and explain the emerging themes of management accounting.

5. Describe the role of management accountants in an organization.

6. Explain the importance of ethical behavior for managers and management accountants.

7. Identify three forms of certification available to management accountants.

KEY TOPICS

The following major topics are covered in this chapter (related learning objectives are listed for each topic).

1. Management accounting information system (learning objective 1)

2. Management accounting and financial accounting (learning objective 2)

3. A brief historical perspective of management accounting (learning objective 3)

4. Emerging themes of management accounting (learning objective 4)

5.	The role of the management accountant (learning objective 5)

6.	Management accounting and ethical conduct (learning objective 6)

7.	Certification (learning objective 7)

## I.	MANAGEMENT ACCOUNTING INFORMATION SYSTEM

Why do managers need accounting information? Have students read the opening scenarios, and then use them to illustrate accounting information's usefulness. PowerPoint transparency (PPT) 1-4 can be used to present management accounting information systems. This transparency is similar to Exhibit 1-1 in the text. Finally, discuss why managers need accounting information using PPT 1-5. The major reasons are:

1.	Managers need accounting information and need to know how to use it.

2.	Accounting information can help managers identify problems, solve problems, and evaluate performance (i.e., accounting information is needed and used in all phases of management, including planning, controlling, and decision making).

3.	Accounting information is used in all organizations: manufacturing, merchandising, and service.

See PPT 1-4 and 1-5

## II.	MANAGEMENT ACCOUNTING AND FINANCIAL ACCOUNTING

Since most students will have recently completed a basic course in financial accounting, the differences between management accounting and financial accounting should be discussed. PPT 1-6 highlights the differences between management and financial accounting. This transparency is similar to Exhibit 1-2 in the text.

See PPT 1-6

## III.	A BRIEF HISTORICAL PERSPECTIVE OF MANAGEMENT ACCOUNTING

The main point to discuss in this section deals with the changes in management accounting over the last 20 years. This section can be used to introduce the emerging themes. A brief discussion or summary of the history is adequate.

IV. EMERGING THEMES OF MANAGEMENT ACCOUNTING

After a brief discussion of the history, students should be informed of the emerging themes of management accounting. These trends are listed below, as well as on PPT 1-7. Many of these themes are covered throughout the text.

1. Customer orientation
2. Cross-functional perspective
3. Global competition
4. Total quality management
5. Time as a competitive element
6. Advances in information technology
7. Advances in the manufacturing environment
8. Growth and deregulation in the service industry
9. Activity-based management

See PPT 1-7

Teaching hint: At this stage only a brief discussion of the trends is appropriate. It is important that students understand that the practice of management accounting is being reshaped and that the changes are some of the more exciting and interesting events in the business world. You may want to emphasize the following quote from Peter Drucker[1]:

> "The most exciting and innovative work in management today is found in accounting theory, with new concepts, new methodology--even what might be called new economic philosophy--rapidly taking shape. And while there is enormous controversy over specifics, the lineaments of the new manufacturing accounting are becoming clearer every day."

Teaching transparency master (TTM) 1-1 can be used to present the quote to your class.

See TTM 1-1

V. THE ROLE OF THE MANAGEMENT ACCOUNTANT

The management accountant is responsible for collecting, processing, and reporting information that will help managers in their planning, controlling, and decision-making activities. This is a good time to discuss what line and staff positions are, as well as who the controller and treasurer are and what they do. PPT 1-8 illustrates an organization chart

---

[1] Peter E. Drucker, "The Emerging Theory of Manufacturing," *Harvard Business Review*, May-June 1990, pp. 94-102.

similar to Exhibit 1-3 from Hansen and Mowen, while PPT 1-9 provides a detailed description of the roles of the controller and treasurer. This detailed description goes beyond the discussion in the text.

See PPT 1-8 and 1-9

VI. MANAGEMENT ACCOUNTING AND ETHICAL CONDUCT

A. Teaching Ethics

Teaching values is considered by many to be an important part of the current educational process. In part, this feeling stems from a number of unethical practices that have been highly publicized. Some examples of moral lapses are reported in the chapter. You may want to cite some with which you are familiar. PPT 1-10 illustrates four groups of ethical issues.

See PPT 1-10

Some believe that teaching ethics to college students is a waste of time. Those holding this view generally believe that by college age it is too late to change the ethical behavior of individuals. Evidence exists, however, that moral reasoning can be taught and that age is not a barrier. Furthermore, learning what is considered acceptable in a business environment is certainly a valid objective. Many — if not most — students will not have a well-developed understanding of "business" ethical issues.

Teaching hint: After discussing the reasons why teaching value judgments is important, ask the students to define ethical behavior. This usually provokes a lively discussion.

B. IMA Code of Ethics

The role of professional codes of ethics should be discussed. Professional associations often provide a well-defined set of ethical standards which helps to define acceptable and unacceptable behavior. PPT 1-11 lists the four standards of the IMA's code of ethics, while PPT 1-12 through 1-15 present each standard in more detail. The resolution of ethical conflict is presented in PPT 1-16. Problems 1-7 through 1-11 provide opportunities to apply the standards. In addition, there are problems and cases throughout the book that provide additional ethical dilemmas.

See PPT 1-11 through 1-16

VII. CERTIFICATION

This section briefly discusses the three major certifications for management accountants. Most students are aware of the CPA but are probably not as knowledgeable about the CMA or CIA. Explaining why these two certifications are viable alternatives to the CPA should prove to be interesting for those who are considering a career in accounting.

Teaching hint: Ask students why certification is needed. You may wish to point out that other professions such as engineering and data processing also have certifications. PPT 1-17 can be used to illustrate the three types of certifications.

See PPT 1-17

VIII. INFORMATION ABOUT WARM-UP EXERCISES, EXERCISES, PROBLEMS, AND CASES

For your convenience, exercises and problems are described below according to coverage of content, learning objective(s), and level of difficulty. The time required to solve the problems is roughly proportional to level of difficulty.

In general, *Basic* exercises/problems are fairly simple and straightforward. The text material is relatively brief; only one or two concepts are covered. Basic exercises and problems should take about 15 to 20 minutes.

Moderate exercises/problems may take longer and involve more concepts. These problems may have a "twist" and require more thought. Moderate exercises and problems may take 20 to 40 minutes.

Challenging problems are more comprehensive and may cover more concepts. The text material is relatively longer and may include some ambiguity. Challenging problems may take 60 to 90 minutes.

Exercise/ Problem	Topical Content (Learning Objective(s))	Level of Difficulty
P1-1	Management Accounting Information System (LO 1)	Basic
P1-2	Employee Empowerment (LO 1)	Moderate
P1-3	The Managerial Process (LO 1)	Moderate
P1-4	Emerging Themes (LO 4)	Basic
P1-5	Role of Management Accountants (LO 5)	Basic
P1-6	Line versus Staff (LO 5)	Basic
P1-7	Ethical Behavior (LO 6)	Basic
P1-8	Ethical Issues (LO 6)	Basic
P1-9	Ethical Issues (LO 6)	Moderate
P1-10	Ethical Behavior (LO 6)	Moderate
P1-11	Ethical Responsibilities (LO 6)	Moderate

CHAPTER 2

BASIC COST CONCEPTS

This chapter is fairly basic, but is also very important because it introduces terminology that is used throughout the text. Students often have difficulty later in the course because they have failed to master the basic cost concepts and definitions discussed in this chapter.

LEARNING OBJECTIVES

After studying Chapter 2, students should be able to:

1. Explain the cost assignment process.

2. Define tangible and intangible products and explain why there are different product cost definitions.

3. Prepare income statements for manufacturing and service organizations.

4. Describe the relationship between activity drivers and cost behavior.

5. Explain the differences between traditional and contemporary management accounting systems.

KEY TOPICS

The following major topics are covered in this chapter (related learning objectives are listed for each topic).

1. Cost assignment: Direct tracing, driver tracing, and allocation (learning objective 1)

2. Product and service costs (learning objective 2)

3. External financial statements (learning objective 3)

4. Activity drivers and cost behavior (learning objective 4)

5. Traditional and contemporary management accounting systems (learning objective 5)

I. COST ASSIGNMENT: DIRECT TRACING, DRIVER TRACING, AND ALLOCATION

This section introduces a variety of terms. Teaching transparencies master (TTM) 2-1 through 2-3 can be used to present some of these concepts. TTM 2-1 discusses five basic terms: cost, opportunity cost, expense, cost object, and activity. Meanwhile, TTM 2-2 presents the concept of traceability, along with the definitions of direct costs and indirect costs. The concept of tracing and methods of tracing (direct and driver) are presented on TTM 2-3. Resource and activity drivers are also discussed on TTM 2-3.

See TTM 2-1 through 2-3

PowerPoint transparency (PPT) 2-3, which is similar to Exhibit 2-2 in the text, can be used to further explain driver tracing. Exhibit 2-1 in the text illustrates the linkage between an activity and potential activity driver. PPT 2-4 is a partial reproduction of this exhibit. Use PPT 2-4 to discuss activity drivers. In addition, a short numerical example can be used to illustrate the assignment of cost through driver tracing. Warm-up exercise 2-1 can be used to discuss drivers.

See PPT 2-3 and 2-4

PPT 2-5 shows how resources are assigned to cost objectives. Allocation can be discussed at this time. PPT 2-5 is a reproduction of Exhibit 2-3 in the text. Discussing Exercise 2-1 at this time will help to differentiate the three methods.

See PPT 2-5

II. PRODUCT AND SERVICE COSTS

Hansen and Mowen discuss four dimensions that differentiate service from tangible products: intangibility, perishability, inseparability, and heterogeneity. TTM 2-4 presents these four dimensions. TTM 2-5 through 2-8 illustrate the derived properties and impact on management accounting of each dimension. You should spend some time discussing these four dimensions.

See TTM 2-4 through 2-8

PPT 2-6 presents the three different product cost definitions and the managerial objectives served by each. This transparency is a reproduction of Exhibit 2-6 in the text. Differentiate between the three approaches.

See PPT 2-6

Some additional terms are presented on TTM 2-9 and 2-10. TTM 2-9 focuses on manufacturing costs, while TTM 2-10 discusses nonmanufacturing costs. Again, these terms are important. Therefore, spend some time discussing these two transparencies.

See TTM 2-9 and 2-10

III.   EXTERNAL FINANCIAL STATEMENTS

External financial statements are presented in TTM 2-11 through 2-13. The first two (2-11 and 2-12) represent a manufacturing firm. TTM 2-11 illustrates a statement of cost of goods manufactured similar to Exhibit 2-8 in the text, while TTM 2-12 presents the income statement of the same manufacturing firm. An income statement for a service firm (Exhibit 2-9 in the text) is illustrated with TTM 2-13. This is a good time to show the flow of costs through the statement of cost of goods manufactured to the income statement.

See TTM 2-11 through 2-13

Teaching hint: Ask the class how the income statements of the merchandising and service firms will differ. Classification of the expenses by function should be emphasized. In addition, the differences between income statements of a manufacturing firm and those of merchandising firms and service firms should be discussed. Merchandising and service firms will not have a schedule of cost of goods manufactured.

IV.   ACTIVITY DRIVERS AND COST BEHAVIOR

Classification of costs by behavior is an important topic for future chapters. This classification provides the foundation for many of the traditional management accounting models. It is also a critical component of activity-based accounting. Students will be exposed to the concept of cost drivers for the first time. At this stage, they need to understand that there are many different factors that drive costs.

Costs that remain unchanged with respect to a cost driver (strictly speaking with respect to any cost driver) are defined as fixed costs.

Costs that vary in direct proportion to a cost driver are defined as variable costs.

Mixed costs have both fixed and variable components. Graphical illustrations are provided in PPT 2-15 and 2-16 for fixed, variable, and mixed costs, respectively.

See PPT 2-15 and 2-16

The number and type of cost drivers are what distinguish traditional management accounting from activity-based accounting. Traditional management accounting systems assume that all costs can be explained by changes in production volume. Activity-based costing systems assume that costs are explained by changes in production volume plus other nonvolume-related cost drivers. Therefore, activity-based costing systems use many more cost drivers than traditional systems. TTM 2-14 discusses the four activity categories of activity-based costing. Warm-up exercises 2-4 and 2-5 can be used to provide numerical examples for describing cost behaviors.

See TTM 2-14

V. TRADITIONAL AND CONTEMPORARY MANAGEMENT ACCOUNTING SYSTEMS

The last section of this chapter can be discussed by using PPT 2-18. This transparency illustrates a comparison of traditional and contemporary cost management systems. Use this transparency to exploit the differences between the two systems. Exercise 2-7 can be used to illustrate the topic further.

See PPT 2-18

VI. INFORMATION ABOUT WARM-UP EXERCISES, EXERCISES, PROBLEMS, AND CASES

For your convenience, exercises and problems are described below according to coverage of content, learning objective(s), and level of difficulty. The time required to solve the problems is roughly proportional to level of difficulty.

In general, *Basic* exercises/problems are fairly simple and straightforward. The text material is relatively brief; only one or two concepts are covered. Basic exercises and problems should take about 15 to 20 minutes.

Moderate exercises/problems may take longer and involve more concepts. These problems may have a "twist" and require more thought. Moderate exercises and problems may take 20 to 40 minutes.

Challenging problems are more comprehensive and may cover more concepts. The text material is relatively longer and may include some ambiguity. Challenging problems may take 60 to 90 minutes.

Exercise/ Problem	Topical Content (Learning Objective(s))	Level of Difficulty
W2-1	Activities and Drivers (LO 1)	Basic
W2-2	Cost of Goods Sold (LO 3)	Basic
W2-3	Cost of Goods Manufactured (LO 3)	Basic
W2-4	Cost Behavior (LO 4)	Basic
W2-5	Cost Behavior (LO 4)	Basic
E2-1	Cost Assignment Methods (LO 1)	Basic
E2-2	Value-Chain Activity (LO 2)	Basic
E2-3	Product Cost Definitions (LO 2)	Basic
E2-4	Cost of Goods Manufactured and Sold (LO 3)	Basic
E2-5	Preparation of Income Statement: Manufacturing Firm (LO 3)	Basic
E2-6	Cost Behavior (LO 4)	Basic
E2-7	Traditional versus Contemporary Management Accounting Systems (LO 5)	Basic
E2-8	Cost of Goods Manufactured and Sold (LO 3)	Moderate
E2-9	Income Statement; Cost Concepts; Service Company (LO 2,3)	Basic
E2-10	Product Cost Definitions (LO 2)	Moderate
E2-11	Activity Classification (LO 4)	Basic
E2-12	Accuracy of Cost Assignments and Cost Behavior (LO 1,4)	Moderate
P2-1	Cost Behavior, Accuracy of Assignment, Unit-Level and Nonunit-Level Drivers (LO 1,4)	Moderate
P2-2	Cost Behavior (LO 4)	Basic
P2-3	Cost Identification (LO 2,4)	Moderate
P2-4	Cost Behavior; Classification and Graphing (LO 4)	Basic
P2-5	Activity Levels and Drivers (LO 4,5)	Basic
P2-6	Contemporary versus Traditional Management Accounting Systems (LO 5)	Basic
P2-7	Income Statement: Cost of Goods Manufactured (LO 3)	Moderate
P2-8	Cost of Goods Manufactured; Cost Identification; Contribution Margin; Solving for Unknowns (LO 2,3,4)	Challenging
P2-9	Income Statement; Cost of Services Provided; Services Attributes (LO 2,3)	Moderate
P2-10	Cost Identification and Analysis; Income Statement (LO 2,3)	Moderate
C2-1	Cost Classification; Income Statements; Unit-based Cost Behavior; Service Organization (LO 2,3,4)	Challenging
C2-2	Cost Information and Ethical Behavior; Service Organization (LO 1)	Challenging
C2-3	Research Assignment (LO 1,3,4)	Challenging
C2-4	Research Assignment (LO 1,3,5)	Challenging

CHAPTER 3

ACTIVITY COST BEHAVIOR

This chapter expands the discussion of cost behavior in Chapter 2; more specifically, it focuses on activity cost behavior. In addition, the resource usage model is presented. This chapter is an important foundation for the activity-based costing system discussed in the next chapter. In addition, several methods to estimate and evaluate the cost equation are discussed.

LEARNING OBJECTIVES

After studying Chapter 3, students should be able to:

1. Define and describe cost behavior and explain the role of the resource usage model in understanding cost behavior.

2. Separate mixed costs into their fixed and variable components using the high-low method, the scatterplot method, and the method of least squares.

3. Evaluate the reliability of a cost equation.

4. Explain the role of multiple regression in assessing cost behavior.

5. Describe the use of managerial judgment in determining cost behavior.

KEY TOPICS

The following major topics are covered in this chapter (related learning objectives are listed for each topic).

1. Cost behavior and the resource usage model (learning objective 1)

2. Methods for separating mixed costs into fixed and variable components (learning objective 2)

3. Reliability of cost formulas (learning objective 3)

4. Multiple regression (learning objective 4)

5. Managerial judgment (learning objective 5)

I. COST BEHAVIOR AND THE RESOURCE USAGE MODEL

The PowerPoint transparencies (PPT) provide a good step-by-step approach for learning objectives 1 through 5 of this chapter. Before proceeding to these transparencies, some basic terms need to be presented. Teaching transparency masters (TTM) 3-1 through 3-3 can be used to illustrate some of these terms.

See TTM 3-1 through 3-3

Cost behavior refers to the way in which costs react to changes in activity level. Usually costs are placed into one of three categories: variable costs, fixed costs, and mixed costs. These categories are convenient, and are reasonably accurate as well, as long as we invoke the concept of relevant range.

Relevant range: The range of activity over which this assumption provides a reasonably accurate representation is called the relevant range. While the cost function may not be linear, we will often assume linearity because the function will appear linear within the relevant range.

Variable cost: A variable cost is a cost that varies in direct proportion to changes in activity level, which is commonly defined as some measure of production or sales activity (e.g., direct labor hours, units produced, and units sold). Activity level can refer to the level of any cost driver (e.g., setup time, number of material moves, etc.) in an activity-based costing system. Total variable costs can be described in equation format to be:

$$TVC = VX$$

where:

TVC = total variable costs
V = variable cost per unit of activity
X = units of activity

Fixed costs: Fixed costs are costs that do not change in total as the activity level changes. Costs are fixed in the short run. The duration of the short run can change depending on the cost under consideration. Total fixed costs can be described in equation format to be:

$$TFC = F$$

where:

TFC = total fixed costs
F = amount of fixed costs

PPT 3-3 can be used to illustrate a variable and fixed cost.

14

See PPT 3-3

Teaching hint: You might emphasize that the variable costs (and later fixed costs) portrayed here are total costs, not average costs. Students often have difficulty with this distinction. Total variable cost increases (decreases) as activity level increases (decreases). Average variable cost stays constant as activity level changes. TTM 3-4 and 3-5 illustrate total versus average variable cost.

See TTM 3-4 and 3-5

Teaching hint: Some students have a hard time with the concept of fixed cost because they equate it to "never changing." However, their experience (living in an inflationary economy) is that costs do change, typically upward. Thus, they think that no cost can ever be fixed. The key point is that a fixed cost does not change because activity level changes; a fixed cost can change for other reasons. For example, property taxes on the factory — a fixed cost with respect to volume — are $1,000 in year 1. In year 2, the property taxes are $1,500 but are still a fixed cost as far as volume is concerned. The distinction between total and average fixed cost is illustrated in TTM 3-6 and 3-7.

See TTM 3-6 and 3-7

Mixed Costs: Costs that have both a fixed and a variable component. Total mixed costs can be described as:

$$TMC = F + VX$$

where:
TMC = the total mixed costs

F, V, and X are defined previously in the chapter.

PPT 3-4 presents a graph of a mixed cost.

See PPT 3-4

Step-variable cost: A step-cost function has the property of displaying a constant level of cost for a range of activity and then jumping to a higher level of cost at some point, where it remains for a similar range of activity. A step-variable cost is simply a step-cost which changes for relatively narrow ranges of activity. PPT 3-5 displays a step-variable cost. This type of cost is usually treated as if it were a pure variable cost because of the narrow ranges of activity.

See PPT 3-5

PPT 3-6 discusses three types of fixed costs. Each of them are presented below.

See PPT 3-6

Committed fixed costs: Costs incurred for the acquisition of long-term capacity, such as plant, equipment, warehouses, vehicles, and salaries of top executives. Many times these committed fixed costs are the result of strategic planning.

Discretionary fixed costs: Costs incurred for the acquisition of short-term capacity, such as training and research and development. The level of these costs can be changed from year to year. Rent payment on a building that can be stopped at any time would be another good example of a discretionary fixed cost.

Step-fixed costs: Step-fixed costs are step-costs with a relatively wide level of activity. The difference between step-variable and step-fixed costs is the range of activity included at each step. For example, a step-variable cost may increase for every 100 units produced, while a step-fixed cost may increase for every 10,000 units produced. A step-fixed cost is usually treated as a fixed cost. PPT 3-7 displays a step-fixed cost.

See PPT 3-7

II. METHODS FOR SEPARATING MIXED COSTS INTO FIXED AND VARIABLE COMPONENTS

The accounting records of a company report the total mixed costs and the associated activity levels. Managers need to know the fixed and variable components of mixed costs. Using the total costs and the associated activity level it is possible to break out the fixed and variable components. There are three methods mentioned in the chapter for doing so: the high-low method, the scatterplot method, and the method of least squares are presented on PPT 3-8. An example for illustrative purposes is presented on PPT 3-9.

See PPT 3-8 and 3-9

A. High-Low Method

When using the high-low method, one selects the two points that will be used for creating the cost formula. The high point is defined as the point with the <u>highest activity</u> and the low point as the point with the <u>lowest activity</u>. Always make sure that the high and low activity points are representative of the rest of the points. A scatterplot would be helpful to see whether the two points are representative of the others. The high-low method is illustrated in PPT 3-10.

See PPT 3-10

Teaching hint: Tell the students that the high-low method is nothing more than finding the equation of a line through two points.

B.   Scatterplot Method

Using the scatterplot method, the manager plots the observations on cost and activity level on a graph. The manager selects two points by visual inspection of the scattergraph and fits a line to these two points. This is accomplished by using the slope-intercept method from basic algebra. The slope is the change in cost divided by the change in activity. Once the slope is known, simply substitute the slope and the values of one of the two points into the linear cost formula ($Y = F + VX$) and solve for the fixed component, F ($F = Y - VX$). PPT 3-11 provides an example to illustrate this method.

See PPT 3-11

C.   Method of Least Squares

The method of least squares identifies the line that fits the points best (sum of squared deviations is minimized). This method is the most sophisticated and provides the user with a measure of goodness of fit, which can be used to assess the usefulness of the cost formula. If the fit is not very good, then a search for additional activity variables may be needed. The students must memorize (or be provided) two formulas in order to use this method. The formulas given in the chapter are chosen (there are alternative forms) because they are easy to use. The method is illustrated in PPT 3-12.

Teaching hint: Very little time should be spent on this method in a beginning managerial class. The students should be aware of it but a thorough discussion is usually made in a second managerial accounting course. Therefore, there is little reason to force a student to memorize the formulas when they can use the regression mode in Lotus 1-2-3.

See PPT 3-12

III.   RELIABILITY OF COST FORMULAS

There are two basic measures for determining reliability of cost formulas: coefficient of determination and coefficient of correlation. PPT 3-13 shows these calculations based on the example.

See PPT 3-13

Teaching hint: While there is not much of a discussion of computer printouts in this manual, the instructor can bypass the calculations and stress computer printouts. In most basic management accounting courses such a move could be helpful to students. Manual calculations can be left for statistics courses.

IV.   MULTIPLE REGRESSION

Generally, covering simple regression in a basic management accounting class is enough, but if you wish to do more, you can use PPT 3-14 to illustrate a model with more than one independent variable. If you wish, you may even provide a computer printout. Again, this is a topic for a statistics course. The discussion of the topic can be done at a higher level in the next management-level course.

See PPT 3-14

V.   MANAGERIAL JUDGMENT

Managerial judgment is a simple approach to classifying costs as variable or fixed. When managers have a deep understanding of the firm and its cost patterns, this method can give good results. If the manager has poor judgment, errors will occur. PPT 3-15 provides an interesting overlay for class discussion.

See PPT 3-15

VI.   INFORMATION ABOUT WARM-UP EXERCISES, EXERCISES, PROBLEMS, AND CASES

For your convenience, exercises and problems are described below according to coverage of content, learning objective(s), and level of difficulty. The time required to solve the problems is roughly proportional to level of difficulty.

In general, *Basic* exercises/problems are fairly simple and straightforward. The text material is relatively brief; only one or two concepts are covered. Basic exercises and problems should take about 15 to 20 minutes.

Moderate exercises/problems may take longer and involve more concepts. These problems may have a "twist" and require more thought. Moderate exercises and problems may take 20 to 40 minutes.

Challenging problems are more comprehensive and may cover more concepts. The text material is relatively longer and may include some ambiguity. Challenging problems may take 60 to 90 minutes.

Exercise/ Problem	Topical Content (Learning Objective(s))	Level of Difficulty
W3-1	Resources Acquired in Advance; Step-Cost Function (LO 1)	Basic
W3-2	Resource Usage Model (LO 1)	Basic
W3-3	Separation of Mixed Costs (LO 2)	Basic
W3-4	Separation of Mixed Costs (LO 2)	Basic
W3-5	Reliability of Equation (LO 3)	Basic
E3-1	Resource Usage Model and Cost Behavior (LO 1)	Basic
E3-2	Resource Supply and Usage; Activity Rates; Service Organization (LO 1)	Basic
E3-3	Step Costs; Relevant Range (LO 1)	Moderate
E3-4	Cost Behavior; Classification and Graphing (LO 1)	Basic
E3-5	Scatterplot Method; Service Setting (LO 2)	Moderate
E3-6	High-Low Method (LO 2)	Moderate
E3-7	Method of Least Squares (LO 2,3)	Moderate
E3-8	High-Low Method; Cost Formulas (LO 2)	Moderate
E3-9	Method of Least Squares; Evaluation of Cost Equation (LO 2,3)	Basic
E3-10	Multiple Regression (LO 4)	Basic
E3-11	Cost Behavior Patterns (LO 1)	Basic
P3-1	Cost Behavior; Resource Usage Model (LO 1)	Moderate
P3-2	Cost Behavior; High-Low Method; Pricing Decision (LO 1,2)	Moderate
P3-3	High-Low Method; Method of Least Squares; Correlation (LO 2,3,5)	Challenging
P3-4	Cost Formulas; Single and Multiple Cost Drivers; Coefficient of Correlation (LO 1,3,4)	Challenging
P3-5	Scattergraph; High-Low Method; Method of Least Squares (LO 2,3)	Challenging
P3-6	Method of Least Squares (LO 1,2,3)	Moderate
P3-7	High-Low Method; Scatterplot (LO 2,5)	Moderate
P3-8	Comparison of Regression Equations (LO 1,2,5)	Challenging
C3-1	Simple and Multiple Regression; Evaluating Reliability of Equation (LO 2,3,4)	Challenging
C3-2	Suspicious Acquisition of Data; Ethical Issues	Challenging

CHAPTER 4

ACTIVITY-BASED COSTING

Technological changes in manufacturing have made the traditional costing method obsolete in many firms. The unit-based cost systems of the 1950's are no longer adequate in measuring product costs because overhead costs have increased while direct labor costs have decreased. This chapter introduces an approach that can improve product costing in many firms.

LEARNING OBJECTIVES

After studying Chapter 4, students should be able to:

1.   Discuss the importance of unit costs.

2.   Define actual and normal costing and explain why normal costing is preferred.

3.   Describe traditional costing approaches.

4.   Explain why traditional costing approaches may produce distorted costs.

5.   Explain how an activity-based cost system can produce more accurate product costs.

6.   Provide a detailed description of how activities are identified and classified so that homogeneous cost pools can be formed.

7.   Describe the role of activity-based costing in a JIT environment.

KEY TOPICS

The following major topics are covered in this chapter (related learning objectives are listed for each topic).

1.   Unit product costs (learning objective 1)

2.   Actual costing and normal costing: Two ways to measure cost (learning objective 2)

3.   Traditional product costing (learning objective 3)

4.   Limitations of traditional cost accounting systems (learning objective 4)

5.   Activity-based product costing: General description (learning objective 5)

6.   Activity identification and classification (learning objective 6)

7.   ABC, JIT, and product costing (learning objective 7)

I.   UNIT PRODUCT COSTS

The first section of the book deals with unit costs. PowerPoint transparency (PPT) 4-4 illustrates that there are two issues in calculating unit costs:

> 1. How to measure costs?

> 2. How to assign costs?

See PPT 4-4

Unit costs are important for a variety of reasons. We need unit costs to calculate inventory values or to calculate cost of goods sold for financial statement purposes. Internally, we need unit costs for decision purposes.

II.   ACTIVITY COSTING AND NORMAL COSTING: TWO WAYS TO MEASURE COST

PPT 4-5 can be used to discuss a conventional product costing system. The problem with traditional product costing pertains to how overhead is assigned.

See PPT 4-5

Teaching hint: Create a simple product costing example and then illustrate the process of assigning costs in a traditional environment to the class. If an actual overhead rate is used, you have an actual system, and if a predetermined rate is used to assign overhead, the system is a normal system.

PPT 4-6 introduces the two approaches to product costing: job-order costing and process costing. Job-order costing and process costing are further discussed in Chapters 5 and 6, respectively.

See PPT 4-6

This section of Hansen and Mowen focuses on actual costing and normal costing. PPT 4-7 can be used to explain the difference between the two systems. The concept of operational accounting is presented on this transparency. Warm-up exercise 4-1 can be used to illustrate the unit costs under both the actual and normal cost system.

See PPT 4-7

III. TRADITIONAL PRODUCT COSTING

PPT 4-5 illustrated a traditional system. Now, you can expand your discussion by focusing on a normal costing system. The next step is to calculate the unit cost for each product using conventional methods to assign overhead costs using plantwide or departmental rates that are based on direct labor hours, machine hours, and other unit-based cost drivers.

Plantwide rates. Teaching transparency master (TTM) 4-1 presents budget and actual information for Belring, Inc. TTM 4-2 presents plantwide calculations (Exhibit 4-3 in text).

See TTM 4-1 and 4-2

Use TTM 4-2 to point out that the regular phones receive nine times as much overhead cost as do the cordless. This is because they use nine times as many direct labor hours. Students can calculate plantwide overhead rates by working Warm-up exercise 4-2.

Departmental rates. TTM 4-3 and 4-4 provide additional information provided in Exhibit 4-5, along with the results for departmental rates (Exhibit 4-6 in text). The rate for the Assembly Department is based on direct labor hours, while the rate for the Fabrication Department is based on machine hours.

See TTM 4-3 and 4-4

TTM 4-4 reveals that departmental rates have failed to improve product-costing accuracy. Thus, departmental rates are not necessarily the solution to the cost-distortion problem. Warm-up exercise 4-3 is a departmental overhead rate problem.

Teaching hint: Ask the students if they think that the plantwide rate provides a fair and accurate assignment of costs. Most will indicate that the cost assignment is unfair since regular phones will be receiving more than their fair share of fabrication and assembly costs. This undercosts the cordless phones and overcosts the regular ones. With this in mind, indicate that moving to departmental rates has been suggested as a way to improve overhead costing accuracy. Ask why the conventional approaches are failing. This should lead to a discussion of product diversity and the relative significance of nonunit-related overhead costs. The products consume the overhead activities in different proportions from those of the unit-based cost drivers. Also, the nonunit-based overhead costs represent a significant proportion of total overhead costs. Finally, ask what approach should be taken for assigning overhead costs. Generally, students will suggest an activity-based approach, allowing the transition to activity costing.

IV. LIMITATIONS OF TRADITIONAL COST ACCOUNTING SYSTEMS

The opening scenario can be used to initiate discussion of the material. What problems were being faced by Sharp Paper Company? Why did the two vice-presidents conclude that the company's costing procedures may be faulty? Discussion of these two questions should elicit some of the common symptoms that companies experience with faulty costing systems. These symptoms, which correspond to Exhibit 4-7 on page 116 of Hansen and Mowen, are illustrated in PPT 4-8 and 4-9.

See PPT 4-8 and 4-9

A. Overhead Assignment: The Source of the Problem

TTM 4-5 presents more data for Belring, Inc. (Exhibit 4-8 in the text). Note to the students that overhead costs have been broken down into setup, material handling, power, and testing costs.

See TTM 4-5

Teaching hint: Ask the students how many costs are traceable to a product if it is the only product being made in a plant. This question prompts students to begin thinking about the issue of traceability. Next, introduce a setting where two products are being made in the same plant. Ask students how product costing differs in this setting.

The discussion should lead to the conclusion that overhead costing is the source of problems with costing accuracy. This is true in multiple-product settings. If a firm focuses and produces only one product, then all overhead is traceable to that single product. For a multiple-product setting, overhead is caused jointly by the products and means must be devised to assign the overhead to each product to determine its unit cost. How overhead is assigned to products is an important issue and, if not given careful attention, can create some significant problems (as the opening scenario illustrates).

V. ACTIVITY-BASED PRODUCT COSTING: GENERAL DESCRIPTION

Activity-based costing traces costs to activities and then to products. It differs from conventional costing on two dimensions. First, costs are traced to activities rather than organizational units. Second, costs are traced to products using both unit-based and nonunit-based cost drivers. PPT 4-10 presents more accurate cost allocations with activity-based costing.

See PPT 4-10

First stage. Activities are identified and the costs of activities are divided into homogeneous cost pools in the first stage of activity-based costing. A **homogeneous cost pool** is a collection of overhead costs that are logically related to the tasks being performed and for which cost variations can be explained by a single activity driver. An overhead rate is computed for each pool. This rate is then used to assign overhead costs to products. PPT 4-11 revisits the types of activities.

See PPT 4-11

Second stage. The second stage uses the pool rates and the level of activity consumed by each product to assign overhead costs to the products. TTM 4-6 and 4-7 present the assignment of costs for the example in the text. These are Exhibits 4-11 and 4-12, respectively. An alternate example for TTM 4-1 through 4-7 would be PPT 4-12 through 4-19.

See TTM 4-6 and 4-7

Comparison with conventional approaches. TTM 4-8 provides a comparison of the unit costs calculated under each of the three approaches. The improvement achieved by activity-based costing should be emphasized.

See TTM 4-8

Teaching hint: This is a good time to continue the discussion pertaining to distorted unit costs. Currently, we think the cost of cordless phones is around $11.00, when in reality the true cost is closer to $21.60. This is a good time to point out that entire markets of high-volume electronic products were given to foreign competition because our product cost system lied to us.

VI. ACTIVITY IDENTIFICATION AND CLASSIFICATION

Activity identification is critical for activity costing. There are four activity categories:

1. Unit-level
2. Batch-level
3. Product-level (sustaining)
4. Facility-level

These four activity categories are presented and defined in TTM 2-14.

See TTM 2-14

After classifying activities into one of the four categories, the costs associated with the unit-level, batch-level, and product-sustaining categories are assigned to products, using cost drivers that reflect the cause and effect relationship between activity consumption and cost. Facility-level costs are viewed as fixed costs and are not traceable to individual products. In practice, most firms allocate these costs to products even though no cost driver is available. Since they are usually a small percentage of total costs, this allocation probably will not have an appreciable effect on the accuracy of individual product costs. The product-cost categories should be reported separately so managers can focus on activities by category and choose those categories for cost reduction that have the greatest potential impact. Exercise 4-12 can be used to help classify activities.

ABC costing promises greater costing accuracy, improved decision making, enhanced strategic planning, and insight concerning activity management. These benefits are not obtained without costs. Firms have operated for decades with the simpler, traditional, unit-based cost systems. Therefore, when to adopt an ABC system becomes an important issue.

Teaching hint: Provide the above background information and ask the students when they think a firm should adopt an ABC system. After allowing for responses, make sure the following points are made. There are three conditions that must be met before an ABC system is adopted. **First**, the nonunit-based costs should be a significant percentage of total overhead costs. **Second**, the consumption ratios of unit-based and nonunit-based activities must differ. **Third**, the benefits of an ABC system must exceed its costs.

This may be a good time to discuss a topic not in the text at this time. **Measurement costs** are the costs associated with the measurements required by the system. **Error costs** are the costs associated with making poor decisions based on inaccurate product costs. The **optimal cost system** is the one that minimizes the sum of measurement costs and error costs. These relationships are portrayed graphically in PPT 4-20. Point out that a more intensive competitive environment has increased error costs over the past 5 to 10 years; and, simultaneously, new information technology has decreased measurement costs. Working together, more complex systems (e.g., an ABC system) are possible--at least for some firms.

See PPT 4-20

Teaching hint: Using a transparency marker, draw new curves on PPT 4-20 that reflect decreased measurement costs and increased error cost. This will visually illustrate the possibility of a more complex cost system.

VII.   ABC, JIT, AND PRODUCT COSTING

The differences between JIT manufacturing and conventional manufacturing should be briefly discussed. PPT 4-21 provides a list of these differences that can be used as the basis for the discussion. The focusing effect of manufacturing cells and the absence of inventories should be emphasized.

After the differences are discussed, the implications for management accounting practice can be presented. The change in the traceability of costs because of the focusing effect of JIT is important. Exercise 4-15 can be used to illustrate product costing in a JIT environment.

VIII. INFORMATION ABOUT WARM-UP EXERCISES, EXERCISES, PROBLEMS, AND CASES

For your convenience, exercises and problems are described below according to coverage of content, learning objective(s), and level of difficulty. The time required to solve the problems is roughly proportional to level of difficulty.

In general, *Basic* exercises/problems are fairly simple and straightforward. The text material is relatively brief; only one or two concepts are covered. Basic exercises and problems should take about 15 to 20 minutes.

Moderate exercises/problems may take longer and involve more concepts. These problems may have a "twist" and require more thought. Moderate exercises and problems may take 20 to 40 minutes.

Challenging problems are more comprehensive and may cover more concepts. The text material is relatively longer and may include some ambiguity. Challenging problems may take 60 to 90 minutes.

Exercise/ Problem	Topical Content (Learning Objective(s))	Level of Difficulty
W4-1	Normal versus Actual Costing (LO 2)	Basic
W4-2	Plantwide Rate (LO 1,3)	Basic
W4-3	Departmental Rates (LO 3)	Basic
W4-4	Activity Product Costs (LO 5,6)	Basic
E4-1	Normal versus Actual Costing (LO 1,2)	Moderate
E4-2	Plantwide Rates; Overhead Variance (LO 1,2,3)	Basic
E4-3	Unit Cost; Plantwide Overhead Rate; Applied Overhead (LO 1,2,3)	Basic
E4-4	Unit Overhead Cost; Predetermined Plantwide Overhead Rate; Applied Overhead (LO 1,2,3)	Basic
E4-5	Unit Overhead Cost; Predetermined Departmental Overhead Rates; Overhead Variance (LO 1,2,3)	Basic
E4-6	Product-Costing Accuracy and Overhead Costs (LO 3,5)	Moderate
E4-7	Multiple versus Single Overhead Rates; Activity Drivers (LO 3,4,5)	Moderate
E4-8	Activity versus Plantwide Overhead Rates; Activity Drivers (LO 4,5)	Moderate

Exercise/ Problem	Topical Content (Learning Objective(s))	Level of Difficulty
E4-9	Activity-based Costing: Homogeneous Cost Pools; Activity Drivers (LO 5,6)	Moderate
E4-10	Conventional Costing; Activity-based Costing; Pricing (LO 5,6)	Moderate
E4-11	Two-Stage Procedure; Activity-based Costing (LO 5,6)	Challenging
E4-12	Classification of Activities (LO 6)	Basic
E4-13	Selection of an ABC System (LO 4,5)	Moderate
E4-14	JIT and Product-Costing Accuracy (LO 7)	Moderate
E4-15	JIT; Traceability of Costs; Product-Costing Accuracy (LO 7)	Moderate
E4-16	Customer-driven Costs (LO 7)	Challenging
P4-1	Activity Drivers and Product-Costing Accuracy (LO 3,4,5)	Challenging
P4-2	Departmental Rates; Product-Costing Accuracy; Pool Rates (LO 3,4,5)	Moderate
P4-3	Traditional Costing versus Activity-based Costing (LO 4,5,6)	Challenging
P4-4	ABC Costing and Cost Behavior (LO 5,6)	Challenging
P4-5	Activity-based Costing: Service Industry (LO 4,5)	Challenging
P4-6	Product-Costing Accuracy; Corporate Strategy; Activity-based Costing (LO 4,5,6)	Challenging
P4-7	JIT and Traceability of Costs (LO 7)	Moderate
P4-8	Cost Assignment and JIT (LO 7)	Moderate
P4-9	ABC and Customer-driven Costs (LO 5)	Challenging
C4-1	Activity-based Costing; Consideration of Customer-driven Costs (LO 5,7)	Challenging
C4-2	Activity-based Product Costing and Ethical Behavior	Challenging

CHAPTER 5

JOB-ORDER COSTING

Product costing is a critical role in the new manufacturing environment and has become a significant factor in the service industries with the impact of deregulation. Nonaccounting majors should realize that understanding the basics of product costing is an important topic covered in the course. This chapter introduces students to the important topic of job-order costing.

LEARNING OBJECTIVES

After studying Chapter 5, students should be able to:

1. Describe the differences between job-order costing and process costing and identify the types of firms that would use each method.

2. Describe the cost flows and prepare the journal entries associated with job-order costing.

3. Identify and set up the source documents used in job-order costing.

KEY TOPICS

The following major topics are covered in this chapter (related learning objectives are listed for each topic).

1. Unit cost in the job-order environment (learning objective 1)

2. The flow of costs through the accounts (learning objective 2)

3. Source documents: Keeping track of individual costs (learning objective 3)

I.   UNIT COST IN THE JOB-ORDER ENVIRONMENT

Provide students with a description of a manufacturing process (from a job-order or process setting) and then ask them to describe how they would determine the cost of each unit produced. After a good discussion, switch to the opposite manufacturing setting and repeat the question. The Applegate Construction Company scenario at the beginning of the chapter can be used as the setting to motivate a discussion that should bring out the essential differences between job-order and process costing. PowerPoint transparency (PPT) 5-6 compares the two methods.

See PPT 5-6

Unit cost is an easy concept to understand, yet many students struggle with it. Warm-up exercises 5-1 or 5-2 can be used to discuss this concept in class. PPT 5-4 can be used to reemphasize the two issues to be addressed by a cost system.

See PPT 5-4

Next, Warm-up exercises 5-3 or 5-4 can be used to revisit the application of overhead issue. PPT 5-7 through 5-12 provide a good overview of the overhead issue. PPT 5-7, 5-9, 5-10, and 5-11 are worth presenting in class.

See PPT 5-7 through 5-12

This may be a good time to discuss the disposal of over- or underapplied overhead. PPT 5-17 and 5-18 may be helpful. In addition, Exercise 5-5 can be used.

See PPT 5-17 and 5-18

II.   THE FLOW OF COSTS THROUGH THE ACCOUNTS

Accountants are concerned with tracing the manufacturing costs from the point of incurrence to the recognition as expenses on the income statement. Teaching transparency masters (TTM) 5-1 and 5-2 provide a general description of the flows. After reviewing the manufacturing cost flows, Exercise 5-4, parts 1 and 3, can be used as a quick check on the students' understanding of the basic concepts. TTM 5-3 provides the solution to this exercise.

See TTM 5-1 through 5-3

Teaching hint: When discussing job-order costing, a simple example of a general contractor can be used. In the example, the company worked on three houses during the year. The following information is generally provided to the students on the board (TTM 5-4), while the solution is presented in TTM 5-5.

Direct materials	
House #1	$ 90,000
House #2	100,000
House #3	30,000
Total direct materials	$220,000

Direct labor	
House #1	$ 65,000
House #2	70,000
House #3	15,000
Total direct labor	$150,000

Overhead is applied at 50 percent of direct labor costs.

Houses #1 and #2 are completed during the period.

House #1 is sold for $200,000 cash.

See TTM 5-4 and 5-5

Unit cost: Once the job is completed, the unit cost is calculated by summing the costs for the job and dividing by the units in the job.

The activity-based costing system from Chapter 4 can be incorporated into job-order costing. Exercise 5-13 can be used to illustrate the application of overhead to jobs using an activity-based costing system. The issue of multiple overhead rates are presented on PPT 5-19 through PPT 5-23. These transparencies provide another example of material present in previous chapters. If you discussed departmental rates and an activity-based costing system in previous chapters, you may wish to overlook this topic at this time.

See PPT 5-19 through 5-23

III.   SOURCE DOCUMENTS: KEEPING TRACK OF INDIVIDUAL COSTS

It is important for students to understand the different documents that are used in a job-order system. The document for collecting all costs that belong to a job is the job-order cost sheet, which identifies the job and collects the materials, labor, and overhead costs for the job. It serves as a subsidiary ledger to the work-in-process account. The total of the costs for all job-cost sheets must equal the total for the controlling work-in-process account. PPT 5-13 illustrates a job-order cost sheet.

See PPT 5-13

A.   Materials Cost

The cost of materials is traced to each job through the use of a materials requisition form. When materials are issued to production, the material requisition form identifies the job, the quantity and type of materials, and the cost of materials. This document is the source document for assigning materials costs to individual job orders. A material requisition form is presented in PPT 5-14.

See PPT 5-14

B.   Labor Cost

Job time tickets are the source documents used to assign labor costs to jobs. When a direct laborer works on a job, he or she fills out a time ticket indicating the time spent on the job, along with his or her wage rate. PPT 5-15 illustrates a job time ticket.

See PPT 5-15

C.   Overhead Cost

Overhead is assigned using predetermined rates. If the rate is based on direct labor hours, then the predetermined rate and the information from the time tickets are used to assign overhead to jobs. If other cost drivers are used (e.g., machine hours) then another document must be created to collect the amount of the activity driver used by each job.

IV.   INFORMATION ABOUT WARM-UP EXERCISES, EXERCISES, PROBLEMS, AND CASES

For your convenience, exercises and problems are described below according to coverage of content, learning objective(s), and level of difficulty. The time required to solve the problems is roughly proportional to level of difficulty.

In general, *Basic* exercises/problems are fairly simple and straightforward. The text material is relatively brief; only one or two concepts are covered. Basic exercises and problems should take about 15 to 20 minutes.

Moderate exercises/problems may take longer and involve more concepts. These problems may have a "twist" and require more thought. Moderate exercises and problems may take 20 to 40 minutes.

Challenging problems are more comprehensive and may cover more concepts. The text material is relatively longer and may include some ambiguity. Challenging problems may take 60 to 90 minutes.

Exercise/ Problem	Topical Content (Learning Objective(s))	Level of Difficulty
W5-1	Unit Cost Calculation (LO 1)	Basic
W5-2	Unit Cost Calculation (LO 1)	Basic
W5-3	Applying Overhead to Jobs Using ABC (LO 2)	Basic
W5-4	Applying Overhead to Jobs Using ABC (LO 2)	Basic
W5-5	Journal Entries (LO 2)	Basic
W5-6	Journal Entries (LO 2)	Basic
W5-7	Nonmanufacturing Costs and the Income Statement (LO 3)	Basic
E5-1	Cost Flows (LO 2)	Moderate
E5-2	Calculating Ending WIP (LO 2)	Moderate
E5-3	Income Statement in Job-Order Firm (LO 2)	Moderate
E5-4	Journal Entries; T-Accounts (LO 2)	Basic
E5-5	Actual and Applied Overhead, Journal Entries, Disposition of Variance (LO 2)	Basic
E5-6	Multiple versus Single Overhead Rates; Activity Drivers (LO 2)	Moderate
E5-7	Journal Entries; T-Accounts (LO 2)	Basic
E5-8	Overhead Assignment: Actual and Normal Activity Compared (LO 2)	Moderate
E5-9	Overhead Applied to Jobs; Departmental Overhead Rates (LO 2)	Basic
E5-10	Unit Cost; Ending Work in Process; Journal Entries (LO 2)	Basic
E5-11	Unit Cost; Journal Entries; Assignment Procedures (LO 2)	Basic
E5-12	Predetermined Overhead Rates; Variances; Cost Flows (LO 2)	Moderate
E5-13	Activity-based Costing and Overhead Rates; Unit Costs (LO 2,3)	Moderate
E5-14	Activity-based Costing and Overhead Rates; Unit Costs (LO 2,3)	Moderate
P5-1	Predetermined Overhead Rates; Overhead Variances; Unit Costs (LO 2)	Moderate
P5-2	Activity-based Costing; Accuracy of Unit Costs; Multiple Overhead Rates Using Activity Drivers versus Single Overhead Rates; Pricing Decisions (LO 2)	Challenging
P5-3	Job Cost Sheets; Journal Entries; Inventories (LO 2,3)	Moderate
P5-4	Job-Order Costing; Housing Construction (LO 2, 3)	Challenging
P5-5	Plantwide Overhead Rate; Departmental Rates; Effects on Job Pricing Decisions (LO 2,3)	Challenging
P5-6	ABC, Departmental Rates, and Pricing Decisions (LO 1,2,3)	Challenging
P5-7	Overhead Rates; Unit Cost (LO 1,2)	Moderate
P5-8	Predetermined Overhead Rate; Departmental Overhead Rates; Job Cost (LO 1,2)	Moderate
P5-9	Departmental Overhead Rates; Job Cost (LO 1,2)	Challenging
P5-10	Activity-based Costing; Job Costs and Prices (LO 2,3)	Challenging
C5-1	Assigning Overhead to Jobs; Ethical Issues (LO 2,3)	Challenging
C5-2	Job-Order Costing: Dental Practice (LO 2,3)	Challenging
C5-3	Job-Order Costing and Pricing Decisions (LO 2,3)	Challenging
C5-4	Research Assignment (LO 1,2,3)	Challenging

CHAPTER 6

PROCESS COSTING

If time permits, coverage of process costing is recommended. It does expose students to a different method of collecting costs for products and provides useful insights in later chapters. The material in this chapter is generally difficult for the students because of the amount of detail. If you wish to hit this lightly, I suggest you focus on the weighted average approach.

LEARNING OBJECTIVES

After studying Chapter 6, students should be able to:

1.   Describe the basic characteristics and cost flows associated with process manufacturing.

2.   Define *equivalent units* and explain their role in process costing. Explain the differences between the weighted average method and the FIFO method of accounting for process costs.

3.   Prepare a departmental production report using the weighted average method.

4.   Explain how process costing is affected by nonuniform application of manufacturing inputs and the existence of multiple processing departments.

5.   Prepare a departmental production report using the FIFO method. (Appendix)

KEY TOPICS

The following major topics are covered in this chapter (related learning objectives are listed after each topic).

1.   Characteristics of process manufacturing (learning objective 1)

2.   The impact of work-in-process inventories on process costing (learning objective 2)

3.   Weighted average costing (learning objective 3)

4.   Multiple inputs and multiple departments (learning objective 4)

5.   Appendix: Production report — FIFO costing (learning objective 5)

I.   CHARACTERISTICS OF PROCESS MANUFACTURING

At this point, it is usually helpful to compare and contrast process costing with job-order costing again. PowerPoint transparency (PPT) 5-6 will be helpful to examine again. Your focus should be on the process costing environment. The opening scenario on pages 200 and 201 of Hansen and Mowen can be used to illustrate how different manufacturing settings require different cost accumulation methods.

See PPT 5-6

This section focuses on the basic characteristics and cost flows associated with process manufacturing. PPT 6-7 illustrates the process costing cost flow, while PPT 6-8 and 6-9 summarize the basic characteristics of process costing. This would be a good time to point out the difference in sequential and parallel processing. See pages 202 and 203 in the text.

See PPT 6-7 through 6-9

II.   THE IMPACT OF WORK-IN-PROCESS INVENTORIES ON PROCESS COSTING

PPT 6-10 presents information on units, while PPT 6-11 illustrates equivalent units. After going over these transparencies, you might note that the percentage of completion is a subjective assessment. Basically, the production manager "eyeballs" ending inventory to come up with a rough estimate of completion. Note that PPT 6-11 illustrates calculations for both weighted average and FIFO. It may be beneficial to explain the differences between the two approaches.

See PPT 6-10 and 6-11

III.   WEIGHTED AVERAGE COSTING

Cost data is presented in PPT 6-12. Both weighted average and FIFO reports are prepared using the data. Teaching transparency master (TTM) 6-1 summarizes the five steps to prepare a production report.

See PPT 6-12 and TTM 6-1

PPT 6-13 through 6-16 illustrate the weighted average method using the example presented. PPT 6-13 presents the analysis of the flow of physical units, while the calculation of equivalent units is illustrated in PPT 6-14. The computation of unit cost is illustrated with PPT 6-15 and the assignment of costs to completed goods and ending inventory, as well as the reconciliation of costs, are illustrated in PPT 6-16. Once the discussion of the five steps is completed, indicate that these steps provide all the essential information for the cost of production report.

See PPT 6-13 through 6-16

Teaching hint: When the students are using the weighted average method, they should ask the following question when calculating equivalent units: "What is the percent of effort provided as of the end of the period on the units worked on during the period?" This way they know they are including some work performed last period in their calculations.

IV.   MULTIPLE INPUTS AND MULTIPLE DEPARTMENTS

There are two remaining complications of process costing that need to be discussed: (1) nonuniform application of manufacturing inputs, and (2) multiple departments.

A.   Nonuniform Application of Manufacturing Inputs

Up to this point, we have assumed that percentage completion applied to all inputs, including materials. What happens when materials and conversion costs are not added uniformly? Materials may be added at either the beginning or the end of a process, while conversion costs are added in a different proportion. Thus, a product that is 60% complete with respect to conversion costs may be 100% complete with respect to materials. This nonuniform application of inputs requires a different approach. The modification is simple. When materials and conversion costs are added nonuniformly, we need to calculate output and unit costs for each category of input. The sum of the unit costs for each input category is the unit cost of the product. TTM 6-2 and 6-3 provide an example illustrating how to adjust to the nonuniform setting.

See TTM 6-2 and 6-3

B.   Multiple Departments

Once the students understand how to treat different categories of inputs, extension to multiple departments is straightforward. Transferred-in goods is simply an additional input category (a type of materials added at the beginning of the process). Besides that, a cost of production report would be prepared for each department.

V.   APPENDIX: PRODUCTION REPORT — FIFO COSTING

This appendix goes through the production costing report using the FIFO method. PPT 6-17 through 6-21 illustrate the FIFO method using our previous weighted average example.

See PPT 6-17 through 6-21

Teaching hint: When the students are using the FIFO method, they should ask the following question when calculating equivalent units: "What is the percent of effort provided <u>during</u> the period on the units worked on during the period?" Here the emphasis is on the work performed during the period.

VI.   INFORMATION ABOUT WARM-UP EXERCISES, EXERCISES, PROBLEMS, AND CASES

For your convenience, exercises and problems are described below according to coverage of content, learning objective(s), and level of difficulty. The time required to solve the problems is roughly proportional to level of difficulty.

In general, *Basic* exercises/problems are fairly simple and straightforward. The text material is relatively brief; only one or two concepts are covered. Basic exercises and problems should take about 15 to 20 minutes.

Moderate exercises/problems may take longer and involve more concepts. These problems may have a "twist" and require more thought. Moderate exercises and problems may take 20 to 40 minutes.

Challenging problems are more comprehensive and may cover more concepts. The text material is relatively longer and may include some ambiguity. Challenging problems may take 60 to 90 minutes.

Exercise/ Problem	Topical Content (Learning Objective(s))	Level of Difficulty
W6-1	Basic Cost Flows (LO 1)	Basic
W6-2	Equivalent Units (LO 2)	Basic
W6-3	Steps in Preparing Cost of Production Report (LO 3)	Basic
W6-4	Cost of Production Report (LO 3)	Basic
W6-5	Nonuniform Inputs (LO 4)	Basic
W6-6	Cost of Production Report; Nonuniform Inputs (LO 3,4)	Basic
W6-7	Nonuniform Inputs; Transferred-in Cost (LO 4)	Basic
W6-8	Appendix Required: FIFO Equivalent Units; Unit Cost (LO 5)	Basic
W6-9	Appendix Required: FIFO Cost of Production Report (LO 5)	Basic
E6-1	Physical Flow; Equivalent Units; Weighted Average Method (LO 1,2,3)	Basic
E6-2	Weighted Average Method; Valuation of Goods Out and Ending Work in Process (LO 3)	Basic
E6-3	Appendix Required: FIFO Method; Value of Goods Transferred Out and Ending Work in Process (LO 5)	Basic
E6-4	Weighted Average Method; Valuation of Goods Transferred Out and Ending Work in Process (LO 3)	Basic
E6-5	Production Report; No Beginning Inventory (LO 3)	Basic
E6-6	Physical Flow; Equivalent Units; Unit Costs, Cost Assignment (LO 2,3)	Moderate

Exercise/ Problem	Topical Content (Learning Objective(s))	Level of Difficulty
E6-7	Equivalent Units — Weighted Average Method (LO 2,3)	Basic
E6-8	Appendix Required: Equivalent Units — FIFO Method (LO 5)	Basic
E6-9	Weighted Average Method; Unit Cost; Valuation of Goods Transferred Out and Ending Work in Process (LO 3)	Basic
E6-10	Appendix Required: FIFO Method; Unit Cost; Valuation of Goods Out and Ending Work in Process (LO 5)	Basic
E6-11	Weighted Average Method; Equivalent Units; Unit Cost; Multiple Departments (LO 2,3,4)	Basic
E6-12	Appendix Required: FIFO Method; Equivalent Units; Unit Cost; Multiple Departments (LO 2,4,5)	Moderate
E6-13	Weighted Average Method; Unit Costs; Inventory Valuation; Cost Reconciliation (LO 3)	Basic
E6-14	Journal Entries; Cost of Ending Inventories (LO 1)	Basic
E6-15	Process Costing: Food Manufacturing (LO 1,2)	Basic
E6-16	Process Costing: Automated Operations (LO 2)	Basic
E6-17	Appendix Required: FIFO Method; Physical Flow; Equivalent Units (LO 5)	Basic
E6-18	Weighted Average Method; Physical Flow; Equivalent Units; Unit Costs; Cost Assignment (LO 1,2,3)	Moderate
E6-19	Appendix Required: FIFO Method; Physical Flow; Equivalent Units; Unit Costs; Cost Assignment (LO 5)	Moderate
E6-20	Weighted Average Method; Equivalent Units; Cost per Unit; Cost of Ending Inventory; Cost of Completed Units (LO 2,3)	Basic
P6-1	Weighted Average Method; Single Department Analysis; One Cost Category (LO 3)	Moderate
P6-2	Appendix Required: FIFO Method; Single Department Analysis; One Cost Category (LO 5)	Moderate
P6-3	Weighted Average Method; Single Department Analysis; Three Cost Categories (LO 3)	Moderate
P6-4	Weighted Average Method; Single Department Analysis; Two Cost Categories (LO 3)	Challenging
P6-5	Appendix Required: FIFO Method; Single Department Analysis; Two Cost Categories (LO 5)	Moderate
P6-6	Weighted Average Method; Single Department Analysis; Transferred-in Goods (LO 3,4)	Moderate
P6-7	Appendix Required: FIFO Method; Single Department Analysis; Transferred-in Goods (LO 4,5)	Moderate
P6-8	Weighted Average Method; Transferred-in Goods (LO 3,4)	Moderate
P6-9	Weighted Average Method; Journal Entries (LO 1,3)	Challenging
P6-10	Appendix Required: FIFO Method; Two Department Analysis (LO 4,5)	Challenging
P6-11	Weighted Average Method; Two Department Analysis (LO 3,4)	Moderate
P6-12	Appendix Required: FIFO Method; Two Department Analysis (LO 4,5)	Moderate

Exercise/ Problem	Topical Content (Learning Objective(s))	Level of Difficulty
P6-13	Weighted Average Method; Multiple Department Analysis (LO 4,5)	Challenging
P6-14	Appendix Required: FIFO Method; Multiple Department Analysis (LO 4,5)	Challenging
P6-15	Production Report (LO 3)	Basic
C6-1	Production Report; Ethical Behavior (LO 3)	Moderate
C6-2	Process Costing versus Alternative Costing Methods; Impact on Resource Allocation Decision (LO 1,3)	Moderate

CHAPTER 7

SUPPORT DEPARTMENT COST ALLOCATION

Allocation of support center costs is an important topic for product costing. In recent years the issue of accurate product costing has assumed considerable importance, and managers need to be fully aware of how products are costed and the limitations associated with those assignments. The introductory scenario discusses a copying department in a large regional public accounting firm.

LEARNING OBJECTIVES

After studying Chapter 7, students should be able to:

1. Describe the difference between support departments and producing departments.

2. Explain five reasons why support department costs may be assigned to producing departments.

3. Calculate charging rates and distinguish between single and dual charging rates.

4. Allocate support-center costs to producing departments using the direct, sequential, and reciprocal methods.

5. Calculate departmental overhead rates.

KEY TOPICS

The following major topics are covered in this chapter (related learning objectives are listed for each topic).

1. An overview of cost allocation (learning objective 1)

2. Objectives of allocation (learning objective 2)

3. Allocating one department's costs to another department (learning objective 3)

4. Choosing a support department cost allocation method (learning objective 4)

5. Departmental overhead rates and product costing (learning objective 5)

I. AN OVERVIEW OF COST ALLOCATION

In Chapter 5, we discussed factory overhead allocation. However, we took the existence of factory overhead cost in a producing department as a given. Chapter 7 asks us to step back and trace these factory overhead costs from incurrence through assignment to units produced. PowerPoint transparency (PPT) 7-4 discusses the steps in determining overhead cost for a unit produced when support departments are present.

See PPT 7-4

Use the opening scenario to introduce the concept of the two categories of departments: support departments and producing departments. Each type of department should be defined and it should be indicated that this chapter is primarily concerned with describing ways of allocating support-department costs to producing departments. Teaching transparency master (TTM) 7-1 provides the definitions and some examples of support and producing departments.

See TTM 7-1

II. OBJECTIVES OF ALLOCATION

In this section you need to discuss why support-department costs are assigned to producing departments. The objectives of allocating support-department costs are:

1. to obtain a mutually agreeable price

2. to compute product-line profitability

3. to predict the economic effects of planning and control

4. to value inventory

5. to motivate managers

PPT 7-5 discusses these objectives.

See PPT 7-5

In addition, Hansen and Mowen state that some basic guidelines should be followed when allocating support-department costs. These guidelines are essentially compatible with the five objectives.

1. As nearly as possible, cost drivers (causal factors) should be used as the basis for cost allocation.

2. Budgeted or expected costs, not actual costs, should be allocated.

3. Costs should be allocated by behavior; fixed costs and variable costs should be allocated separately.

III. ALLOCATING ONE DEPARTMENT'S COSTS TO ANOTHER DEPARTMENT

Although it may not be possible to identify a method of allocating support-department costs that satisfies all the objectives of allocation, the three fundamental principles noted above should be followed in allocating support costs. Support costs should be allocated using factors that explain or relate to the consumption of the services. Examples of support activities and some possible causal factors are given in PPT 7-7.

See PPT 7-7

Teaching hint: It would be helpful to tell students that there should be a strong relationship between the cost pool and the cost driver. If we have a change in the cost driver, we should see a predictable change in the cost pool.

Allocating budgeted costs ensures that the inefficiencies (or efficiencies) of one manager are not passed on to another manager. Therefore, budgeted costs, not actual costs, should be allocated to producing departments. You should probably discuss this point carefully.

Hansen and Mowen suggest that separate allocation rates should be found for fixed and variable support costs. TTM 7-2 discusses the allocation of variable support costs, while fixed support costs are discussed in TTM 7-3.

See TTM 7-2 and 7-3

A numerical example will help illustrate these concepts. PPT 7-12 provides a good problem for illustrating the allocation based on cost behavior. PPT 7-13 presents the allocation of variable and fixed costs. Exercise 7-4 would be a good problem to illustrate the dual rates further.

See PPT 7-12 and 7-13

IV. CHOOSING A SUPPORT DEPARTMENT COST ALLOCATION METHOD

There are three methods commonly used to allocate support costs: (1) the direct method; (2) the sequential (or step) method; and (3) the reciprocal method. The first two are covered in the main body of the chapter and the third is covered in the appendix. (Many choose to defer coverage of the reciprocal method to cost accounting.) PPT 7-14 presents the three methods of allocation. It is important for students to realize that no matter which method of support-department cost allocation is used, total factory overhead costs remain unchanged. That is, the different allocation methods simply split up the costs differently among the producing departments.

See PPT 7-14

Teaching hint: Encourage students to sum the direct overhead costs of both producing and support departments prior to allocation, then sum the overhead costs of the producing department after allocation. The two sums should be identical (barring rounding errors).

The direct method assumes no interactions between the support departments. Therefore, support-department costs are allocated only to producing departments, never to other support departments. PPT 7-15 provides an example of a support department allocation. The direct method solution is provided on PPT 7-16.

See PPT 7-15 and 7-16

The sequential method recognizes that interactions do occur but assumes that they occur in a sequential manner, where the sequence is assumed to follow the degree of support rendered. This method assumes one-way relationships between the support departments (i.e., A provides services to B, but B does not provide services to A). The sequential solution to the numerical example is provided on PPT 7-17.

See PPT 7-17

The reciprocal method provides the most complete approach to dealing with support-department interactions. This method assumes two-way relationships between the support departments. For example, Personnel uses the services of Maintenance and Maintenance uses the services of Personnel. What is the total cost associated with the Personnel Department? It would be Personnel's direct costs plus the cost of cleaning the Personnel office which is "hidden" in the direct costs of Maintenance. Determining the degree to which the two departments increase each other's costs can be determined only by solving a system of simultaneous equations.

V. DEPARTMENTAL OVERHEAD RATES AND PRODUCT COSTING

When all costs are allocated from the support departments to the production departments, overhead rates can be calculated for each production department. These calculations are similar to overhead calculations discussed in earlier chapters.

VI. INFORMATION ABOUT WARM-UP EXERCISES, EXERCISES, PROBLEMS, AND CASES

For your convenience, exercises and problems are described below according to coverage of content, learning objective(s), and level of difficulty. The time required to solve the problems is roughly proportional to level of difficulty.

In general, *Basic* exercises/problems are fairly simple and straightforward. The text material is relatively brief; only one or two concepts are covered. Basic exercises and problems should take about 15 to 20 minutes.

Moderate exercises/problems may take longer and involve more concepts. These problems may have a "twist" and require more thought. Moderate exercises and problems may take 20 to 40 minutes.

Challenging problems are more comprehensive and may cover more concepts. The text material is relatively longer and may include some ambiguity. Challenging problems may take 60 to 90 minutes.

Exercise/ Problem	Topical Content (Learning Objective(s))	Level of Difficulty
W7-1	Single Charging Rate (LO 3)	Basic
W7-2	Dual Charging Rates (LO 3)	Basic
W7-3	Changes in the Use of the Support Department and the Impact on Fixed-Cost Allocation (LO 3)	Basic
W7-4	Allocating Support-Department Cost Using the Direct Method (LO 4)	Basic
W7-5	Allocating Support-Department Cost Using the Sequential Method (LO 4)	Basic
W7-6	Allocating Support-Department Cost Using the Reciprocal Method (LO 4)	Basic
W7-7	Computing Departmental Overhead Rates and Product Cost (LO 5)	Basic
E7-1	Classifying Departments as Producing or Support (LO 1)	Basic
E7-2	Identifying Causal Factors (LO 1)	Basic
E7-3	Actual versus Budgeted Costs (LO 3,4)	Basic
E7-4	Fixed- and Variable-Cost Allocation (LO 3,4)	Basic
E7-5	Direct Method and Overhead Rates (LO 4,5)	Basic
E7-6	Sequential Method (LO 4,5)	Basic
E7-7	Reciprocal Method (LO 4,5)	Basic

Exercise/ Problem	Topical Content (Learning Objective(s))	Level of Difficulty
E7-8	Direct Method (LO 4,5)	Basic
E7-9	Sequential Method (LO 4,5)	Basic
E7-10	Allocation: Fixed and Variable Costs (LO 3)	Basic
E7-11	Allocation: Budgeted Fixed and Variable Costs (LO 3)	Basic
E7-12	Fixed-Cost Allocation; Variable Base (LO 3)	Basic
E7-13	Reciprocal Method (LO 4)	Basic
E7-14	Direct Method; Overhead Rates (LO 4,5)	Basic
E7-15	Sequential Method; Overhead Rates (LO 4,5)	Basic
E7-16	Reciprocal Method; Overhead Rates (LO 4,5)	Basic
E7-17	Allocation: Fixed and Variable Costs (LO 3)	Basic
P7-1	Direct Method; Variable versus Fixed; Costing and Performance Evaluation (LO 3,4)	Moderate
P7-2	Comparison of Methods of Allocation (LO 4)	Moderate
P7-3	Comparison of Methods of Allocation (LO 4,5)	Moderate
P7-4	Comparison of Ranking of Support Departments Using the Sequential Method (LO 4,5)	Moderate
P7-5	Predetermined Rates; Allocation for Performance Evaluation (LO 3)	Moderate
P7-6	Sequential and Direct Methods (LO 4,5)	Challenging
P7-7	Reciprocal Method; Cost of Operating a Support Department (LO 4)	Challenging
P7-8	Direct Method; Sequential Method; Overhead Rates (LO 4,5)	Moderate
P7-9	Fixed- and Variable-Cost Allocation (LO 3)	Moderate
P7-10	Support Department Cost Allocation; Plantwide Overhead Rate versus Departmental Rates; Effects on Pricing Decisions (LO 4,5)	Challenging
C7-1	Allocation; Pricing; Ethical Behavior (LO 1,2)	Challenging
C7-2	Managerial Decision Case: Direct Method; Settlement of a Contract Dispute (LO 4,5)	Challenging
C7-3	Research Assignment	Challenging

CHAPTER 8

BUDGETING FOR PLANNING AND CONTROL

Budgeting is one topic that most students can relate to since they are involved with their own personal budgets. Students may benefit by reading the scenario at the beginning of the chapter.

LEARNING OBJECTIVES

After studying Chapter 8, students should be able to:

1. Define *budgeting* and discuss its role in planning, control, and decision making.

2. Define and prepare the *master budget*, identify its major components, and explain the interrelationships of the various components.

3. Identify and discuss the key features that a budgetary system should have to encourage managers to engage in goal-congruent behavior.

4. Describe budgets for merchandising and service firms and zero-base budgeting.

KEY TOPICS

The following major topics are covered in this chapter (related learning objectives are listed after each topic).

1. Description of budgeting (learning objective 1)

2. Preparing the budget (learning objective 2)

3. Using budgets for performance evaluation (learning objective 3)

4. Other types of budgets (learning objective 4)

I.   DESCRIPTION OF BUDGETING

First discuss what a budget is and the role it plays in an organization. Start by asking students the following two questions: What is a budget? What are the purposes of budgeting? Planning and control will emerge as two major purposes. Budgets are the means used to translate the goals and objectives of an organization into operational terms.

By comparing actual outcomes with planned outcomes, budgets also can be used to control. It is important for students to understand that budgets are the outgrowth of strategic planning and that they play a vital role in implementing strategic plans. The planning and control purposes of budgeting (Exhibit 8-1) are shown in the flow chart in PowerPoint transparency (PPT) 8-3. Teaching transparency Masters (TTM) 8-1 and 8-2 give an example that can be used to show how budgeting, planning, and control interrelate.

See PPT 8-3, TTM 8-1 and 8-2

The purposes of budgeting are listed in PPT 8-4.

See PPT 8-4

Once the planning and control functions of budgeting are understood, these concepts can be used as the basis for illustrating the notion of responsibility accounting. TTM 8-3 defines responsibility accounting and also offers definitions of the major types of responsibility centers.

See TTM 8-3

II.   PREPARING THE BUDGET

PPT 8-5 presents the two dimensions of budgeting: how the budget is prepared, and how the budget is used to implement an organization's plans. The preparation is referred to as the mechanics of budgeting and the implementation as the behavioral dimension. Most budgets are for a one-year period and are broken down into monthly and quarterly segments. Some companies practice continuous budgeting, which is a moving 12-month budget. As a month expires, another month is added. The master budget is a comprehensive financial plan made up of various individual budgets. In addition, the master budget can be divided into operating and financial budgets, as illustrated on PPT 8-6.

See PPT 8-5 and 8-6

Problem 8-1 can be used to illustrate the operating budgets in class. A more complete problem may be Problem 8-7. Often I will present a cash budget problem in addition to stressing cash collections and disbursements. Exercise 8-9 will stress cash collections, and Exercise 8-12 can be used to illustrate cash budgets further.

III. USING BUDGETS FOR PERFORMANCE EVALUATION

Budgets are used to judge a manager's performance (by comparing actual outcomes with planned outcomes). Bonuses, salary increases, and promotions are often tied to budgetary performance. Clearly, budgets can have a significant effect on the behavior of managers. Whether the effect is positive or negative depends on how budgets are used. Hopefully, budgets will promote goal congruence and, simultaneously, create a drive in managers to achieve the organization's goals. Although no one has yet developed the perfect budgetary system, there are key features that a sound budgetary system should possess. These features are presented in TTM 8-4 and 8-5. Warm-up exercise 8-7 can be used to illustrate flexible budgets.

See TTM 8-4 and 8-5

IV. OTHER TYPES OF BUDGETS

The traditional approach to budgeting is the incremental approach, which starts with last year's budget and adds or subtracts from that budget to reflect changing assumptions for the coming year. Zero-base budgeting is an alternative approach which may not take the prior year's budgeted level for granted. Each activity or operation is justified on the basis of its need or usefulness to the organization.

In order to translate the concepts of zero-base budgeting into practice requires four steps. TTM 8-6 presents these steps.

See TTM 8-6

V. INFORMATION ABOUT WARM-UP EXERCISES, EXERCISES, PROBLEMS, AND CASES

For your convenience, exercises and problems are described below according to coverage of content, learning objective(s), and level of difficulty. The time required to solve the problems is roughly proportional to level of difficulty.

In general, *Basic* exercises/problems are fairly simple and straightforward. The text material is relatively brief; only one or two concepts are covered. Basic exercises and problems should take about 15 to 20 minutes.

Moderate exercises/problems may take longer and involve more concepts. These problems may have a "twist" and require more thought. Moderate exercises and problems may take 20 to 40 minutes.

Challenging problems are more comprehensive and may cover more concepts. The text material is relatively longer and may include some ambiguity. Challenging problems may take 60 to 90 minutes.

Exercise/ Problem	Topical Content (Learning Objective(s))	Level of Difficulty
W8-1	Sales Budget (LO 2)	Basic
W8-2	Production Budget (LO 2)	Basic
W8-3	Purchases Budget (LO 2)	Basic
W8-4	Direct Labor Budget and Overhead Budget (LO 2)	Basic
W8-5	Cash Receipts Budget (LO 2)	Basic
W8-6	Cash Budget (LO 2)	Basic
W8-7	Flexible Budget (LO 3)	Basic
E8-1	Sales Budget (LO 1,2)	Basic
E8-2	Production Budget (LO 2)	Basic
E8-3	Direct Materials Purchases Budget (LO 2)	Basic
E8-4	Production Budget (LO 2)	Basic
E8-5	Direct Materials Purchases Budget (LO 2)	Basic
E8-6	Direct Labor Budget (LO 2)	Basic
E8-7	Sales Budget (LO 2)	Basic
E8-8	Purchases Budget (LO 2)	Basic
E8-9	Cash Receipts Budget (LO 2)	Basic
E8-10	Production Budget; Direct Materials Purchases Budget (LO 2)	Basic
E8-11	Overhead Budget; Flexible Budgeting (LO 2,3)	Basic
E8-12	Cash Budget (LO 2)	Basic
E8-13	Flexible Budget (LO 2,3)	Basic
E8-14	Performance Report (LO 3)	Basic
E8-15	Budgeted Cash Collections; Budgeted Cash Payments (LO 2)	Basic
E8-16	Zero-Base Budgeting (LO 4)	Basic
E8-17	Participative versus Imposed Budgeting (LO 3)	Moderate
E8-18	Flexible Budgeting (LO 3)	Basic
E8-19	Cash Receipts Budget (LO 2)	Basic
E8-20	Cash Payments Schedule (LO 2)	Moderate
P8-1	Operating Budget; Comprehensive Analysis (LO 2)	Challenging
P8-2	Cash Budget; Pro Forma Balance Sheet (LO 2)	Moderate
P8-3	Participative Budgeting; Not-for-Profit Setting (LO 3)	Moderate
P8-4	Cash Budgeting (LO 2)	Basic
P8-5	Revision of Operating Budget; Pro Forma Statements for Income and Cost of Goods Sold (LO 2)	Moderate
P8-6	Performance Reporting; Behavioral Considerations (LO 1,3)	Moderate
P8-7	Master Budget; Comprehensive Review (LO 2)	Challenging
P8-8	Flexible Budgeting (LO 2,3)	Moderate
P8-9	Budgeting and Behavioral Consequences (LO 1,3)	Moderate
P8-10	Purchases Budget; Direct Labor Budget; Cash Budget; Flexible Budget (LO 2,3)	Moderate
P8-11	Flexible Budgeting (LO 3)	Moderate
P8-12	Importance of Cash Budget, Cash Budget (LO 1,2)	Moderate

Exercise/ Problem	Topical Content (Learning Objective(s))	Level of Difficulty
C8-1	Budgetary Performance; Rewards; Ethical Behavior (LO 3)	Moderate
C8-2	Cash Budget (LO 2)	Challenging
C8-3	Participative Budgeting (LO 3)	Challenging
C8-4	Research Assignment	Challenging

CHAPTER 9

STANDARD COSTING: A MANAGERIAL CONTROL TOOL

This chapter is usually difficult for students to understand. Besides that, it has become less relevant in the new manufacturing environment.

LEARNING OBJECTIVES

After studying Chapter 9, students should be able to:

1. Explain how unit standards are set and why standard cost systems are adopted.

2. Explain the purpose of a standard cost sheet.

3. Describe the basic concepts underlying variance analysis and explain when variances should be investigated.

4. Compute the materials and labor variances and explain how they are used for control.

5. Compute the variable and fixed overhead variances and explain their meanings.

6. Prepare journal entries for materials and labor variances and describe the accounting for overhead variances. (Appendix)

KEY TOPICS

The following major topics are covered in this chapter (related learning objectives are listed for each topic).

1. Unit standards (learning objective 1)

2. Standard product costs (learning objective 2)

3. Variance analysis: General description (learning objective 3)

4. Variance analysis: Materials and labor (learning objective 4)

5. Variance analysis: Overhead costs (learning objective 5)

6. Appendix: Accounting for variances (learning objective 6)

I. UNIT STANDARDS

A. Introduction

Cost control. The opening scenario illustrates that many prosperous companies tend to ignore the need for cost control. As conditions become more competitive and profits are being squeezed, it suddenly becomes easy to be cost conscious. In reality, even prosperous firms should be cost conscious. By exerting control over costs in prosperous times, the ability to weather more demanding times is improved. Comparing actual amounts with budgeted amounts is one approach to control. Developing unit standards can enhance control.

Unit standards. Unit standards are of two types: quantity standards and price standards. Quantity standards are concerned with how much of an input should be used and price standards with how much should be paid per unit of input. There are two reasons frequently mentioned for adopting a standard cost system (these are also illustrated in PowerPoint transparency (PPT) 9-4):

   1.   To improve planning and control.
   2.   To facilitate product costing.

See PPT 9-4

Planning and control is enhanced because the budget (total) variance can be decomposed into quantity and price variances. Further, product costs are known before the fact (at least what they should be) and this is very helpful for bidding and cost-plus pricing decisions. PPT 9-5 summarizes the major points and compares standard costing with normal and actual costing.

See PPT 9-5

Teaching hint: Point out that the use of variances at the operational level is generally discouraged for the advanced manufacturing environment. Using variances at the operational level may actually impede the effectiveness of a JIT system. It is also useful to indicate that standard cost systems are widely used--and that many firms using standard costing do calculate and report variances at the operational level. Although many academics are questioning the value of detailed variances at the operational level, their continued use suggests some utility--or at least the belief in their utility.

B. Development of Standards

There are two types of standards mentioned in the text: ideal and currently attainable. **Ideal standards** demand maximum efficiency and can be achieved only if everything operates perfectly. **Currently attainable standards** are achievable under efficient operating conditions. Conventional wisdom favors currently attainable standards because ideal standards are too demanding and can prove to be frustrating to workers and managers. PPT 9-3 provides an overlay for illustrating these terms.

See PPT 9-3

In developing quantitative standards, there are three potential sources of input that can be used: (1) historical experience, (2) engineering studies, and (3) input from operating personnel. In setting price standards for materials, factors that must be considered include market forces, discounts, freight, and quality. For labor, we must consider such factors as market forces, trade unions, payroll taxes, and qualifications. Teaching transparency master (TTM) 9-1 summarizes these concepts.

See TTM 9-1

II. STANDARD PRODUCT COSTS

The standard cost sheet provides the unit quantity and price standards and the standard cost per unit. PPT 9-6 illustrates a standard cost sheet.

See PPT 9-6

Teaching hint: At this point, it is probably a good idea to reinforce the ideas underlying the development of standards. Ask how the standard of two pounds of material per unit was developed. Then ask the same question about the price of $1.50. Next, using information from this sheet, compute the standard quantity of materials allowed and the standard hours allowed (for the actual output). Often students have difficulty distinguishing between unit standards and the inputs allowed, which are based on unit standards and actual output. Make sure that students understand the difference.

III. VARIANCE ANALYSIS: GENERAL DESCRIPTION

A. General Description

Breakdown of total variance. Start by describing the total budget variance and how it can be broken down into price and usage variances. TTM 9-2 presents a three-pronged representation of this decomposition.

See TTM 9-2

Favorable and unfavorable variances. A **favorable variance** occurs whenever the usage or prices are less than the standard usage or prices. **Unfavorable variances** occur when the opposite holds.

Investigation of variances. Whether variances are good or bad depends on if they are large enough to be significant and why they occurred. An investigation is required to find out why a variance occurred and who is responsible for it when these variances are significant. Investigating, however, is costly, and should be undertaken only if the benefits from corrective action exceed the costs of investigating and taking corrective action. Since it is difficult to estimate the costs and benefits of investigation, managers may investigate only if the variance is outside some predetermined acceptable range. The top and bottom measures are referred to as upper and lower control limits. These limits are determined by taking the standard and adding or subtracting the allowable deviation. TTM 9-3 summarizes these points.

See TTM 9-3

IV.   VARIANCE ANALYSIS: MATERIALS AND LABOR

PPT 9-7 illustrates the computation of materials variances. The variances are calculated using formulas and the diagram. In addition, the person responsible for the variance is identified. The labor variances are presented on PPT 9-8.

See PPT 9-7 and 9-8

Teaching hint: Discuss the issue of responsibility as the computation of each variance is described. Explain why the normal assignment of responsibility can change as the variance is analyzed. Also, ask when a manager might decide to change the standard after an investigation has been completed. Remember, one reason for a variance can be that the standard is too tight or too loose.

V.   VARIANCE ANALYSIS: OVERHEAD COSTS

Total overhead variance. Applied overhead in a standard cost system is SOR x SH, where SOR is the standard overhead rate. The **total overhead variance** is the difference between the actual overhead and the applied overhead. Like the materials and labor variances, this total variance can be broken down into component variances. First, overhead is divided into variable and fixed overhead categories, then two variances are computed for each category.

Variable overhead variances. The variable overhead variances are the **variable overhead budget (spending) variance (price variance)** and the **variable overhead efficiency variance (quantity variance)**. These variances are found in a similar manner to material and labor variances. Variable overhead variances are presented on PPT 9-9.

See PPT 9-9

Fixed overhead variances. The fixed overhead variances are the **fixed budget (spending) variance** and the **fixed volume variance**. Since these costs are not variable in nature, the calculations of the variances are different from the material, labor, and variable overhead variances. Fixed overhead variances are presented on PPT 9-10.

See PPT 9-10

Teaching hint: As the variances are discussed, point out that the two variances will always add up to the total under or overapplied overhead variance. By breaking the variances down into two pieces, a manager gains more knowledge about why the total variance occurred. This can then produce better planning and control.

VI. APPENDIX: ACCOUNTING FOR VARIANCES

The journal entries described assume that all inventories are carried at standard. The general form of entries is supplied on PPT 9-11 through 9-17. It is assumed that overhead variances are not journalized but are reported on a periodic basis as part of a performance report. At the end of the year, actual and applied overhead accounts are closed out and any resulting variance is disposed of by closing it to cost of goods sold if immaterial or by prorating it among Work in Process, Finished Goods, and Cost of Goods Sold if material. Of course, disposition of material and labor variances follow essentially the same pattern.

See PPT 9-11 through 9-17

VII. INFORMATION ABOUT WARM-UP EXERCISES, EXERCISES, PROBLEMS, AND CASES

For your convenience, exercises and problems are described below according to coverage of content, learning objective(s), and level of difficulty. The time required to solve the problems is roughly proportional to level of difficulty.

In general, *Basic* exercises/problems are fairly simple and straightforward. The text material is relatively brief; only one or two concepts are covered. Basic exercises and problems should take about 15 to 20 minutes.

Moderate exercises/problems may take longer and involve more concepts. These problems may have a "twist" and require more thought. Moderate exercises and problems may take 20 to 40 minutes.

Challenging problems are more comprehensive and may cover more concepts. The text material is relatively longer and may include some ambiguity. Challenging problems may take 60 to 90 minutes.

Exercise/ Problem	Topical Content (Learning Objective(s))	Level of Difficulty
W9-1	Standard Quantities (LO 2)	Basic
W9-2	Performance Report (LO 3)	Basic
W9-3	Materials and Labor Variances (LO 4)	Basic
W9-4	Variable Overhead Variances (LO 5)	Basic
W9-5	Fixed Overhead Variances (LO 5)	Basic
E9-1	Setting Standards and Assigning Responsibility (LO 1)	Moderate
E9-2	Computation of Inputs Allowed; Materials and Labor (LO 2)	Basic
E9-3	Materials and Labor Variances (LO 4)	Basic
E9-4	Overhead Variances (LO 5)	Basic
E9-5	Decomposition of Budget Variances; Materials and Labor (LO 4)	Moderate
E9-6	Appendix Required: Materials and Labor Variances; Journal Entries (LO 4,6)	Basic
E9-7	Overhead Application; Overhead Variances (LO 5)	Basic
E9-8	Investigation of Variances (LO 3)	Basic
E9-9	Appendix Required: Overhead Application; Overhead Variances; Journal Entries (LO 5,6)	Moderate
E9-10	Materials, Labor, and Overhead Variances (LO 4,5)	Moderate
E9-11	Appendix Required: Journal Entries (LO 6)	Basic
E9-12	Variances, Evaluation, and Behavior (LO 1)	Basic
E9-13	Straightforward Computation of Variances: Materials and Labor (LO 4)	Basic
E9-14	Appendix Required: Refer to E9-13 (LO 6)	Basic
E9-15	Incomplete Data (LO 2,4,5)	Moderate
P9-1	Basics of Variance Analysis: Variable Inputs (LO 3,4)	Moderate
P9-2	Setting Standards; Materials and Labor Variances (LO 1,2,4)	Moderate
P9-3	Setting a Direct Labor Standard; Learning Effects (LO 1,2)	Moderate
P9-4	Appendix Required: Basic Variance Analysis; Revision of Standards (LO 3,4,5,6)	Challenging
P9-5	Appendix Required: Unit Costs; Multiple Products; Variance Analysis; Journal Entries (LO 2,4,5,6)	Challenging
P9-6	Incomplete Data; Overhead Analysis (LO 2,4,5)	Challenging
P9-7	Control Limits; Variance Investigation (LO 3,4,5)	Moderate
P9-8	Appendix Required: Flexible Budget; Standard Cost Variances; T-Accounts; (LO 3,4,5,6)	Moderate
P9-9	Control Limits; Variance Investigation (LO 3,4)	Moderate
P9-10	Standard Costing: Planned Variances (LO 2,4)	Challenging

Exercise/ Problem	Topical Content (Learning Objective(s))	Level of Difficulty
P9-11	Standard Cost Sheet; Incomplete Data; Variance Analysis (LO 2,4,5)	Challenging
C9-1	Standard Costing (LO 1,2,3)	Moderate
C9-2	Establishment of Standards; Variance Analysis (LO 1,2,4)	Challenging
C9-3	Standard Costing and Ethical Behavior	Challenging
C9-4	Research Assignment	Challenging

CHAPTER 10

ACTIVITY-BASED MANAGEMENT

Activity-based management is a fairly new topic in management accounting textbooks. This chapter is important in order to understand the new environment in management accounting. The scenario to Chapter 10 is a good place for students to start. In addition, students should be comfortable with the topics from Chapters 3 and 4.

LEARNING OBJECTIVES:

After studying Chapter 10, students should be able to:

1. Compare and contrast traditional responsibility accounting with contemporary responsibility accounting.

2. Explain process value analysis.

3. Describe the role of financial measures of activity performance.

4. Discuss the role of nonfinancial measures of performance.

KEY TOPICS

The following major topics are covered in this chapter (related learning objectives are listed for each topic).

1. Responsibility accounting (learning objective 1)

2. Process value analysis (learning objective 2)

3. Financial measures of activity performance (learning objective 3)

4. Nonfinancial measures of activity performance (learning objective 4)

I.   RESPONSIBILITY ACCOUNTING

The responsibility accounting system for a stable environment is referred to as traditional responsibility accounting. The traditional system was developed when most firms were operating in relatively stable environments. Contemporary responsibility accounting, on the other hand, is the responsibility accounting system that is emerging for those firms operating in dynamic environments. PowerPoint transparencies (PPT) 10-4 and 10-5 illustrate the four responsibility elements for each of the two approaches. These are similar to Exhibits 10-1 and 10-2 in the textbook. An element-by-element comparison of these two approaches provides some key insights about the differences between the two environments.

See PPT 10-4 and 10-5

Limitations of traditional responsibility accounting are presented on PPT 10-3. This is similar to Exhibit 10-3 in the textbook.

See PPT 10-3

Teaching hint: Ask students how this view of responsibility accounting differs from the traditional view. This question should provide the opportunity for some good discussion. Exercise 10-4 can be used effectively here.

The focus is on eliminating waste in a world-class manufacturer. Consequently, managers must determine whether an activity is a value-added or nonvalue-added activity. Activity-based management (ABM) is a systemwide, integrated approach that focuses management attention on activities. Activity-based management has two dimensions: a cost dimension and a control dimension. PPT 10-6 presents the two-dimensional ABM model similar to Exhibit 10-4 in the textbook.

See PPT 10-6

II.   PROCESS VALUE ANALYSIS

A.   Activity Analysis

Activity analysis is the process of identifying, describing, and evaluating the activities an organization performs. There are four potential outcomes of activity analysis, which are described in teaching transparency masters (TTM) 10-1. The fourth outcome is the most important and refers to activity management.

See TTM 10-1

As mentioned earlier, the focus in the new manufacturing environment is on elimination of nonvalue-added activities. A **nonvalue-added activity** is one that is unnecessary or necessary but inefficient and improvable. **Value-added activities**, on the other hand, are necessary activities carried out with perfect efficiency. TTM 10-2 summarizes many of the above concepts and provides examples of nonvalue-added and value-added activities.

See TTM 10-2

There are four ways activity management can reduce costs: activity elimination, activity selection, activity reduction, and activity sharing. PPT 10-9 provides an opportunity for class discussion.

See PPT 10-9

B.   Activity Performance Measurement

Assessing how well activities (and processes) are performed is fundamental to management's efforts to improve profitability. Activity performance measures exist in both financial and nonfinancial forms. These measures are designed to assess how well an activity was performed and the results achieved. They are also designed to reveal if constant improvement is being realized. Measures of activity performance center on three major dimensions (PPT 10-11):

1. Efficiency
2. Quality
3. Time

See page 397 for a discussion of each item.

See PPT 10-11

III.   FINANCIAL MEASURES OF ACTIVITY PERFORMANCE

A.   Value and Nonvalue-added Cost Reporting

Cost Reporting. Performance reports should highlight the costs of nonvalue-added costs. By highlighting these costs, managers can focus on measures to reduce them and to eventually eliminate them. In effect, value-added activities and costs correspond to the traditional notion of ideal standards and costs. Although ideal standards were criticized earlier as being unsuitable because they tend to frustrate workers and managers, this outlook assumed that they would be used as standards that must be achieved currently (immediately). Continual improvement assumes a company will work towards the ideal and to search for ways of becoming more efficient. Managers will know the potential for improvement when nonvalue-added costs are identified and reported.

Fundamental to identifying value- and nonvalue-added costs is the identification of cost drivers for each activity. Once cost drivers are identified, ideal levels, or optimal standards for each cost driver, can be identified. TTM 10-3 and 10-4 provide the computational formulas for value-added and nonvalue-added costs and an example of a value- and nonvalue-added cost report. These transparencies are Exhibits 10-5 and 10-6 in the textbook.

63

See TTM 10-3 and 10-4

## B.	Trend Reporting

Reporting trends in actual costs is becoming a key part of the control system in the new manufacturing environment. The emphasis is on improvement and trend reporting allows managers to assess whether improvement is occurring. This is especially important for nonvalue-added costs. The idea is to eliminate these costs by aggressive activity management. TTM 10-5 presents Exhibit 10-7 which illustrates a simple trend report for nonvalue-added costs.

See TTM 10-5

## C.	The Role of Interim (Currently Attainable) Standards

Cost Reduction and Standards. As managers attempt to move toward the ideal level, standards that are achievable within a given period may be desirable. Currently attainable standards can be modified so that they reflect the targeted reduction in nonvalue-added costs for the coming period. Comparing actual costs with the currently attainable standard is equivalent to evaluating how well the current year's goals for improvement have been met. Here the targeted reduction is motivated internally—by desires to increase efficiency for the sake of efficiency and the resulting cost savings. See TTM 10-6 and 10-7 for an illustration of setting currently attainable standards (modified as described).

See TTM 10-6 and 10-7

## D.	Benchmarking

Another approach to standard setting that is used to help identify opportunities for activity improvement is called benchmarking. Benchmarking uses best practices as the standard for evaluating activity performance. Within an organization, different units (e.g., different plant sites) that perform the same activities are compared. PPT 10-19 provides information on benchmarking.

See PPT 10-19

## E.	Drivers and Behavioral Effects

Fundamental to the identification of nonvalue-added costs is the identification of cost drivers. Their selection, however, along with the emphasis on elimination of nonvalue-added costs, carries with it some strong behavioral ramifications. For example, using number of setups as the cost driver may encourage a manager to reduce the number of setups by simply producing larger lot sizes, creating unnecessary inventories. Using setup time as the cost driver, however, may encourage a manager to search for ways to reduce setup time, a desirable outcome.

F.   Activity Flexible Budgeting

This topic can be discussed using PPT 10-14 through 10-18. PPT 10-14 presents projected costs and cost behaviors for 100,000 units. PPT 10-15 presents a flexible budget under traditional costing, while PPT 10-16 illustrates a flexible budget under ABC. Fixed activity variances and variance analysis for variable activity costs are illustrated on PPT 10-17 and 10-18, respectively.

See PPT 10-14 through 10-18

Teaching hint: Problem 10-10 can be used as part of the lecture to help students grasp the effects different cost drivers can have on behavior.

G.   Life Cycle Cost Budgeting

Product life cycle is the time a product exists from conception to abandonment. **Life-cycle costs** are all the costs associated with the product for its entire life cycle. These costs consist of three major elements: developing costs, production costs, and logistics support costs. **Life-cycle cost management** focuses on managing value-chain activities so that a long-term competitive advantage is created. TTM 10-8 provides these definitions.

See TTM 10-8

Target Costs. A related but conceptually distinct approach is that of target costs. Here the target cost (standard) is motivated by outside factors. The target cost is defined as the difference between sales price needed to capture a predetermined market share and the desired profit per unit.

Teaching hint: Emphasize the importance of life-cycle cost management. From a life-cycle point of view, product cost consists of all life-cycle costs, not just manufacturing costs. Furthermore, 90 percent or more of the life-cycle costs are committed (not incurred) by the end of the development stage. This can be illustrated by showing the cost commitment curve in PPT 10-20 (see Exhibit 10-13). Also mention that life-cycle cost management is particularly important for products with short life cycles—and then ask why this is so. The information from Exhibits 10-14 and 10-15 are presented in PPT 10-21 through 10-23.

See PPT 10-20 through 10-23

IV.   NONFINANCIAL MEASURES OF ACTIVITY PERFORMANCE

There is a greater emphasis on operating measures (physical measures of input and output) in the new manufacturing environment. There is also an increased emphasis on timely control. Feedback is often on a real-time basis. Because of the potential savings as well as the effect on a firm's competitive position, the following areas have received special control emphasis: quality, inventory, materials cost, productivity, delivery performance, and machine performance.

Quality. Operational measures of quality include defects per unit, number of defective units/total units produced, the percentage of external failures, and pounds of scrap/total pounds of materials issued.

Inventory. Inventory is controlled through the use of a JIT purchasing and manufacturing approach and through the use of a Kanban system. Operational measures such as inventory turnover rates, days of inventory, and number of inventoried items play a role in controlling inventory.

Materials costs. Materials cost is controlled through supplier selection and long-term contracting, with special attention being paid to reliability, quality, and price.

Productivity. Productivity concerns how efficient inputs are used in producing outputs. Operational measures of productivity include output/materials, output/labor hours, output/kilowatt hours, and output/persons employed.

Delivery Performance. Delivery performance is measured by on-time delivery percentage, cycle time/velocity, and manufacturing cycle efficiency (MCE).

Machine Performance. Equipment is categorized as either nonbottleneck or bottleneck equipment. Machine availability is a crucial measure for nonbottleneck equipment whereas machine utilization is the critical measure for bottleneck equipment.

TTM 10-9 provides a summary of potential operational measures.

See TTM 10-9

Teaching hint: Of the above operational measures, the delivery performance measures are the most computationally demanding. Cycle time, velocity, and MCE all should be defined and illustrated. TTM 10-10 and 10-11 can be used for this purpose.

See TTM 10-10 and 10-11

V. INFORMATION ABOUT WARM-UP EXERCISES, EXERCISES, PROBLEMS, AND CASES

For your convenience, exercises and problems are described below according to coverage of content, learning objective(s), and level of difficulty. The time required to solve the problems is roughly proportional to level of difficulty.

In general, *Basic* exercises/problems are fairly simple and straightforward. The text material is relatively brief; only one or two concepts are covered. Basic exercises and problems should take about 15 to 20 minutes.

Moderate exercises/problems may take longer and involve more concepts. These problems may have a "twist" and require more thought. Moderate exercises and problems may take 20 to 40 minutes.

Challenging problems are more comprehensive and may cover more concepts. The text material is relatively longer and may include some ambiguity. Challenging problems may take 60 to 90 minutes.

Exercise/ Problem	Topical Content (Learning Objective(s))	Level of Difficulty
W10-1	Value- and Nonvalue-added Cost Report (LO 2)	Basic
W10-2	Activity Flexible Budgeting and Variance Analysis (LO 3)	Basic
W10-3	MCE; Cycle Time (LO 4)	Basic
E10-1	Labor Efficiency Variance; Ethical Issues; Incentives (LO 1)	Basic
E10-2	Limitations of Traditional Control Measures (LO 1)	Basic
E10-3	Traditional versus Contemporary Responsibility Accounting (LO 1)	Basic
E10-4	Contemporary versus Traditional Responsibility Accounting (LO 1)	Basic
E10-5	Driver Analysis; Activity Analysis (LO 2)	Moderate
E10-6	Calculation of Value-added and Nonvalue-added Costs; Unused Capacity (LO 2,3)	Moderate
E10-7	Cost Report; Value-added and Nonvalue-added Costs (LO 2, 3)	Basic
E10-8	Trend Report: Nonvalue-added Costs (LO 2,3)	Basic
E10-9	Activity Analysis, Activity Drivers, Driver Analysis, and Behavioral Effects (LO 3)	Moderate
E10-10	Cycle Time and Conversion Cost per Unit (LO 4)	Basic
E10-11	Cycle Time and Velocity; MCE (LO 4)	Basic
P10-1	Continuous Improvement; Performance Measurement (LO 1, 4)	Moderate
P10-2	Activity-based Management; Nonvalue-added Costs; Target Costs (LO 2,3)	Moderate
P10-3	Value-added and Interim Standards; Nonvalue-added Costs; Volume Variance; Unused Capacity (LO 3)	Moderate
P10-4	Benchmarking and Nonvalue-added Costs (LO 3,4)	Moderate
P10-5	Flexible Budgeting; Single Cost Driver versus Multiple Cost Drivers (LO 3)	Moderate
P10-6	Life-Cycle Cost Management (LO 3)	Moderate
P10-7	Cycle Time and Velocity; Conversion Cost per Unit; MCE (LO 4)	Moderate
P10-8	MCE (LO 2,4)	Basic
P10-9	Traditional versus Contemporary Responsibility Accounting (LO 1)	Moderate
P10-10	Flexible Budgeting; Multiple Cost Drivers; Variance Analysis (LO 3)	Challenging

Exercise/ Problem	Topical Content (Learning Objective(s))	Level of Difficulty
P10-11	Cycle Time; Velocity; Product Costing (LO 4)	Challenging
C10-1	Ethical Considerations	Challenging
C10-2	Research Assignment	Challenging

CHAPTER 11

QUALITY COSTS AND PRODUCTIVITY: MEASUREMENT, REPORTING, AND CONTROL

This chapter focuses on the measurement and control of quality costs, and does a good job of discussing a topic that is not presented in most first-level management accounting textbooks. It provides an excellent bridge to understanding the new manufacturing environment of a world-class manufacturer. The opening scenario provides an interesting discussion of the quality issues being faced by Ladd Lighting Corporation.

LEARNING OBJECTIVES

After studying Chapter 11, students should be able to:

1.   Identify and describe the four types of quality costs.

2.   Prepare a quality cost report and explain the difference between the conventional view of acceptable quality level and the view espoused by total quality control.

3.   Explain why quality cost information is needed and how it is used.

4.   Explain what productivity is and calculate the impact of productivity changes on profits.

KEY TOPICS

The following major topics are covered in this chapter (related learning objectives are listed for each topic).

1.   Measuring the costs of quality (learning objective 1)

2.   Reporting quality cost information (learning objective 2)

3.   Using quality cost information (learning objective 3)

4.   Productivity: Measurement and control (learning objective 4)

I. MEASURING THE COSTS OF QUALITY

A. Quality Defined

The costs of quality, actually mostly poor quality, are often cited as being 20 to 30 percent of sales for most American companies. By improving quality, these costs can be drastically reduced--to as low as two to four percent of sales. Thus, having good quality can mean a significant increase in profitability, even when the market share is simply maintained. When one considers the possibility of increasing market share because of improved quality, the possibility of even greater profitability exists. Quality is the degree or grade of excellence. In other words, quality is a relative measure of goodness. There are two types of quality: quality of design and quality of conformance. Teaching transparency masters (TTM) 11-1 provides the definitions and examples of both types.

See TTM 11-1

B. Costs of Quality Defined

Of the two types of quality, quality of conformance is the type that offers cost savings and potential increases in market share. The **costs of quality** are costs that exist because poor quality may or does exist. There are four categories of quality costs illustrated on PowerPoint transparency (PPT) 11-4: **prevention, appraisal, internal failure, and external failure**. Examples of these costs are provided on PPT 11-5 and 11-6.

See PPT 11-4 through 11-6

II. REPORTING QUALITY COST INFORMATION

The quality control department has often been the unit responsible for reporting quality costs. With the new emphasis on quality, however, firms are beginning to assign this responsibility to the accounting department. The reasoning is simple. First, cost reports from the same department responsible for ensuring quality are not objective enough. Second, the accounting department has the expertise and system for collecting and disseminating cost information. Why duplicate?

A. Quality Cost Report

A quality cost report lists the costs by category and by specific type within each category. It also expresses the costs as a percentage of sales, providing the relative magnitude of the costs. PPT 11-8 provides a typical quality cost report.

See PPT 11-8

The quality cost report provides some very useful information. First, by providing the costs as a percentage of sales, the potential increase in profits from improving quality can be assessed. Second, the amount being spent in each category is given. This information is very useful because the optimal level of quality costs is achieved by identifying the optimal balance between failure costs and prevention and appraisal costs. The manager can make adjustments and hopefully move toward the optimal levels by knowing the amounts being spent in each category. Since there are no mathematical formulas describing these relationships, the assessment must necessarily be subjective. A pie chart can also be used to display the relative amounts in each category. PPT 11-9 provides a pie chart illustration of quality costs.

See PPT 11-9

B. Optimal Distribution

AQL. The conventional view of quality costs assumes that there is an optimal balance between prevention and appraisal costs and failure costs. At this optimal level a certain number of defective units will exist. This level of defective units is defined as the **acceptable quality level (AQL).** PPT 11-10 provides a traditional quality cost graph that illustrates the trade-offs between the two categories of costs and provides a visual demonstration of AQL. PPT 11-12 discusses some considerations for controlling quality costs.

See PPT 11-10 and 11-12

Zero defects. For firms operating in the advanced manufacturing environment, quality is a critical competitive dimension. It has been discovered that quality costs can be managed differently than what is implied by the traditional AQL model. In reality, defects can be reduced below the AQL level and, simultaneously, quality costs can be reduced. The optimal level of quality is defined as where **zero defects** are produced. TTM 11-2 illustrates the zero-defect graph.

See TTM 11-2

Teaching hint: With TTM 11-2 shown on the screen, explain how a supplier selection program can be used to reduce total quality costs. Initially, a supplier selection program will entail additional prevention and appraisal costs and a reduction in failure costs. However, once the desired quality level is achieved and the supplier relationships are on a sound footing, many of the prevention and appraisal activities can be eliminated. The result is a movement downward on the zero-defect cost graph.

III.   USING QUALITY COST INFORMATION

The principal objective of reporting quality costs is to improve and facilitate managerial planning, control, and decision making. The utility of quality cost information should be discussed. Scenarios A and B in the chapter can be used as the framework for this discussion. Problems 11-3 and 11-4 are both useful for teaching the decision and planning utility of quality cost information.

Reporting quality costs is not enough to ensure that they are being controlled. For control to occur, a standard or plan must exist against which actual outcomes can be compared. For quality costs, then, we must have some idea of what they should be. The ultimate objective is to attain a quality level corresponding to zero defects. At this level, virtually all the quality costs are prevention and appraisal costs. PPT 11-13 discusses the types of quality performance reports.

See PPT 11-13

Interim reports. In addition to measuring progress toward the ultimate goal, managers should also have reports that measure performance in the interim. These interim reports measure the progress with respect to a current period standard. PPT 11-14 provides an example an interim report.

See PPT 11-14

Trend reports. Trend reports are also desirable. Performance can be gauged with respect to last year's quality costs (one-year trend report, see PPT 11-15) The trend over several years also provides useful information. Typically, however, multiple-year trends is a plot of quality costs as a percentage of sales for the years involved. This plot can be for total costs or for each cost category. PPT 11-16 and 11-17 provide multi-period total quality costs as a percent of sales in table and graph form, respectively. PPT 11-18 and 11-19 provides trend analysis for individual quality costs as a percent of sales in table and graph form, respectively.

See PPT 11-15 through 11-19

In practical terms, many quality experts suggest that quality costs ought to be about two to three percent of sales. This level then gives a firm a target to work towards. By comparing actual quality costs with the 2.5 percent-of-sales standard, a manager can assess progress toward the "optimal" goal.

IV. PRODUCTIVITY: MEASUREMENT AND CONTROL

A. Productivity Measurement Defined

Productivity is concerned with the efficient production of output. Thus, the relationship between inputs and outputs is critical. Total productive efficiency is where both technical and price efficiency are achieved. Productivity improvement programs attempt to move toward a state of total productive efficiency. **Productivity measurement** attempts to measure productivity changes so that efforts to improve productivity can be evaluated.

Teaching hint: Productivity improvement is achieved by improving technical and/or price efficiency. Thus, it is important that students understand technical and price efficiency. TTM 11-3 through 11-5 provide definitions of each and show how improvement for each category can be realized.

See TTM 11-3 through 11-5

B.   Partial Productivity Measurement

Productivity measures can be developed for each input separately or for all inputs jointly. **Partial productivity measurement** is measuring productivity for one input at a time. It is usually measured by dividing output by input. An **operational productivity measure** exists when both output and input are measured in physical quantities. By comparing partial measures of the current period with those of a prior period (called a **base period**), changes in the productivity of individual inputs can be assessed. TTM 11-6 and 11-7 summarize these concepts and illustrate the computation of partial measures.

See TTM 11-6 and 11-7

C.   Total Productivity Measurement

Profits change from the base period to the current period. Some of that profit change is attributable to productivity changes. Assessing the amount of profit change attributable to productivity change is defined as **profit-linked productivity measurement.** Interest in profit-linked productivity measurement is strong. For example, over 50 large companies have used some version of a profit-linked productivity measure developed by the American Productivity Center (the profit-linked measure described in the text is an improved version of this measure). Students should understand that profit-linked productivity measurement is a practical and important topic.

Profit-linked productivity measurement follows the **profit-linkage rule.** This rule is reproduced and its application is illustrated in TTM 11-8 and 11-9.

See TTM 11-8 AND 11-9

Teaching hint: Emphasize the fact that a profit-linked measure is a total productivity measure. It therefore captures the tradeoffs that occur as productivity changes are made. Ask the students to calculate the partial operational measures for the example described in TTM 11-7. Then ask then to decide--using only these measures--whether productivity has improved or declined. The power of a total measure then should be clearly evident to the students.

V. INFORMATION ABOUT WARM-UP EXERCISES, EXERCISES, PROBLEMS, AND CASES

For your convenience, exercises and problems are described below according to coverage of content, learning objective(s), and level of difficulty. The time required to solve the problems is roughly proportional to level of difficulty.

In general, *Basic* exercises/problems are fairly simple and straightforward. The text material is relatively brief; only one or two concepts are covered. Basic exercises and problems should take about 15 to 20 minutes.

Moderate exercises/problems may take longer and involve more concepts. These problems may have a "twist" and require more thought. Moderate exercises/problems may take 20 to 40 minutes.

Challenging problems are more comprehensive and may cover more concepts. The text material is relatively longer and may include some ambiguity. Challenging problems may take 60 to 90 minutes.

Exercise/ Problem	Topical Content (Learning Objective(s))	Level of Difficulty
W11-1	Hidden Quality Costs (LO 1)	Basic
W11-2	Quality Cost Report (LO 2)	Basic
W11-3	Productivity Analysis (LO 4)	Basic
E11-1	Quality Cost Classification (LO 1)	Basic
E11-2	Quality Improvement and Profitability (LO 2,4)	Basic
E11-3	Quality Costs: Profit Improvement and Distribution across Categories (LO 2,3)	Basic
E11-4	Trade-offs among Quality Cost Categories; Total Quality Control (LO 2)	Basic
E11-5	Quality Cost Report; Taguchi Loss Function (LO 2)	Basic
E11-6	Taguchi Loss Function (LO 2)	Basic
E11-7	Multiple-Year Trend Reports (LO 2)	Basic
E11-8	Productivity Measurement; Partial Measures (LO 4)	Basic
E11-9	Interperiod Measurement of Productivity; Basic Computations (LO 4)	Basic
E11-10	Productivity Measurement: Trade-offs (LO 4)	Basic
E11-11	Productivity Measurement: Technical and Price Efficiency Illustrated (LO 4)	Moderate
E11-12	Productivity and Quality (LO 4)	Moderate
E11-13	Basics of Productivity Measurement (LO 4)	Basic
P11-1	Classification of Quality Costs (LO 1)	Basic
P11-2	Quality Cost Summary (LO 2)	Moderate
P11-3	Quality Costs; Pricing Decisions; Market Share (LO 3)	Challenging
P11-4	Quality Costs; Profitability Analysis (LO 2,3)	Challenging
P11-5	Quality Cost Report; Quality Cost Categories (LO 1,2)	Moderate

Exercise/ Problem	Topical Content (Learning Objective(s))	Level of Difficulty
P11-6	Distribution of Quality Costs (LO 2)	Moderate
P11-7	Trend Analysis; Quality Costs (LO 2)	Moderate
P11-8	Productivity Measurement; Basics (LO 4)	Basic
P11-9	Productivity Measurement (LO 4)	Moderate
P11-10	Productivity Measurement: Partial and Total Measures; Price Recovery (LO 4)	Moderate
P11-11	Quality and Productivity; Interaction; Use of Operational Measures (LO 4)	Challenging
P11-12	Productivity; Trade-offs; Price Recovery (LO 4)	Moderate
C11-1	Quality Cost Performance Reports (LO 4)	Moderate
C11-2	Quality Performance and Ethical Behavior	Moderate

CHAPTER 12

DECENTRALIZATION: RESPONSIBILITY ACCOUNTING, PERFORMANCE EVALUATION, AND TRANSFER PRICING

This chapter deals with the divisional setting. In this chapter, Hansen and Mowen discuss decentralization, performance measurement, management compensation and transfer pricing. These issues are presented in the scenario at the beginning of the chapter.

LEARNING OBJECTIVES

After studying Chapter 12, students should be able to:

1.   Define responsibility accounting and describe four types of responsibility centers.

2.   Explain why firms choose to decentralize.

3.   Compute and explain return on investment (ROI) and residual income (RI).

4.   Discuss methods of evaluating and rewarding managerial performance.

5.   Explain the role of transfer pricing in a decentralized firm.

KEY TOPICS

The following major topics are covered in this chapter (related learning objectives are listed for each topic).

1.   Responsibility accounting (learning objective 1)

2.   Decentralization (learning objective 2)

3.   Measuring the performance of investment centers (learning objective 3)

4.   Measuring and rewarding the performance of managers (learning objective 4)

5.   Transfer pricing (learning objective 5)

I.   RESPONSIBILITY ACCOUNTING

There are four major issues that are present in the divisional setting. Decentralization is discussed in the next section, followed by performance measurement. Management compensation is in section IV, while transfer pricing is discussed in the last two sections of the chapter. PowerPoint transparency (PPT) 12-3 discusses the major issues of decentralization, while responsibility accounting is illustrated on PPT 12-4.

See PPT 12-3 and 12-4

II.   DECENTRALIZATION

Reviewing the introductory scenario is an excellent way to begin discussion. This scenario brings out four major issues: decentralization, performance measurement, management compensation, and transfer pricing. Ask students what it means to decentralize. Next ask them why an organization would choose to decentralize. Seven reasons for decentralization are listed in PPT 12-5.

See PPT 12-5

III.   MEASURING THE PERFORMANCE OF INVESTMENT CENTERS

Even though an organization may decentralize, it does not give up control of the subunits. There are three types of responsibility centers that are usually created in a decentralized firm: cost centers, profit centers, and investment centers. Cost centers and profit centers are usually controlled through the use of a budgetary system. This section focuses on investment centers. PPT 12-6 presents methods to measure the performance of investment centers.

See PPT 12-6

Performance measures for investment centers usually attempt to assess how well the investment dollar is being utilized. This is done by relating operating profits to assets employed. This measure of profitability is known as return on investment (ROI) and is defined as follows:

$$ROI = \frac{operating\ income}{average\ operating\ assets}$$

The formula can also be broken down into the product of margin and turnover. PPT 12-7 defines ROI, breaks it into margin and turnover, and illustrates its computation. PPT 12-8 and 12-9 present an ROI example and calculations. PPT 12-10 lists and illustrates the advantages of using ROI as a performance measure. PPT 12-11 lists and illustrates the disadvantages of ROI. The overlays are designed to produce discussion.

See PPT 12-7 through 12-11

Residual income is the difference between operating income and the minimum required return for an investment. The measure was originally created to encourage managers to invest in projects that would increase a company's profitability. PPT 12-12 applies residual income to the same example used in PPT 12-8, which was used to show that managers may turn down profitable investments to maintain their divisional ROI. The outcome is now different and explains why a significant number of firms have added residual income as a supplementary performance measure. PPT 12-13 compares ROI and RI measures, while PPT 12-14 presents some features of residual income measures.

See PPT 12-12 through 12-14

Measuring the performance of subsidiaries in a multinational firm is complicated by environmental conditions. Because managers are subject to differing environmental factors, the performance of one subsidiary is not directly comparable with that of another. Thus, it has been suggested that the performance of managers be evaluated apart from the performance of the subsidiary itself. Teaching transparency masters (TTM) 12-1 lists general categories of environmental factors affecting multinational firms. These items are discussed in detail in Chapter 13.

See TTM 12-1

IV.   MEASURING AND REWARDING THE PERFORMANCE OF MANAGERS

It is important to determine what factors are under the manager's control. These are the factors to use when determining managerial compensation. Since each manager is different and certain behavior is needed in order to have congruence between the goals of a manager and the owners, compensation plans are important. A well-structured incentive pay plan can help encourage goal congruence between the two parties.

Managerial rewards generally include incentives tied to performance. These rewards include salary increases, bonuses based on reported income, stock options, and noncash compensation.

Income-based compensation can encourage dysfunctional behavior, such as postponing needed maintenance in years when income is down or deferring revenues in years the maximum bonus has been received. PPT 12-16 discusses management compensation.

V.   TRANSFER PRICING

Transfer pricing affects the transferring divisions and overall firm through its impact on divisional performance measures, firm-wide profits, and divisional autonomy. The price charged for a good transferred from one division to another is called the transfer price. The price chosen is important because it affects the profitability of both the selling division (through revenues) and the buying division (it's an input cost).

The trick is to find a transfer price that simultaneously satisfies three objectives: accurate performance evaluation, goal congruence, and divisional autonomy. These are presented on PPT 12-17. Using an opportunity costing approach, it is possible to identify the minimum and maximum transfer prices and use these to determine whether an internal transfer ought to occur. If an outside, perfectly competitive market exists for the intermediate good, then the minimum price = the maximum price and the firm is indifferent to an internal transfer. If an internal transfer does occur, then the optimal transfer price is market price. If the outside market is not perfectly competitive and if the minimum price < the maximum price, then a transfer ought to occur and the minimum and maximum prices identify a negotiation set. In this case, negotiated transfer prices should be used. Cost-based transfer prices are used but have little theoretical justification. Some possible explanations for their use can be offered, however. Full cost may be used because the impact of the transfer on the transferring division's profits is immaterial and the costs of negotiation can be avoided (it is cost-beneficial to use the simple full cost approach). Full cost plus markup may be the outcome of negotiation. This formula could be used until the original conditions change so that renegotiation is mandated. PPT 12-18 discusses several transfer pricing approaches, while PPT 12-19 and 12-20 illustrate a transfer pricing problem.

See PPT 12-17 through 12-20

VI.   INFORMATION ABOUT WARM EXERCISES, EXERCISES, PROBLEMS, AND CASES

For your convenience, exercises and problems are described below according to coverage of content, learning objective(s), and level of difficulty. The time required to solve the problems is roughly proportional to level of difficulty.

In general, *Basic* exercises/problems are fairly simple and straightforward. The text material is relatively brief; only one or two concepts are covered. Basic exercises and problems should take about 15 to 20 minutes.

Moderate exercises/problems may take longer and involve more concepts. These problems may have a "twist" and require more thought. Moderate exercises/problems may take 20 to 40 minutes.

Challenging problems are more comprehensive and may cover more concepts. The text material is relatively longer, and may include some ambiguity. Challenging problems may take 60 to 90 minutes.

Exercise/ Problem	Topical Content (Learning Objective(s))	Level of Difficulty
W12-1	Unit-Cost Calculation (LO 3)	Basic
W12-2	ROI of Individual Projects (LO 3)	Basic
W12-3	Rate of Return on Residual Income (LO 3)	Basic
W12-4	Stock Options (LO 4)	Basic
W12-5	Transfer Pricing (LO 5)	Basic
E12-1	ROI; Margin; Turnover (LO 3)	Basic
E12-2	ROI; Margin; Turnover (LO 3)	Basic
E12-3	ROI and Investment Decisions (LO 3)	Basic
E12-4	Residual Income and Investment Decisions (LO 3)	Basic
E12-5	Transfer Pricing; Outside Market with Full Capacity (LO 5)	Basic
E12-6	Transfer Pricing; Idle Capacity (LO 5)	Basic
E12-7	ROI; Margin; Turnover (LO 3)	Basic
E12-8	ROI and Residual Income (LO 3)	Basic
E12-9	Transfer Pricing and Autonomy (LO 5)	Basic
E12-10	Margin; Turnover; ROI (LO 3)	Basic
E12-11	Residual Income (LO 3)	Basic
E12-12	Transfer Pricing (LO 5)	Moderate
E12-13	Stock Options (LO 4)	Moderate
E12-14	Bonuses and Stock Options (LO 4)	Moderate
E12-15	ROI; Residual Income (LO 3,4)	Moderate
P12-1	Setting Transfer Prices — Market Price versus Full Cost (LO 5)	Moderate
P12-2	Transfer Pricing with Idle Capacity (LO 3,5)	Basic
P12-3	ROI Calculations with Varying Assumptions (LO 3)	Moderate
P12-4	Market Price versus Full Cost Plus (LO 2,3,4,5)	Challenging
P12-5	Full Cost Plus Pricing and Negotiation (LO 5)	Moderate
P12-6	Transfer Pricing: Various Computations (LO 5)	Moderate
P12-7	Transfer Pricing: Custom-made Subassembly (LO 3,5)	Moderate
P12-8	Transfer Pricing and ROI: Various Computations (LO 3,5)	Moderate
P12-9	Transfer Pricing (LO 5)	Challenging
P12-10	Managerial Performance Evaluation (LO 3,4)	Moderate
P12-11	Management Compensation (LO 4)	Challenging
C12-1	ROI and Residual Income; Ethical Considerations	Moderate
C12-2	Transfer Pricing; Behavioral Considerations	Moderate
C12-3	Research Assignment	Challenging

CHAPTER 13

INTERNATIONAL ISSUES IN MANAGEMENT ACCOUNTING

The scenario in this chapter illustrates some of the issues faced by firms selling abroad. This chapter is relevant because of global competition faced by many firms.

LEARNING OBJECTIVES

After studying Chapter 13, students should be able to:

1. Explain the role of the management accountant in the international environment.

2. Discuss the varying levels of involvement that firms can undertake in international trade.

3. Explain the ways management accountants can manage foreign currency risk.

4. Explain why multinational firms choose to decentralize.

5. Explain how environmental factors can affect performance evaluation in the multinational firm.

6. Discuss the role of transfer pricing in the multinational firm.

7. Discuss ethical issues that affect firms operating in the international environment.

KEY TOPICS

The following major topics are covered in this chapter (related learning objectives are listed for each topic).

1. Management accounting in the international environment (learning objective 1)

2. Levels of involvement in international trade (learning objective 2)

3. Foreign currency exchange (learning objective 3)

4. Decentralization (learning objective 4)

5. Measuring performance in the multinational firm (learning objective 5)

6. Transfer pricing and the multinational firm (learning objective 6)

7. Ethics in the international environment (learning objective 7)

I.   MANAGEMENT ACCOUNTING IN THE INTERNATIONAL ENVIRONMENT

The business environment, which exists in the United States, is not universal. There are differences in customs, marketing practices, legal systems, etc. Where does the management accountant fit into the global business environment? The remainder of the chapter discusses this issue. PowerPoint transparency (PPT) 13-4 presents an illustration of these issues.

See PPT 13-4

II.   LEVELS OF INVOLVEMENT IN INTERNATIONAL TRADE

A multinational corporation (MNC) is one that "does business in more than one country in such a volume that its well-being and growth rest in more than one country." A company may be involved in both importing (bring product in from a foreign country) or exporting (shipping to a foreign country) activities.

Companies that import may have a tariff (or duty) added to the goods. A tariff (or duty) is a tax imposed by the federal government. Payment of tariffs can be delayed if a company locates a production facility in a foreign trade zone, which is an area near a customs port of entry that is physically on U. S. soil but considered to be outside U. S. commerce. Tariffs are paid when the finished product leaves the zone.

Multinational corporations may also do business internationally through wholly owned subsidiaries or joint ventures. Many U. S. firms are outsourcing technical and professional jobs. Outsourcing is the payment by a firm for a business function that was formerly done in-house. A special case of a joint venture is the maquiladora, which is a manufacturing plant located in Mexico that processes imported materials and reexports them to the United States. PPT 13-5 provides an overlay for this section.

See PPT 13-5

III.   FOREIGN CURRENCY EXCHANGE

A.   Managing Transaction Risk

When a company becomes an MNC, exchange rates between foreign currency and domestic currency become an issue. Currency risk management is the firm's management of its transaction, economic, and translation exposure due to exchange rate fluctuations. There are a number of risks associated with exchange rates. PPT 13-6 presents the different kinds of foreign currency exchange risks. An example of transaction risk is presented on PPT 13-7.

See PPT 13-6 and 13-7

B.   Managing Economic Risk

Economic risk refers to the possibility that a firm's present value of future cash flows will be affected by exchange fluctuations. When the dollar strengthens, a foreign firm will become more "competitive" in American markets; when the dollar weakens, American exports become relatively cheaper to foreign customers. Hedging is one potential way to manage economic risk. An example of economic risk is illustrated on PPT 13-8.

See PPT 13-8

C.   Managing Translation Risk

Translation risk is the degree to which a firm's financial statements are exposed to exchange rate fluctuations. The key point to make here is that translating foreign currencies into dollars can give false impressions about what is taking place. An example of translation risk is presented on PPT 13-9.

See PPT 13-9

IV.   DECENTRALIZATION

This would be a good time to review PPT 13-10, which discuss the advantages of decentralization in the MNC. In addition, I would suggest why this would improve the company's response to local laws, languages, customs, etc.

See PPT 13-10

V.   MEASURING PERFORMANCE IN THE MULTINATIONAL FIRM

This section discusses measuring performance in a multinational firm. A manager should be evaluated on factors over which he or she exercises control. In addition, comparing divisions from different countries is very difficult because of environmental factors, which are listed on teaching transparency masters (TTM) 13-1.

See TTM 13-1

The authors suggest that multiple measures of performance should be used. Residual income and ROI has a short-run focus. Therefore, top management could look at such factors as market share, customer complaints, personnel turnover ratios, and personnel development. PPT 13-11 illustrates measuring performance in the MNC.

See PPT 13-11

VI. TRANSFER PRICING AND THE MULTINATIONAL FIRM

In a multinational firm, transfer pricing will have an affect on performance evaluation as well as on calculation of income taxes. Both of these are discussed below.

A. Performance Evaluation

In a multinational firm the transfer price is often dictated by the parent corporation. Consequently, the use of ROI and net income are suspect because they are not under the control of divisional managers.

B. Income Taxes and Transfer Pricing

Multinational companies will mandate transfer prices to shift costs to high-tax countries and to shift revenues to low-tax countries. PPT 13-12 reproduces Exhibit 13-3. In addition, PPT 13-13 presents acceptable transfer pricing methods according to IRS regulations.

See PPT 13-12 and 13-13

VII. ETHICS IN THE INTERNATIONAL ENVIRONMENT

Ethics in a foreign country is different from ethics in the United States. I suggest you read through the discussion and present some differences that may occur from one country to another. The chapter ends with the following two questions:

> Is the action right legally?

> Is the action right morally?

To be competitive in a foreign market, an American firm will have to work within the system, but should do so within the mission of the company.

VIII. INFORMATION ABOUT WARM-UP EXERCISES, EXERCISES, PROBLEMS, AND CASES

For your convenience, exercises and problems are described below according to coverage of content, learning objective(s), and level of difficulty. The time required to solve the problems is roughly proportional to level of difficulty.

In general, *Basic* exercises/problems are fairly simple and straightforward. The text material is relatively brief; only one or two concepts are covered. Basic exercises and problems should take about 15 to 20 minutes.

Moderate exercises/problems may take longer and involve more concepts. These problems may have a "twist" and require more thought. Moderate exercises and problems may take 20 to 40 minutes.

Challenging problems are more comprehensive and may cover more concepts. The text material is relatively longer and may include some ambiguity. Challenging problems may take 60 to 90 minutes.

Exercise/ Problem	Topical Content (Learning Objective(s))	Level of Difficulty
W13-1	Payment of Duty and Duty-Related Carrying Cost (LO 2)	Basic
W13-2	Foreign Trade Zone Cost Savings (LO 2)	Basic
W13-3	Exchange Gain and Losses (LO 3)	Basic
W13-4	Hedging (LO 3)	Basic
W13-5	Transfer Pricing (LO 6)	Basic
W13-6	Transfer Pricing (LO 6)	Basic
E13-1	Preparation for Becoming a Management Accountant in an MNC (LO 1)	Basic
E13-2	Foreign Trade Zones (LO 2)	Basic
E13-3	Currency Exchange (LO 3)	Basic
E13-4	Exchange Gains and Losses (LO 3)	Basic
E13-5	Hedging (LO 3)	Basic
E13-6	Currency Exchange Rates (LO 3)	Basic
E13-7	Divisional Performance Evaluation in the MNC (LO 5)	Basic
E13-8	Transfer Pricing in the MNC (LO 6)	Basic
E13-9	Transfer Pricing (LO 6)	Basic
P13-1	Decentralization in the MNC (LO 4)	Moderate
P13-2	Exporting, Maquiladoras, Foreign Trade Zones (LO 2)	Moderate
P13-3	Foreign Currency Exchange, Hedging (LO 3)	Moderate
P13-4	Transfer Pricing (LO 6)	Moderate
P13-5	Transfer Pricing (LO 6)	Moderate
P13-6	Involvement in International Trade (LO 2)	Moderate
C13-1	Transfer Pricing and Ethical Issues	Challenging
C13-2	Transfer Pricing; International Setting; Tax Implications	Challenging
C13-3	Research Assignment	Challenging

CHAPTER 14

VARIABLE COSTING AND SEGMENTAL REPORTING:
TRADITIONAL AND ABC APPROACHES

Coverage of this chapter expands on material outlined briefly in Chapter 2. Here, we use the variable-costing income statement as a way to organize information on cost behavior. A variety of management decision-making applications are presented.

LEARNING OBJECTIVES

After studying Chapter 14, students should be able to:

1. Explain the differences between variable and absorption costing.

2. Explain how variable costing is useful in evaluating the performance of managers.

3. Prepare a segmented income statement based on a variable-costing approach and explain how this format can be used with activity-based costing to assess customer profitability.

4. Explain how variable costing can be used in planning and control.

KEY TOPICS

The following major topics are covered in this chapter (related learning objectives are listed for each topic).

1. Variable costing and absorption costing: An analysis and comparison (learning objective 1)

2. Variable costing and performance evaluation of managers (learning objective 2)

3. Variable costing and segmented reporting (learning objective 3)

4. Variable costing for planning and control (learning objective 4)

I. VARIABLE COSTING AND ABSORPTION COSTING: AN ANALYSIS AND COMPARISON

The opening scenario can be used to convey the idea that there are different ways of assigning product costs and that some ways may be more useful for managerial purposes than other ways. The two product-costing approaches often used are <u>variable costing</u> and <u>absorption costing</u>. Define and discuss how the unit cost is computed under each approach. Most of the discussion up to this point in time has pertained to absorption costing (sometimes referred to as full costing). This chapter is focused on variable costing (sometimes referred to as direct costing). Absorption costing is used for financial accounting and tax preparation, but it is not adequate for internal decision makers. Variable costing is preferred by managerial accountants, but it cannot be used for financial statements or tax purposes. Teaching transparency masters (TTM) 14-1 illustrates the classification of costs as product or period costs under absorption and variable costing.

See TTM 14-1

A. Inventory Valuation

TTM 14-2 provides a numerical example that illustrates how the unit cost is computed for each method. Ask your class why the valuation of the finished goods inventory differs. Emphasize that the only difference between the two methods is how they treat fixed overhead.

See TTM 14-2

B. Income Statements

Using data from TTM 14-2, absorption-costing and variable-costing income statements can be prepared. These statements appear in TTM 14-3. In discussing the two statements, point out that expenses are classified by function for the absorption-costing approach and by behavior for the variable-costing approach. Before showing TTM 14-3, ask the students why the two income figures differ. If they have difficulty with this question, ask them how the two approaches differ. Again ask why the value of the finished goods inventory differs under the two approaches. You might also ask how much fixed overhead is expensed on the income statements for each of the two approaches. At this point, it may help to discuss the relationships between production, sales, and income. This usually helps them visualize how the flow of fixed overhead into and out of inventory can create differences between the two incomes. A good approach is to place the production and sales relationships on the board first and ask the students to predict the income relationships. This information is in Exhibit 14-5 of the textbook.

See TTM 14-3

Exercise 14-2 can be used to check the students' grasp of the basic concepts. The solution for this exercise is provided in TTM 14-4 and 14-5.

See TTM 14-4 and 14-5

II.   VARIABLE COSTING AND PERFORMANCE EVALUATION OF MANAGERS

Students should understand that variable costing cannot be used for external reporting but that it has some definite advantages for internal reporting. Performance evaluation, segment reporting, and planning and control are some reasons for variable costing.

This section discusses how variable-costing income provides a better measure of managerial performance than does absorption-costing income. Use Exercise 14-3 to illustrate this important concept. The solution is given in TTM 14-6 and 14-7.

See TTM 14-6 and 14-7

III.   VARIABLE COSTING AND SEGMENTED REPORTING

Segmented reporting relies on variable costing. It should be pointed out that managers need more detailed information than what appears on financial statements prepared for external users. Specifically, managers need information about segments for decision making and evaluation purposes. Segments are any profit-making unit or activity within an organization. Thus segments can be divisions, plants, products, territories, etc. Exercise 14-5 can be used to show the advantages of variable-costing segmented reports. The solution to this exercise is given in TTM 14-8. As the solution is presented, ask students what information they are using. Then ask if this information would be available on an absorption-costing income statement.

See TTM 14-8

IV.   VARIABLE COSTING FOR PLANNING AND CONTROL

Variable costing facilitates planning and control. What costs should be at various levels of activity can be predicted more accurately when the cost behavior is known. This enables better planning and more reasonable comparisons of actual costs with planned costs.

V.   INFORMATION ABOUT WARM-UP EXERCISES, EXERCISES, PROBLEMS, AND CASES

For your convenience, exercises and problems are described below according to coverage of content, learning objective(s), and level of difficulty. The time required to solve the problems is roughly proportional to level of difficulty.

In general, *Basic* exercises/problems are fairly simple and straightforward. The text material is relatively brief; only one or two concepts are covered. Basic exercises and problems should take about 15 to 20 minutes.

Moderate exercises/problems may take longer and involve more concepts. These problems may have a "twist" and require more thought. Moderate exercises and problems may take 20 to 40 minutes.

Challenging problems are more comprehensive and may cover more concepts. The text material is relatively longer and may include some ambiguity. Challenging problems may take 60 to 90 minutes.

Exercise/ Problem	Topical Content (Learning Objective(s))	Level of Difficulty
W14-1	Inventory Valuation under Absorption and Variable Costing (LO 1)	Basic
W14-2	Income Statements Prepared According to Absorption and Variable Costing (LO 1)	Basic
W14-3	Reconciling the Difference Between Absorption-Costing Income and Variable-Costing Income (LO 1)	Basic
W14-4	Segmented Reporting (LO 3)	Basic
W14-5	Customer Profitability (LO 3)	Basic
E14-1	Unit Costs; Inventory Valuation; Variable and Absorption Costing (LO 1)	Basic
E14-2	Income Statements; Variable and Absorption Costing (LO 1)	Basic
E14-3	Income Statements and Firm Performance: Variable and Absorption Costing (LO 1,2)	Basic
E14-4	Absorption Costing; Variable Costing; Reconciliation with Fixed Overhead Variance (LO 1)	Basic
E14-5	Segmented Income Statements; Product-Line Analysis (LO 3,4)	Basic
E14-6	Product-Line Analysis with Complementary Effects (LO 3,4)	Moderate
E14-7	Absorption Costing; Variable Costing; Income Statements; Inventory Valuations; Income Reconciliation (LO 1)	Basic
E14-8	Variable Costing; Absorption Costing; Income Statements; Inventory Valuation; Underapplied Fixed Overhead (LO 1)	Basic
E14-9	Customer Profitability (LO 3)	Moderate
E14-10	Segmented Income Statements; Absorption Costing; Variable Costing; Regional Analysis (LO 3,4)	Moderate
E14-11	Unit Cost; Inventory Valuation; Absorption and Variable Costing; Contribution Margin (LO 1,4)	Basic
E14-12	Net Income; Absorption and Variable Costing (LO 1)	Basic
E14-13	Inventory Valuation under Absorption and Variable Costing; Variable-Costing Net Income (LO 1)	Basic
E14-14	Calculating Unit and Total Costs under Absorption Costing (LO 1)	Moderate
E14-15	Inventory Valuation and Net Income under Variable Costing (LO 1)	Basic

Exercise/ Problem	Topical Content (Learning Objective(s))	Level of Difficulty
E14-16	Variable and Absorption Costing (LO 1)	Basic
P14-1	Variable- and Absorption-Costing Income Statements (LO 1)	Moderate
P14-2	Variable Costing and Break-even Analysis (LO 1,4)	Moderate
P14-3	Variable Costing; Targeted Net Income (LO 4)	Moderate
P14-4	Segment Analysis; Addition of a New Product (LO 3)	Challenging
P14-5	Income Statements; Variable Costing; Absorption Costing (LO 1)	Moderate
P14-6	Sales; Income Behavior; Variable Costing; Absorption Costing (LO 1)	Moderate
P14-7	Variable Costing; Absorption Costing; Income Statements; Inventory Valuations (LO 1)	Moderate
P14-8	Segmented Income Statements; Analysis of Proposals to Improve Profits (LO 2,3)	Moderate
P14-9	Performance Evaluation; Absorption Costing Compared with Variable Costing (LO 2)	Challenging
P14-10	Absorption Costing and Performance Evaluation (LO 2)	Moderate
P14-11	Comparison of Variable and Absorption Costing; Predetermined Overhead Rates (LO 1)	Moderate
P14-12	Segmented Income Statements; Adding and Dropping Product Lines (LO 2,3)	Moderate
P14-13	Comprehensive Review Problem: Variable Costing, Absorption Costing, Segmented Reporting (LO 1,3)	Challenging
C14-1	Ethical Issues; Absorption Costing; Performance Measurement (LO 1,2)	Basic
C14-2	Variable Costing versus Absorption Costing (LO 1,2,3,4)	Challenging

CHAPTER 15

COST-VOLUME-PROFIT ANALYSIS: A MANAGERIAL PLANNING TOOL

Cost-volume-profit (CVP) analysis can be used to illustrate how managers use accounting data for planning and decision making. Students who enjoy solving puzzles will probably enjoy the discussion of CVP. A more complete analysis of the subject material can be taught by using simple algebra.

LEARNING OBJECTIVES

After studying Chapter 15, students should be able to:

1. Determine the number of units that must be sold to break even or to earn a targeted profit.

2. Determine the amount of revenue required to break even or to earn a targeted profit.

3. Apply cost-volume-profit analysis in a multiple-product setting.

4. Prepare a profit-volume graph and a cost-volume-profit graph and explain the meaning of each.

5. Explain the impact of risk, uncertainty, and changing variables on cost-volume-profit analysis.

6. Discuss the impact of activity-based costing on cost-volume-profit analysis.

KEY TOPICS

The following major topics are covered in this chapter (related learning objectives are listed for each topic).

1. Break-even point in units (learning objective 1)

2. Break-even point in sales dollars (learning objective 2)

3. Multiple-product analysis (learning objective 3)

4. Graphical representation of CVP relationships (learning objective 4)

5. Changes in the CVP variables (learning objective 5)

6. CVP analysis and activity-based costing (learning objective 6)

I. BREAK-EVEN POINT IN UNITS / II. BREAK-EVEN POINT IN SALES DOLLARS

CVP analysis focuses on prices, revenues, volumes, costs, profits, and sales. Many questions involving these six areas can be addressed by CVP analysis. Teaching transparency masters (TTM) 15-1 illustrates some of these questions. PowerPoint transparency (PPT) 15-4 illustrates the benefits of CVP.

See TTM 15-1 and PPT 15-4

Start teaching this area by presenting a series of graphs. First, put separate graphs on the board for total variable costs and total fixed costs. Then, combine these graphs into a third graph and refer to it as a total cost curve. Now, introduce the total revenue graph. Finally, combine the total cost and total revenue graphs into one graph and refer to it as the CVP graph (See Exhibit 15-5). Discuss the basics of the CVP graph. TTM 15-2 can be used for this discussion.

See TTM 15-2

TTM 15-3 presents a simple example, along with the calculations of the break-even points in units and sales dollars using the units-produced approach. A variable-costing income statement and the sales revenue approach are illustrated in TTM 15-4.

See TTM 15-3 AND 15-4

The following questions can be addressed using the same example.

1. What sales in units and dollars are needed to obtain a targeted profit before taxes of $20,000? TTM 15-5 addresses this issue.

2. What sales in units and dollars are needed to obtain a targeted profit after taxes of $24,000? TTM 15-6 and 15-7 address this issue.

3. What sales in dollars is needed to obtain a targeted profit before taxes equal to 20 percent of sales? TTM 15-8 addresses this issue.

4. What sales in dollars is needed to obtain a targeted profit after taxes equal to 6 percent of sales? TTM 15-9 and 15-10 address this issue.

See TTM 15-5 through 15-10

PPT 15-6 through 15-12 present another example.

See PPT 15-6 through 15-12

III. MULTIPLE-PRODUCT ANALYSIS

Students have been taught virtually all the concepts needed to do multiple-product analysis. Therefore, the following example can be put on the board to study multiple-product analysis:

Product	Mix	Price/Unit	VC/Unit
A	3	$ 10	$ 6
B	2	8	5

Total fixed expenses = $180,000

Ask the students how many units of A and how many units of B must be sold to break even. It doesn't take them long to realize that the problem is more complicated than the single-product setting. Explain that the methodology developed for CVP analysis is for a single-product setting. To apply this methodology we must convert the multiple-product problem into a single-product problem. Ask your students how this might be done. Usually, someone will suggest defining the single product as the mix consisting of three units of A and 2 units of B. TTM 15-11 provides the solution to this example. A second example is presented in PPT 15-13 through 15-15.

See TTM 15-11 and PPT 15-13 through 15-15

Teaching hint: Some students worry that they won't choose the "correct" sales mix numbers. You might emphasize that it is the proportion which is important. Solve the above problem using a sales mix of 30 units of A and 20 units of B, or 6 units of A and 4 units of B, to show that the same break-even point is reached.

To illustrate the utility of the sales revenue approach, put the following income statement on the board, and indicate that it corresponds to the statement associated with products A and B.

Sales	$690,000
Less: Variable expenses	420,000
Contribution margin	$270,000
Less: Fixed expenses	180,000
Income before taxes	$ 90,000

Ask the students to compute the revenues needed to break even. This should be a simple task and most should produce the answer of $460,000. Show that this corresponds to the revenues that would be produced by selling 30,000 units of A and 20,000 units of B. The process, however, is much simpler than the units-sold approach.

IV.   GRAPHICAL REPRESENTATION OF CVP RELATIONSHIPS

This section discusses the cost-volume-profit and profit-volume graphs. The CVP graph was presented in TTM 15-2. The profit-volume graph is presented in TTM 15-12. You may wish to discuss the following before pointing out the profit-volume graph.

$$\text{Income (I)} = \text{Total Revenues (R)} - \text{Total Costs (C)}$$

$$I = R - TC$$

$$I = PX - F - VX$$

$$I = (P-V)X - F$$

Therefore; the slope of the profit line is the contribution margin per unit and the Y-intercept is a negative fixed cost.

See TTM 15-12

There are a number of limitations of CVP analysis mentioned by Hansen and Mowen. These limitations are presented on TTM 15-13.

See TTM 15-13

V.   CHANGES IN THE CVP VARIABLES

This section briefly discusses margin of safety and the operating leverage. Margin of safety is defined as the difference between sales (actual or expected) and the break-even volume. TTM 15-14 shows a simple example of the margin of safety in sales.

See TTM 15-14

Operating leverage is concerned with the relative mix of fixed and variable costs. This tradeoff affects the amount by which profits will change as sales fluctuate and is measured by the degree of operating leverage (CM/Profit) using a given level of sales as the reference point. Once the degree of operating leverage (DOL) is computed, the percentage change in profits is computed by multiplying the percentage change in profits by the DOL. TTM 15-15 illustrates the degree of operating leverage.

See TTM 15-15

An important tool is sensitivity analysis, a "what-if" technique that examines the impact of changes in underlying assumptions on an answer. Spreadsheets can effortlessly handle the many computations.

VI. CVP ANALYSIS AND ACTIVITY-BASED COSTING

CVP analysis changes slightly under ABC. PPT 15-18 and 15-19 illustrate the calculations.

See PPT 15-18 and 15-19

VII. INFORMATION ABOUT WARM-UP EXERCISES, EXERCISES, PROBLEMS, AND CASES

For your convenience, exercises and problems are described below according to coverage of content, learning objective(s), and level of difficulty. The time required to solve the problems is roughly proportional to level of difficulty.

In general, *Basic* exercises/problems are fairly simple and straightforward. The text material is relatively brief; only one or two concepts are covered. Basic exercises and problems should take about 15 to 20 minutes.

Moderate exercises/problems may take longer and involve more concepts. These problems may have a "twist" and require more thought. Moderate exercises and problems may take 20 to 40 minutes.

Challenging problems are more comprehensive and may cover more concepts. The text material is relatively longer and may include some ambiguity. Challenging problems may take 60 to 90 minutes.

Exercise/ Problem	Topical Content (Learning Objective(s))	Level of Difficulty
W15-1	Breakeven in units (LO 1)	Basic
W15-2	Contribution Margin Ratio, Variable Cost Ratio, Breakeven in Sales Revenue (LO 2)	Basic
W15-3	Multiple-Product Breakeven (LO 3)	Basic
W15-4	Margin of Safety and Degree of Operating Leverage (LO 5)	Basic

Exercise/ Problem	Topical Content (Learning Objective(s))	Level of Difficulty
W15-5	CVP and Activity-based Costing (LO 6)	Basic
E15-1	Units Sold; After-Tax Profit; Margin of Safety (LO 2,5)	Basic
E15-2	Contribution Margin; Unit Amounts (LO 1,2)	Basic
E15-3	CVP; Margin of Safety (LO 2,5)	Basic
E15-4	CVP (LO 1,2)	Basic
E15-5	Contribution Margin; CVP; Net Income; Margin of Safety (LO 1,2,5)	Basic
E15-6	Sales Revenue Approach; Variable Cost Ratio; Contribution Margin Ratio; Margin of Safety (LO 2,5)	Basic
E15-7	CVP Analysis with Target Profits (LO 2)	Basic
E15-8	Operating Leverage (LO 5)	Basic
E15-9	CVP Analysis with Multiple Products (LO 3)	Basic
E15-10	Contribution Analysis (LO 1,2)	Basic
E15-11	Changes in Break-even Points with Changes in Unit Prices (LO 1,2)	Basic
E15-12	CVP and Profit-Volume Graphs (LO 4)	Basic
E15-13	Basic CVP Concepts (LO 1,2)	Moderate
E15-14	CVP; Before- and After-Tax Targeted Net Income (LO 1,2)	Basic
E15-15	Multiproduct Breakeven (LO 3)	Moderate
P15-1	Basic CVP Concepts (LO 1,2,5)	Moderate
P15-2	Multiple-Product Analysis; Changes in Sales Mix (LO 3)	Moderate
P15-3	CVP Equation; Basic Concepts; Solving for Unknowns (LO 1,2)	Moderate
P15-4	CVP Analysis with Multiple Services (LO 3)	Challenging
P15-5	Basics of the Sales Revenue Approach (LO 2,5)	Moderate
P15-6	CVP Analysis: Sales Revenue Approach; Pricing; After-Tax Profit Target (LO 2)	Moderate
P15-7	CVP with Multiple Products; Sales Mix Changes; Changes in Fixed and Variable Costs (LO 3)	Moderate
P15-8	Multiple Products; Break-even Analysis; Operating Leverage (LO 3,5)	Basic
P15-9	Multiproduct Breakeven (LO 3)	Basic
P15-10	CVP; Margin of Safety (LO 2,5)	Basic
P15-11	Multiplant Breakeven (LO 2,3)	Challenging
P15-12	CVP Analysis and Assumptions (LO 2,6)	Challenging
C15-1	Ethics and a CVP Application (LO 1)	Challenging
C15-2	Service Organization; Multiple Products; Breakeven; Pricing and Scheduling Decisions (LO 1,2,3)	Challenging

CHAPTER 16

TACTICAL DECISION MAKING: RELEVANT COSTING, THE ACTIVITY RESOURCE USAGE MODEL, AND PRICING

This chapter deals with relevant information and how it is used in short-run decisions.

LEARNING OBJECTIVES

After studying Chapter 16, students should be able to:

1. Describe and explain the tactical decision-making model.

2. Explain how the activity resource usage model is used in assessing relevancy.

3. Apply the tactical decision-making concepts in a variety of business situations.

4. Choose the optimal product mix when faced with one constrained resource.

5. Explain the impact of cost on pricing decisions.

6. Use linear programming to find the optimal solution to a problem of multiple constrained resources. (Appendix)

KEY TOPICS

The following major topics are covered in this chapter (related learning objectives are listed for each topic).

1. Tactical decision making (learning objective 1)

2. Relevancy, cost behavior, and the activity resource usage model (learning objective 2)

3. Illustrative examples of relevant cost application (learning objective 3)

4. Product mix decisions (learning objective 4)

5. Pricing (learning objective 5)

6. Appendix: Linear programming (learning objective 6)

I. TACTICAL DECISION MAKING

Fundamental to the decision process described in the chapter is the understanding of relevant and irrelevant costs. Start by reviewing the introductory case dealing with Tidwell Products. Once the two alternatives are identified, indicate that, all other things being equal, the company should choose the least costly alternative.

Then, indicate that in choosing the least costly alternative only those costs that are relevant to the decision should be considered. This provides a natural framework for defining and illustrating relevant costs. PowerPoint transparency (PPT) 16-6 provides the definition. PPT 16-7 presents the types of decisions illustrated in this chapter.

See PPT 16-6 and 16-7

The activity resource usage model and assessing relevancy is illustrated on PPT 16-8 through 16-10. These transparencies cover the material in Exhibit 16-2 in the textbook. PPT 16-8 focuses on the acquired as used and needed costs, while acquired in advance costs (short term) are illustrated on PPT 16-9. Finally, acquired in advance costs (multi-period capacity) is discussed with PPT 16-10.

See PPT 16-8 through 16-10

II. RELEVANCY, COST BEHAVIOR, AND THE ACTIVITY RESOURCE USAGE MODEL

PPT 16-4 and 16-5 list the six steps that describe the decision-making model. Covering these steps and using the opening scenario (or your own example) to illustrate each step is recommended. As step six is covered, the limitations of the decision model should be detailed. Essentially, students should understand that the quantitative analysis is but one of several inputs required for the decision. The next section discusses relevant information, cost behavior, and the activity resource usage model.

See PPT 16-4 and 16-5

III. ILLUSTRATIVE EXAMPLES OF RELEVANT COST APPLICATION

We all are aware of the need of quantitative numbers to make decisions, but there is a need to examine qualitative factors. Many times it is difficult to quantify qualitative factors, such as quality of materials, late orders, customer relations, etc. Qualitative factors are very important when making decisions. We will examine qualitative factors in Exercise 16-5 in the next section.

There are four major types of relevant costing decisions mentioned in this section: make or buy, keep or drop, special order, and sell or process further. Exercises 16-3 through 16-6 can be used to illustrate each of the decision types. The next section and the appendix deal with product mix decisions. Teaching transparency masters (TTM) 16-1 through 16-5 provide solutions to each of these exercises. The solution to 16-5 uses incremental unit costs to illustrate an alternative approach.

See TTM 16-1 through 16-5

IV. PRODUCT MIX DECISIONS

The product mix decision is broken up into two categories: (1) one constrained resource and (2) multiple constrained resources. This section addresses the one constrained resource problems, while the Appendix deals with the multiple constraint resources. Ask students how many units of each product they would produce. Some may recognize that the product with the highest contribution margin per unit of scarce resource should be produced. TTM 16-6 provides an example for a one constrained resource.

See TTM 16-6

V. PRICING

PPT 16-20 presents two approaches to pricing: (1) market-driven prices and (2) cost prices. Some types of costs are presented in PPT 16-21. PPT 16-22 through 16-24 present an example and determine selling price.

See PPT 16-20 through 16-24

VI. APPENDIX: LINEAR PROGRAMMING

The multiple constrained resource setting requires linear programming. An elementary introduction is available in the Appendix to the chapter for a two-variable setting. TTM 16-7 and 16-8 provide an illustrative example.

See TTM 16-7 and 16-8

VII. INFORMATION ABOUT WARM-UP EXERCISES, EXERCISES, PROBLEMS, AND CASES

For your convenience, exercises and problems are described below according to coverage of content, learning objective(s), and level of difficulty. The time required to solve the problems is roughly proportional to level of difficulty.

In general, *Basic* exercises/problems are fairly simple and straightforward. The text material is relatively brief; only one or two concepts are covered. Basic exercises and problems should take about 15 to 20 minutes.

Moderate exercises/problems may take longer and involve more concepts. These problems may have a "twist" and require more thought. Moderate exercises and problems may take 20 to 40 minutes.

Challenging problems are more comprehensive and may cover more concepts. The text material is relatively longer and may include some ambiguity. Challenging problems may take 60 to 90 minutes.

Exercise/ Problem	Topical Content (Learning Objective(s))	Level of Difficulty
W16-1	Make-or-Buy Decision (LO 3)	Basic
W16-2	Keep-or-Drop Decision (LO 3)	Basic
W16-3	Special-Order Decision (LO 3)	Basic
W16-4	Sell at Split-off or Process Further Decision (LO 3)	Basic
W16-5	Product Mix Decision with One Constrained Resource(LO 4)	Basic
W16-6	Cost-based Pricing Decision (LO 5)	Basic
W16-7	Linear Programming Decision (LO 6)	Basic
E16-1	Lease Decision; Relevance of Book Value (LO 1,2,3)	Basic
E16-2	Keep or Buy; Sunk Costs (LO 1,2,3)	Basic
E16-3	Make or Buy (LO 1,2,3)	Basic
E16-4	Keep or Drop; Product Substitutes (LO 1,2,3)	Basic
E16-5	Special-Order Decision; Qualitative Aspects (LO 1,2,3)	Basic
E16-6	Sell or Process Further; Basic Analysis (LO 1,2,3)	Basic
E16-7	Product Mix Decision; Single Constraint (LO 4)	Basic
E16-8	Appendix Required: Product Mix; Multiple Constraints (LO 5,6)	Moderate
E16-9	Buy or Keep; Identification of Relevant Costs and Benefits (LO 2,3)	Basic
E16-10	Keep or Drop; Complementary Effects (LO 2,3)	Basic
E16-11	Special Order (LO 2,3)	Basic
E16-12	Product Mix Decision; Single Constraint (LO 4)	Basic
E16-13	Effect of Opportunity Cost on Pricing Decision (LO 1,2)	Moderate
E16-14	Make or Buy (LO 2,3)	Basic
E16-15	Comparison of Alternatives (LO 1,2,3)	Moderate
E16-16	Special Order (LO 2,3)	Moderate
E16-17	Relevant Costs (LO 1,2,3)	Basic
P16-1	Make or Buy; Qualitative Considerations (LO 1,2,3)	Moderate
P16-2	Sell or Process Further (LO 1,2,3)	Moderate
P16-3	Keep or Drop (LO 1,2,3)	Moderate
P16-4	Accept or Reject a Special Order (LO 2,3)	Moderate
P16-5	Keep or Drop a Division (LO 2,3)	Moderate
P16-6	Plant Shutdown or Continue to Operate; Qualitative Considerations (LO 2,3)	Challenging

Exercise/ Problem	Topical Content (Learning Objective(s))	Level of Difficulty
P16-7	Appendix Required: Product Mix Decision; Single and Multiple Constraints; Basics of Linear Programming (LO 4,6)	Moderate
P16-8	Keep or Drop; Product Mix (LO 2,3)	Challenging
P16-9	Appendix Required: Product Mix Decisions (LO 4,6)	Challenging
P16-10	Make or Buy (LO 2,3)	Challenging
P16-11	Make or Buy (LO 1,2,3)	Challenging
P16-12	Make or Buy (LO 1,2,3)	Challenging
C16-1	Make or Buy: Ethical Considerations (LO 1,2,3,6)	Challenging
C16-2	Centralize versus Decentralize (LO 1,2,3)	Challenging
C16-3	Research Assignment	Challenging

CHAPTER 17

CAPITAL INVESTMENT DECISIONS

This chapter covers the basic capital budgeting models. Taxes are considered later in the chapter. The focus of the chapter is on learning how to apply the models.

LEARNING OBJECTIVES

After studying Chapter 17, students should be able to:

1. Explain what a capital investment decision is and distinguish between independent and mutually exclusive capital investment decisions.

2. Compute the payback period and accounting rate of return for a proposed investment and explain their roles in capital investment decisions.

3. Use net present value analysis for capital investment decisions involving independent projects.

4. Use the internal rate of return to assess the acceptability of independent projects.

5. Explain the role and value of postaudits.

6. Explain why NPV is better than IRR for capital investment decisions involving mutually exclusive projects.

7. Convert gross cash flows to after-tax cash flows

8. Describe capital investment in the advanced manufacturing environment.

KEY TOPICS

The following major topics are covered in this chapter (related learning objectives are listed for each topic).

1. Types of capital investment decisions (learning objective 1)

2. Nondiscounting models (learning objective 2)

3. Discounting models: The net present value method (learning objective 3)

4. Internal rate of return (learning objective 4)

5. Postaudit of capital projects (learning objective 5)

6. Mutually exclusive projects (learning objective 6)

7. Computation and adjustment of cash flows (learning objective 7)

8. Capital investment: The advanced manufacturing environment (learning objective 8)

I. **TYPES OF CAPITAL INVESTMENT DECISIONS**

The opening scenario illustrates what capital budgeting is about and reveals the importance of both qualitative and quantitative factors. Begin by quickly reviewing the scenario and presenting a definition of capital budgeting. Next indicate that capital budgeting decisions are concerned with two types of projects: **independent projects** and **mutually exclusive projects**. Teaching transparency master (TTM) 17-1 provides the definitions to capital budgeting and these types of projects.

See TTM 17-1

II. **NONDISCOUNTING MODELS**

Managers must have some basic criteria for accepting or rejecting proposed investments when making capital budgeting decisions. Hansen and Mowen discuss four basic methods that can be used by managers to assist in making these decisions. These methods can be categorized as nondiscounting models and discounting models. There are two methods for each category. Since nondiscounting models are the simplest and can be used to motivate the use of discounting models, they are discussed first. The discounting models are discussed later in the chapter.

A. **Payback Period**

The **payback period** is the time required for a firm to recover its original investment. This method continues to be widely used, although it is rarely used by itself. The fact that it continues to be used, however, suggests that it must convey some useful information to management. When the cash flows of a project are assumed to be even, the following formula can be used.

$$\text{Payback period} = \frac{\text{Original investment}}{\text{Annual cash flow}}$$

TTM 17-2 provides the definition, an illustrative application, some possible reasons why the method continues to be used, and its major deficiencies. This transparency examines annual cash flows that are uneven.

See TTM 17-2

B. Accounting Rate of Return

The accounting rate of return measures the return on a project in terms of income, as opposed to using the project's cash flow. The accounting rate of return is computed by the following formula:

$$\text{Accounting rate of return} = \frac{\text{Average income}}{\text{Investment}}$$

Average income can be found by adding the net income for each year and dividing this total by the number of years. Investment can be defined as original investment or average investment, where the latter is found by adding the original investment to the salvage value and dividing this total by two. The definition, an illustrative application, possible reasons for continued use, and deficiencies of the accounting rate of return are provided by TTM 17-3.

See TTM 17-3

III. DISCOUNTING MODELS: THE NET PRESENT VALUE METHOD

A. Future Value

The payback period and the accounting rate of return both ignore the time value of money. Specifically, they fail to acknowledge the fact that a dollar received today is worth more than a dollar received one year (or further) in the future. The reason that a dollar received today is worth more than one received tomorrow is because it can be invested to earn a return. The Appendix discusses time value of money.

Thus, the **future value** of a dollar invested today is the original dollar plus the return (or interest). The interest can be either simple or compound. The interest is simple if it is paid each interest period and it is compound interest if the interest remains invested so that interest is earned on interest. Compound interest is assumed. TTM 17-4 illustrates the computation of future value.

See TTM 17-4

B. Present Value

For capital budgeting decisions, managers need to know how to convert future cash flows into present values (i.e., how much must be invested now to earn some future amount). This can be computed by solving for P in the equation developed for future value.

This process of computing the present value of a future amount is called discounting, which can be done either by using the equation directly for computing the present value or by using tabled discount factors (these tables appear at the end of the chapter). There are two tables of discount factors: one to compute the present value of individual amounts and one for computing the present value of a uniform series of cash flows. TTM 17-5 and 17-6 illustrate the computation of present value using the tabled values.

See TTM 17-5 and 17-6

Teaching hint: Work several scenarios in front of the class using Exhibit 17B-1 in the Appendix. Each example becomes a little more difficult. For example, work the following types of problems:

1. How much will I need to deposit today in a fund paying 24 percent, compounded annually, in order to have $10,000 at the end of four years?

2. How much will I need to deposit today in a fund paying 24 percent, compounded semi-annually, in order to have $10,000 at the end of four years?

3. How much will I need to deposit today in a fund paying 24 percent, compounded quarterly, in order to have $10,000 at the end of four years?

4. How much will I need to deposit today in a fund paying 10 percent, compounded annually, in order to be able to withdraw $1,000 at the end of year 1, $3,000 at the end of year 2, and $5,000 at the end of year 3?

5. How much will I need to deposit today in a fund paying 10 percent, compounded annually, in order to be able to withdraw $2,000 annually for the next five years?

First solve these five problems using Exhibit 17B-1, then discuss how to use Exhibit 17B-2 to simplify the calculations for the last problem.

C.   Net Present Value

Net present value (NPV) is the difference between the present value of a project's future cash flows and the present value of the project's cost. Present value is computed using the cost of capital (required rate of return). The **cost of capital** (required rate of return) is the weighted average of the returns expected by those contributing the investment funds. The NPV method is defined and discussed in TTM 17-7 and 17-8. TTM 17-9 defines and illustrates the cost of capital.

See TTM 17-7 through 17-9

IV.   INTERNAL RATE OF RETURN

The **internal rate of return (IRR)** is defined as the interest rate that sets the present value of future cash flows equal to the investment (the point where NPV = 0). The IRR method is defined and discussed in TTM 17-10. Exercise 17-8 is recommended for a more detailed illustration of IRR.

See TTM 17-10

V.   POSTAUDIT OF CAPITAL PROJECTS

Essentially, postaudits are designed to compare the actual performance of a capital investment with its expected performance. The outcome of a postaudit may result in corrective actions or even abandonment of the project (as the company described in the scenario did).

VI.   MUTUALLY EXCLUSIVE PROJECTS

In choosing among competing projects, IRR may lead to the wrong choice whereas NPV is consistent in providing the correct signal. An example illustrating this outcome is provided in TTM 17-11 and 17-12. Because NPV consistently selects the wealth-maximizing alternative and IRR does not, NPV is generally preferred to IRR for choosing among competing projects.

See TTM 17-11 and 17-12

For mutually exclusive projects, the NPV method is recommended. There are three steps associated with this approach: (1) assessing the cash- flow pattern for each project, (2) computing the NPV, and (3) selecting the project with the largest NPV. Before presenting examples for the NPV method, the issues surrounding cash flows should be discussed. These issues have been broken down into two major categories: (1) forecasting cash flows, and (2) conversion of gross cash flows to after-tax cash flows. The next section focuses on these issues.

VII. COMPUTATION AND ADJUSTMENT OF CASH FLOWS

A. Forecasting Cash Flows

Soundness of Assumptions. Although no formal models of forecasting are discussed, students should understand that forecasting is a critical part of the capital budgeting process. The assumptions underlying the forecast should be understood. Both technical and planning assumptions should be made explicit. **Technical assumptions** deal with the statistical models used to forecast future cash flows. **Planning assumptions** relate to the marketing and production strategies associated with the project.

Sensitivity Analysis. Sensitivity analysis is important because of the uncertainty involved in forecasting future cash flows. Considerable insight can be gained about the attractiveness of a project by altering the values of key variables and assessing the effect on the initial outcome. An example illustrating sensitivity analysis is provided in TTM 17-13.

See TTM 17-13

Effects of Inflation. The effect inflation will have on the forecast should also be described. The cost of capital should reflect a real rate of return plus an inflationary component, while future cash flows should be restated to reflect the expected inflation rate. Since the cost of capital reflects an inflationary component at the time NPV analysis is performed, restating future cash flows to reflect inflation is the key adjustment. An example illustrating how to adjust future cash flows for inflation is provided in TTM 17-14.

See TTM 17-14

B. Computation of After-Tax Cash Flows

Operating cash flows can be computed in one of two ways: (1) the income approach, and (2) the decomposition approach.

Income Approach. Operating cash flows can be computed directly by adding noncash expenses to after-tax net income. The income approach is defined and illustrated in TTM 17-15.

See TTM 17-15

Decomposition Approach. Operating cash flows can also be computed by calculating the after-tax cash flows for each *item* of the income statement. The decomposition approach is defined and illustrated in TTM 17-16. This approach is very useful since it allows computation of after-tax cash flows without preparation of an income statement. It also can be used in a spreadsheet format.

See TTM 17-16

Teaching hint: Once the general details of the two procedures are discussed, the role of depreciation should be discussed. As the after-tax cash flow computations are shown, the role of depreciation in generating cash flows could be described. Begin by asking students how depreciation, a noncash expense, can be part of an after-tax cash flow computation. Shielding revenues from taxation should be the response. Some students may see this immediately. Many will not. TTM 17-17 and 17-18 illustrate the shielding effect of depreciation.

See TTM 17-17 and 17-18

Depreciation and Tax Laws. TTM 17-19 through 17-21 summarize the current tax laws that pertain to depreciation.

Teaching hint: After displaying TTM 17-19 through 17-21, ask the students which of the two methods would be preferred: straight line with a half-life convention or MACRS. Most will select MACRS. Ask them to explain why.

See TTM 17-19 through 17-21

There is a need for rationing whenever a firm does not have enough capital funds to do all projects with a positive NPV. The net present value index can be used to ration capital funds. Integer programming models are used when partial investments are not allowed. This approach is not discussed in this textbook because of the advanced nature of the methodology. Capital rationing is illustrated in TTM 17-22 for independent projects with partial investment allowed.

See TTM 17-22

VIII.   CAPITAL INVESTMENT: THE ADVANCED MANUFACTURING ENVIRONMENT

All the discounting methodology continues to be fully applicable; however, more attention must be paid to inputs.

A.   Tangible and Intangible Benefits

Operating cash flows should reflect both tangible and intangible benefits. Companies considering automation should ask the following, "What will be the impact on cash flows if the investment is not made?" This question should be answered assuming the competitors are or are not making similar investments.

B. Salvage Value

Salvage value should be explicitly considered. It may mean the difference between acceptance or rejection. TTM 17-23 provides an example that illustrates points A, B, and C.

C. Discount Rate

In addition to the increasing importance of intangible benefits, it is also becoming more critical to use the correct discount rate. Many times firms will use required rates of return that are well above their cost of capital, which creates a bias against long-term projects that may offer larger cash flows in later years.

See TTM 17-23

IX. INFORMATION ABOUT WARM-UP EXERCISES, EXERCISES, PROBLEMS, AND CASES

For your convenience, exercises and problems are described below according to coverage of content, learning objective(s), and level of difficulty. The time required to solve the problems is roughly proportional to level of difficulty.

In general, *Basic* exercises/problems are fairly simple and straightforward. The text material is relatively brief; only one or two concepts are covered. Basic exercises and problems should take about 15 to 20 minutes.

Moderate exercises/problems may take longer and involve more concepts. These problems may have a "twist" and require more thought. Moderate exercises and problems may take 20 to 40 minutes.

Challenging problems are more comprehensive and may cover more concepts. The text material is relatively longer and may include some ambiguity. Challenging problems may take 60 to 90 minutes.

Exercise/ Problem	Topical Content (Learning Objective(s))	Level of Difficulty
W17-1	Payback Period; ARR (LO 2)	Basic
W17-2	NPV (LO 3)	Basic
W17-3	IRR; Even Cash Flows (LO 4)	Basic
W17-4	Mutually Exclusive Projects (LO 5)	Basic
W17-5	After-tax Cash Flows (LO 6)	Basic
E17-1	Basic Concepts (LO 1,2,3,4)	Basic
E17-2	Payback; Accounting Rate of Return; NPV; IRR (LO 1,2,3,4)	Moderate
E17-3	Payback; Accounting Rate of Return; Present Value; NPV; IRR (LO 1,2,3,4)	Moderate
E17-4	NPV; Accounting Rate of Return; Payback (LO 1,2,3)	Moderate

Exercise/ Problem	Topical Content (Learning Objective(s))	Level of Difficulty
E17-5	NPV: Basic Concepts (LO 3)	Basic
E17-6	NPV; Cost of Capital; Basic Concepts (LO 3)	Basic
E17-7	Solving for Unknowns (LO 3,4)	Moderate
E17-8	NPV versus IRR (LO 6)	Basic
E17-9	Computation of After-Tax Cash Flows (LO 7)	Basic
E17-10	MACRS; NPV (LO 7)	Basic
E17-11	Discount Rates: Advanced Manufacturing Environment (LO 8)	Moderate
E17-12	Quality; Market Share; Advanced Manufacturing Environment (LO 8)	Moderate
P17-1	Basic NPV Analysis (LO 1,3)	Basic
P17-2	NPV Analysis (LO 1,3)	Basic
P17-3	Basic IRR Analysis (LO 1,4)	Moderate
P17-4	NPV; IRR; Uncertainty (LO 1,3)	Challenging
P17-5	Review of Basic Capital Investment Procedures (LO 1,2,3,4)	Moderate
P17-6	Replacement Decision; Basic NPV Analysis (LO 1,6,7)	Moderate
P17-7	Lease versus Buy (LO 1,6,7)	Moderate
P17-8	Competing Investments; NPV; Basic Analysis (LO 1,6,7)	Basic
P17-9	Capital Investment; Advanced Manufacturing Environment (LO 7,8)	Moderate
P17-10	Postaudit; Sensitivity Analysis (LO 5,6,7)	Moderate
P17-11	Capital Investment; Discount Rates; Intangible Benefits; Time Horizon; Advanced Manufacturing Environment (LO 7,8)	Challenging
P17-12	Inflation and Capital Investment (LO 3,4)	Moderate
C17-1	Capital Investment and Ethical Behavior (LO 3)	Moderate
C17-2	Managerial Decision Case: Payback; NPV; IRR; Effect of Differences in Sales on Project Viability (LO 2,3,4)	Challenging
C17-3	Cash Flows; NPV; Choice of Discount Rate; Advanced Manufacturing Environment (LO 1,6,7,8)	Challenging
C17-4	Research Assignment	Challenging

CHAPTER 18

INVENTORY MANAGEMENT

The coverage of the material in this chapter is less vital than other chapters.

LEARNING OBJECTIVES

After studying Chapter 18, students should be able to:

1. Describe the traditional inventory management model.

2. Describe JIT inventory management.

3. Describe the theory of constraints and explain how it can be used to manage inventory.

KEY TOPICS

The following major topics are covered in this chapter (related learning objectives are listed for each topic).

1. Traditional inventory management (learning objective 1)

2. JIT inventory management (learning objective 2)

3. Theory of constraints (learning objective 3)

I. TRADITIONAL INVENTORY MANAGEMENT

There are three basic costs associated with inventory when it is purchased from an outside supplier. These are:

1. Ordering costs
2. Carrying costs
3. Stockout costs

Teaching transparency master (TTM) 18-1 provides the definitions and examples of each cost. Ordering costs are replaced by setup costs when the goods are produced internally.

See TTM 18-1

A. Inventory: Why is It Needed?

Why is inventory needed? TTM 18-2 lists some of the reasons commonly offered for keeping inventory. These reasons are still valid for many organizations.

See TTM 18-2

Teaching hint: It may be appropriate to briefly discuss JIT concepts at this time. Students should be aware that traditional approaches to inventory have changed greatly.

B. Economic Order Quantity (EOQ)

A firm that keeps inventory must address the following two questions:

1.   How much inventory should be ordered (or produced)?

2.   When should the order be placed (or the setup done)?

PowerPoint transparency (PPT) 18-6 presents these two questions.

See PPT 18-6

The economic order quantity (EOQ) model will need to be used to answer both questions in a traditional firm. The amount ordered (produced) depends on the trade-off between ordering (setup) costs and carrying costs. PPT 18-4 and 18-5 graphically illustrate inventory when purchasing outside or producing internally, respectively.

See PPT 18-4 and 18-5

Minimizing carrying costs favors ordering or producing in small lot sizes, whereas minimizing ordering costs (setup costs) favors large, infrequent orders (long, infrequent production runs). The quantity that minimizes total ordering (setup) and carrying costs is defined as the **economic order quantity**. TTM 18-3 presents the total cost equation for inventory and the equation for economic order quantity. TTM 18-4 and 18-5 provide an illustrative application.

See TTM 18-3 through 18-5

C. Reorder Point

The second question deals with the reorder point, which is the point in time a new order should be placed (or another setup started). The reorder point is based on how many units are left in inventory. The activity needed for replacement should begin when inventory drops to a certain level. The reorder point is easily computed as follows when the rate of usage is known with certainty:

Reorder point = Rate of usage x Lead time

Determining the reorder point is more difficult when there is uncertainty in the lead time or usage. Many firms respond to this uncertainty by building in a buffer known as safety stock. The reorder point incorporating safety stock is computed as follows:

Reorder point = (Average rate of usage x Lead time) + Safety stock

TTM 18-6 defines and illustrates the reorder point when demand is certain while TTM 18-7 illustrates it when demand is uncertain. TTM 18-8 illustrates the reorder point in graph form.

See TTM 18-6 through 18-8

II.   JIT INVENTORY MANAGEMENT

A.   Inventories

The traditional approach to inventory management assumes that inventories are needed and supplies reasons to justify the need. Increased competition based on product diversity, quality, specialized features, and shorter life cycles have led many firms to reject the traditional EOQ model in favor of the JIT model. JIT can offer greater cost efficiency and more flexibility to respond to customer demands. PPT 18-11 compares traditional versus JIT inventory procedures.

See PPT 18-11

Teaching hint: Place TTM 18-2 on the screen once again to review the conventional wisdom for inventories. Then indicate that JIT responds to these reasons in a much different way than the conventional approach. The difference can create higher quality, more flexibility, and greater cost efficiency. How JIT responds to the traditional reasons for inventory is summarized in TTM 18-9 and 18-10, which also provide the opportunity to discuss JIT purchasing. It should be made clear to the students that lowering inventories to insignificant levels is the *ideal* goal in the JIT environment. Most firms should be able to lower their inventory levels.

See TTM 18-9 and 18-10

B.   Kanban System

The Kanban system is used to ensure that parts or materials are available when needed. The **Kanban system** is an information system that controls production by using markers or cards. It is responsible for ensuring that the necessary products are produced (or acquired) in the necessary quantities at the necessary time. It is the heart of the JIT system.

The basic Kanban system uses three cards: a withdrawal Kanban, a production Kanban, and a vendor Kanban. A **withdrawal Kanban** specifies the quantity that a subsequent process should withdraw from the preceding process. A **production Kanban** specifies the quantity that the preceding process should produce. **Vendor Kanbans** are used to notify suppliers to deliver more parts. These items are listed on PPT 18-12. The **Kanban system** is further illustrated with PPT 18-13 to 18-16.

See PPT 18-12 through 18-16

III.   THEORY OF CONSTRAINTS

Three measures of organizational performance for the theory of constraint is presented in PPT 18-17. Meanwhile, the five steps to improve performances is discussed on PPT 18-18. Finally, a brief flow chart is shown on PPT 18-19 illustrating the **Drum-Buffer-Rope System**.

See PPT 18-17 through 18-19

IV.   INFORMATION ABOUT WARM-UP EXERCISES, EXERCISES, PROBLEMS, AND CASES

For your convenience, exercises and problems are described below according to coverage of content, learning objective(s), and level of difficulty. The time required to solve the problems is roughly proportional to level of difficulty.

In general, *Basic* exercises/problems are fairly simple and straightforward. The text material is relatively brief; only one or two concepts are covered. Basic exercises and problems should take about 15 to 20 minutes.

Moderate exercises/problems may take longer and involve more concepts. These problems may have a "twist" and require more thought. Moderate exercises and problems may take 20 to 40 minutes.

Challenging problems are more comprehensive and may cover more concepts. The text material is relatively longer and may include some ambiguity. Challenging problems may take 60 to 90 minutes.

Exercise/ Problem	Topical Content (Learning Objective(s))	Level of Difficulty
W18-1	Inventory Costs (LO 1)	Basic
W18-2	EOQ (LO 1)	Basic
W18-3	Reorder Point (LO 1)	Basic
W18-4	Optimal Mix (LO 3)	Basic
E18-1	Ordering and Carrying Costs (LO 1)	Basic
E18-2	Economic Order Quantity (LO 1)	Basic
E18-3	Economic Order Quantity (LO 1)	Basic
E18-4	Reorder Point (LO 1)	Basic
E18-5	EOQ with Setup Costs; Reorder Point; Production Scheduling (LO 1)	Basic
E18-6	Safety Stock (LO 1)	Basic
E18-7	Reasons for Carrying Inventory (LO 1,2,3)	Basic
E18-8	Kanban Cards (LO 2)	Basic
E18-9	JIT Limitations (LO 2)	Basic
E18-10	Product Mix Decision; Single Constraint (LO 3)	Basic
E18-11	Drum-Buffer-Rope System (LO 3)	Basic
P18-1	EOQ and Reorder Point (LO 1)	Moderate
P18-2	EOQ with Safety Stock (LO 1)	Basic
P18-3	EOQ; Safety Stock; Lead Time; Batch Size and JIT (LO 1,2)	Moderate
P18-4	Kanban System; EDI (LO 2)	Challenging
P18-5	Product Mix Decision; Single and Multiple Constraints (LO 3)	Moderate
P18-6	Optimal Product Mix Decisions (LO 3)	Moderate
P18-7	Identifying and Exploiting Constraints; Constraint Elevation (LO 3)	Challenging
P18-8	Theory of Constraints; Internal Constraints (LO 3)	Moderate
P18-9	TOC; Internal and External Constraints (LO 3)	Challenging
C18-1	Ethical Issues	Moderate

Peter Drucker made the following comment:*

"The most exciting and innovative work in management today is found in accounting theory, with new concepts, new methodology--even what might be called new economic philosophy--rapidly taking shape. And while there is enormous controversy over specifics, the lineaments of the new manufacturing accounting are becoming clearer every day."

*Peter E. Drucker, "The Emerging Theory of Manufacturing," *Harvard Business Review*, May-June 1990, pp. 94-102.

BASIC COST CONCEPTS
(Definitions)

1.   **COST:** The cash or cash-equivalent value sacrificed for goods and services that are expected to bring a current or future benefit to the organization.

2.   **OPPORTUNITY COST:** The benefit given up or sacrificed when one alternative is chosen over another.

   > *EXAMPLE: Wages or salary foregone by attending college instead of working.*

3.   **EXPENSE:** An expired cost, a cost used up in the production of revenues.

   > *EXAMPLE: Cost of materials in a product that was sold.*

4.   **COST OBJECT:** Any item such as products, customers, departments, projects, activities, and so on, for which costs are measured and assigned.

   > *EXAMPLE: A bicycle is a cost object when you are determining the cost to produce a bicycle.*

5.   **ACTIVITY:** This is a basic unit of work performed within an organization.

   > *EXAMPLE: Setting up equipment, moving materials, maintaining equipment, designing products, etc.*

BASIC COST CONCEPTS

(Definitions)

6. **TRACEABILITY:** The relationship of costs to cost objects can be exploited to help increase the accuracy of cost assignments. Costs are directly or indirectly associated with cost objects.

7. **DIRECT COSTS:** Those costs that can be easily and accurately traced to a cost object.

> *EXAMPLE: The salary of a supervisor of a department, where the department is defined as the cost object.*

8. **INDIRECT COSTS:** Those costs that cannot be easily and accurately traced to a cost object.

> *EXAMPLE: The salary of a plant manager, where departments within the plant are defined as the cost objects.*

METHODS OF TRACING

TRACING: The actual assignment of costs to a cost object using an observable measure of the resources consumed by the cost object. Tracing costs to cost objects can occur in the following two ways:

> **DIRECT TRACING:** The process of identifying and assigning costs to a cost object that are specifically or physically associated with the cost object.

> **DRIVER TRACING:** The use of drivers to assign costs to cost objects. Driver tracing uses two types of drivers for tracing costs to cost objects: resource drivers and activity drivers.

>> **RESOURCE DRIVERS:** These drivers measure the demands placed on resources by activities and are used to assign the cost of resources to activities.

>> **ACTIVITY DRIVERS:** These drivers measure the demands placed on activities by cost objects and are used to assign the cost of activities to cost objects.

INTERFACE OF SERVICES WITH MANAGEMENT ACCOUNTING

1. Intangibility

2. Perishability

3. Inseparability

4. Heterogeneity

INTANGIBILITY

Derived Properties	Impact on Management Accounting
Services cannot be stored	No inventory
No patent protection	Strong ethical code*
Cannot display or communicate services	
Prices difficult to set	Demand for more accurate cost assignment*

Many of these effects are also true of tangible products.

PERISHABILITY

Derived Properties	Impact on Management Accounting
Services benefits expire quickly	No inventory
Services may be repeated often for one customer	Need for standards and consistent high quality *

* Many of these effects are also true of tangible products.

INSEPARABILITY

Derived Properties	Impact on Management Accounting
Customer directly involved with production of service	Costs often accounted for by customer type*
Centralized mass production of services is difficult	Demand for measurement and control of quality to maintain consistency*

Many of these effects are also true of tangible products.

HETEROGENEITY

Derived Properties	Impact on Management Accounting
Wide variation in service product is possible	Productivity and quality measurement and control must be ongoing* Total quality management is critical*

* Many of these effects are also true of tangible products.

FUNCTIONAL CLASSIFICATION OF COSTS

1.   **MANUFACTURING COSTS** (product costs): Costs associated with the production function in the plant or factory.

 a. **DIRECT MATERIALS**: The cost of materials that become part of the product. These costs are directly traceable to the product.

 EXAMPLE: *The cost of tires on an automobile.*

 b. **DIRECT LABOR:** The cost of labor used to convert raw materials to a finished product. This cost is directly traceable to the product.

 EXAMPLE: *Wages of assembly-line workers.*

 c. **OVERHEAD:** All other manufacturing costs.

 EXAMPLE: *Plant depreciation, utilities, property taxes, indirect materials, indirect labor, etc.*

 d. **PRIME COST:** The sum of direct labor cost and direct materials cost.

 e. **CONVERSION COST:** The sum of direct labor cost and overhead cost.

2. **NONMANUFACTURING COSTS** (period costs): Costs associated with the functions of selling and administration.

    a.   **SELLING COSTS:** Those costs necessary to market and distribute a product or service.

        EXAMPLE: *Commissions, storage costs, and freight.*

    b.   **ADMINISTRATIVE COSTS:** All costs associated with the general administration of the organization that cannot be reasonably assigned to either marketing or production.

        EXAMPLE: *Legal fees, salary of the chief executive officer.*

Statement of Cost of Goods Manufactured
For the Year Ended December 31, 1998

Direct Materials:

Beginning inventory	$ 400,000	
Add: Purchases	900,000	
Materials available	$1,300,000	
Less: Ending inventory	100,000	
Direct materials used		$ 1,200,000
Direct labor		700,000

Manufacturing Overhead:

Indirect labor	$ 255,000	
Depreciation	345,000	
Rent	100,000	
Utilities	75,000	
Property taxes	25,000	
Maintenance	100,000	900,000
Total manufacturing costs added		$ 2,800,000
Add: Beginning work in process		400,000
Total manufacturing costs		$ 3,200,000
Less: Ending work in process		800,000
Cost of goods manufactured		$ 2,400,000

Income Statement: Manufacturing Organization
For the Year Ended December 31, 1998

Sales		$4,000,000
Less cost of goods sold:		
Beginning finished goods inventory	$ 500,000	
Add: Cost of goods manufactured	2,400,000	
Goods available for sale	$2,900,000	
Less: Ending finished goods inventory	300,000	
		2,600,000
Gross margin		$1,400,000
Less operating expenses:		
Selling expenses	$ 600,000	
Administrative expenses	300,000	
		900,000
Income before taxes		$ 500,000

Income Statement: Service Organization
For the Year Ended December 31, 1998

Sales			$300,000
Less expenses:			
Cost of services sold:			
Beginning WIP		$ 5,000	
Direct materials	$ 40,000		
Direct labor	80,000		
Overhead	100,000	220,000	
		$225,000	
Less: Ending WIP		(10,000)	215,000
Gross margin			$ 85,000
Less operating expenses:			
Selling expenses		$ 8,000	
Administrative expenses		22,000	(30,000)
Income before taxes			$ 55,000

ACTIVITY CATEGORIES

1. **UNIT-LEVEL ACTIVITIES** are those that are performed each time a unit is produced.

   Examples: *Power and machine hours are used each time a unit is produced. Direct materials and direct labor activities are also unit-level activities, even though they are not overhead costs.*

2. **BATCH-LEVEL ACTIVITIES** are those that are performed each time a batch of products is produced.

   Examples: *Setups, inspections, production scheduling, and material handling.*

3. **PRODUCT-LEVEL (SUSTAINING) ACTIVITIES** are those that are performed as needed to support the various products produced by a company. These activities consume inputs that develop products or allow products to be produced and sold.

   Examples: *Engineering changes, maintenance of equipment, and expediting.*

4. **FACILITY-LEVEL ACTIVITIES** are those that sustain a factory's general manufacturing processes.

   Examples: *plant management, landscaping, maintenance, security, property taxes, and plant depreciation.*

BASIC TERMS

1. **Activity capacity** is the ability to perform activities.

2. **Practical capacity** is the efficient level of activity performance.

3. **Resources** are economic inputs that are consumed in performing activities.

BASIC TERMS

4. **Resource spending** is the cost of acquiring capacity to perform an activity.

5. **Resource usage** is the amount of activity capacity used in producing the activity output.

BASIC TERMS

6. **Resources supplied as used and needed** are resources that are acquired from outside sources, where the terms of acquisition do not require any long-term commitment for any given amount of the resource.

    Examples: materials and energy

7. **Resources supplied in advance of usage** are resources acquired by the use of either an explicit or implicit contract to obtain a given quantity of resource, regardless of whether the quantity of the resource available is fully used or not.

    Examples: equipment and supervision

TOTAL VERSUS AVERAGE VARIABLE COST

EXAMPLE: Suppose that Porter Pottery Company makes mugs. Each mug requires 1/4 lb. of clay at $2 per lb. If Porter manufactures 5,000 mugs, total cost of clay is $2,500 (5,000 x $2 x .25). If Porter manufactures 10,000 mugs, total cost of clay is $5,000 (10,000 x $2 x .25). The average cost of clay per mug stays at $.50 (.25 x $2) no matter how many mugs are made.

Total Variable Cost

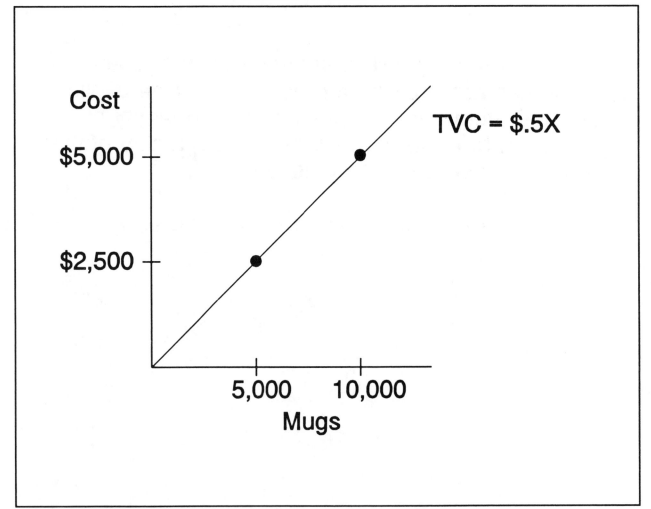

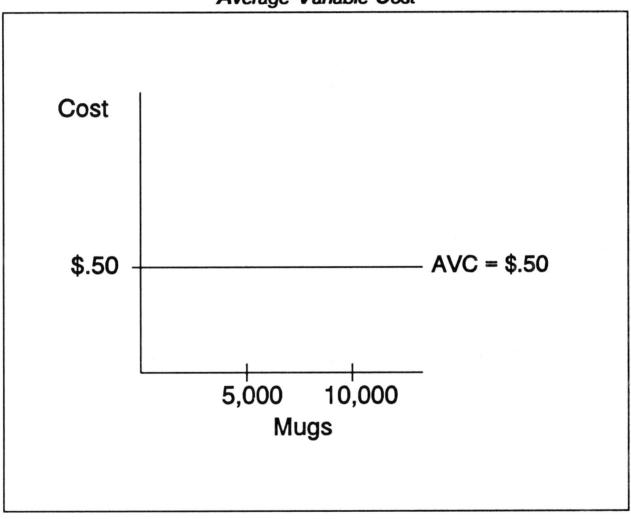

Average Variable Cost

TOTAL FIXED VERSUS AVERAGE FIXED COST

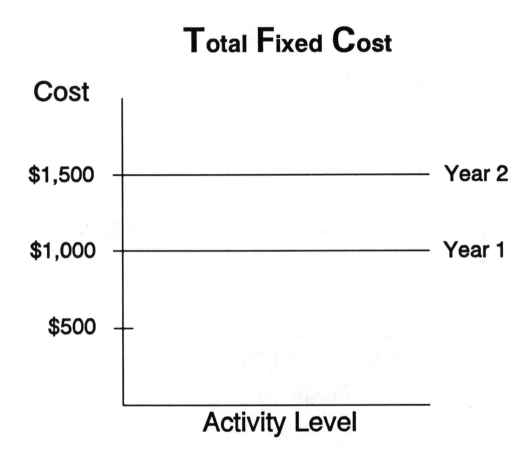

Total Fixed Cost

TTM 3-7 compares total fixed cost with average fixed cost.

Total versus Average Fixed Cost

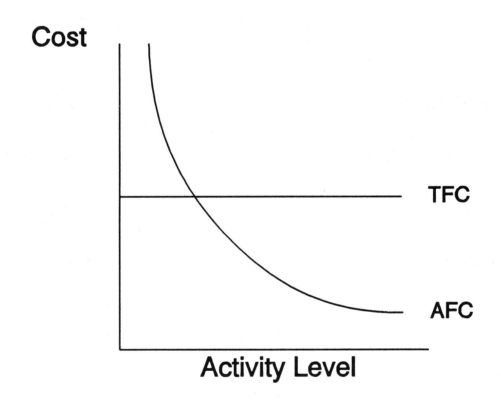

BELRING, INC.

Belring, Inc. produces two telephones: a cordless and a regular model.

The company had the following actual and budgeted data:

Budgeted overhead	$360,000
Expected activity (DLH)	100,000
Actual activity (DLH)	100,000
Actual overhead	$380,000

	Cordless	Regular
Units produced	10,000	100,000
Prime costs	$78,000	$738,000
Direct labor hours	10,000	90,000

Predetermined
Overhead rate = $360,000/100,000 = $3.60 per DLH

UNIT-COST COMPUTATION: PLANTWIDE RATE

	Cordless	Regular
Prime costs	$ 78,000	$ 738,000
Overhead costs:		
$3.60 x 10,000	36,000	
$3.60 x 90,000		324,000
Total manufacturing costs	$114,000	$1,062,000
Units of production	10,000	100,000
Unit cost (total costs/units)	$11.40	$10.62

DEPARTMENTAL DATA

	Fabrication	Assembly
Budgeted overhead	$252,000	$108,000
Expected and actual activity (DLH):		
Cordless	7,000	3,000
Regular	13,000	77,000
	20,000	80,000
Expected and actual activity (MH):		
Cordless	4,000	1,000
Regular	36,000	9,000
	40,000	10,000

Fabrication Rate = $252,000/40,000 = $6.30 per MH

Assembly Rate = $108,000/80,000 = $1.35 per DLH

UNIT COST COMPUTATION: DEPARTMENTAL RATES

	Cordless	Regular
Prime costs	$ 78,000	$ 738,000
Overhead costs:		
($1.35 x 3,000) + ($6.30 x 4,000)	29,250	
($1.35 x 77,000) + ($6.30 x 36,000)		330,750
Total manufacturing costs	$107,250	$1,068,750
Units of production	10,000	100,000
Unit cost (total costs/units	$10.73	$10.69

MORE PRODUCT COSTING DATA FOR BELRING, INC.

Activity usage measures:

	Cordless	Regular	Total
Units produced per year	10,000	100,000	--
Prime costs	$78,000	$738,000	$816,000
Direct labor hours	10,000	90,000	100,000
Machine hours	5,000	45,000	50,000
Production runs	20	10	30
Number of moves	60	30	90

Additional cost data (overhead activities):

Activity	Activity Cost
Setup	$120,000
Material handling	60,000
Power	100,000
Testing	80,000
Total	$360,000

FIRST-STAGE PROCEDURE: ACTIVITY-BASED COSTING

Batch-level Pool:

Setup costs	$120,000
Material-handling costs	60,000
Total costs	$180,000
Production runs	30
Pool rate (cost per run)	$6,000

Unit-level Pool:

Power cost	$100,000
Testing cost	80,000
Total costs	$180,000
Machine hours	50,000
Pool rate (cost per machine hour)	$3.60

UNIT COST COMPUTATION: ACTIVITY-BASED COSTING

	Cordless	Regular
Prime costs	$ 78,000	$738,000
Overhead costs:		
Batch-level pool:		
($6,000 x 20)	120,000	
($6,000 x 10)		60,000
Unit-level pool:		
($3.60 x 5,000)	18,000	
($3.60 x 45,000)		162,000
Total manufacturing costs	$216,000	$960,000
Units of production	10,000	100,000
Unit cost (total costs/units)	$21.60	$9.60

UNIT COST COMPARISONS

	Cordless	Regular
Activity-based costing	$21.60	$9.60
Plantwide rate	$11.40	$10.62
Departmental rate	$10.73	$10.69

JOB-ORDER COSTING: SPECIFIC COST FLOW DESCRIPTION

I. **Direct materials**

   A. Raw Materials account is debited for the cost of materials purchased.

   B. Raw Materials is credited for the cost of materials issued to jobs.

   Work in Process is debited for the cost of materials issued to jobs.

Raw Materials		Work in Process	
(A)	(B)	(B)	

II. **Direct labor**

   C. Wages Payable is credited for direct labor.

   Work in Process is debited for the cost of direct labor.

Wages Payable		Work in Process	
	(C)	(C)	

III. **Overhead**

   D. Overhead Control is credited for applied overhead.

   Work in Process is debited for applied overhead.

   E. Overhead Control is debited for actual overhead.

Overhead Control		Work in Process	
(E)	(D)	(D)	

IV. Transfer of Completed Goods

F.   Credit Work in Process for the cost of goods manufactured.
Debit Finished Goods for the cost of goods manufactured.

Work in Process		Finished Goods	
(B)	(F)	(F)	
(C)			
(D)			

V. Recognition of expense

G.   Credit Finished Goods for value of units sold.
Debit Cost of Goods Sold for value of units sold.

Finished Goods		Cost of Goods Sold	
	(G)	(G)	

EXERCISE 5-4

a.	Raw Materials	32,475	
	Accounts Payable		32,475
b.	Work in Process	27,000	
	Raw Materials		27,000
c.	Work in Process	26,250	
	Wages Payable		26,250
d.	Overhead Control	19,950	
	Misc. Payable		19,950
e.	Work in Process	21,000	
	Overhead Control		21,000
f.	Finished Goods	37,500	
	Work in Process		37,500
h.	Cost of Goods Sold	6,240	
	Finished Goods		6,240
	Accounts Receivable	7,800	
	Sales Revenue		7,800

GENERAL CONTRACTOR EXAMPLE — DATA

Direct Materials	House #1	$ 90,000
	House #2	100,000
	House #3	30,000
		$220,000

	House #1	$ 65,000
Direct Labor	House #2	70,000
	House #3	15,000
		$150,000

— Overhead is applied at 50 percent of DLC.

— Houses #1 and #2 are completed during the period.

— House #1 is sold for $200,000 cash.

GENERAL CONTRACTOR EXAMPLE — SOLUTION

Work in Process

(1) DM	220,000		
(2) DL	150,000	(4)	187,500
(3)	75,000	(5)	205,000
House #3	52,500		

Finished Goods

(4)	187,500		
(5)	205,000	(6)	187,500
House #2	205,000		

Cost of Goods Sold

(6)	187,500	
House #1	187,500	

House #1

(1)	90,000	(2)	65,000	(3)	32,500
					187,500

House #2

(1)	100,000	(2)	70,000	(3)	35,000
					205,000

House #3

(1)	30,000	(2)	15,000	(3)	7,500
					52,500

STEPS FOR COSTING OUT PRODUCTION IN PROCESS COSTING

1. Analysis of the flow of physical units

2. Calculation of equivalent units

3. Computation of unit cost

4. Valuation of inventories (goods transferred out and ending work in process)

5. Cost reconciliation

NONUNIFORM INPUTS: AN ILLUSTRATIVE EXAMPLE

Materials are added at the beginning of the process.

Units in process, May 1, 60% complete	2,000
Units completed and transferred out	10,000
Units in process, May 31, 40% complete	1,000

Costs:

	BWIP Cost	Cost Added
Materials	$300	$3,000
Conversion Costs	600	4,600

Step I - Physical Flow:

Units to account for

Units, BWIP	2,000
Units started	9,000
Total	11,000

Units accounted for

Units completed	10,000
Units, EWIP	1,000
Total	11,000

Step II - Equivalent Units (Weighted Average):

	Materials	Conversion
Units completed	10,000	10,000
EWIP	1,000	400
Total equivalent units	11,000	10,400

Step III - Unit Cost

Unit Cost = $3,300/11,000 + $5,200/10,400
           = $0.30 (materials) + $0.50 (conversion)
           = $0.80

Step IV - Valuation of Inventories

Goods transferred out
     $0.80 x 10,000 = $8,000

     EWIP: ($0.30 x 1,000) + ($0.50 x 400) = $500

Step V - Cost Reconciliation

Costs assigned
Goods transferred	$8,000
EWIP	500
	$8,500

Costs to account for
BWIP	$ 900
Costs added	7,600
Total	$8,500

SUPPORT AND PRODUCING DEPARTMENTS

I. Support Departments: Units within an organization that provide essential support services for producing departments.

Examples: *Laundry, power, maintenance, materials handling, grounds, and engineering.*

II. Producing Departments: Units within an organization that are directly responsible for manufacturing or creating the products and services sold to customers.

Examples: *Services: auditing, tax, management advisory. Manufacturing: machining and assembly.*

ALLOCATION BY COST BEHAVIOR

I. Variable Costs

1. **Rate Determination**. At the beginning of the year, the company determines what the variable cost per unit of service **should be** (a budgeted rate, not an actual rate, is used to assign variable costs).

2. **Budgeted Usage**. Each producing department determines its expected or budgeted usage of the service for the year.

3. **Actual Usage Measurement**. The actual units of service used by each producing department are measured.

4. **Allocation**. Variable support costs are allocated by multiplying the budgeted rate by the usage:

   a. Product costing:
   Allocation = Budgeted Rate x Budgeted Usage

   b. Performance evaluation:
   Allocation = Budgeted Rate x Actual Usage

II. Fixed Costs

1. **Determination of Budgeted Fixed Support Costs**. The fixed support costs that **should be** incurred for a period need to be identified.

2. **Computation of Allocation Ratio**. Using practical or normal capacity of each producing department, compute an allocation ratio as follows:

    Allocation Ratio = Producing Department Capacity/Total Capacity

3. **Allocation**. The fixed support costs are allocated in proportion to each producing department's original service needs:

    Allocation = Allocation Ratio x Budgeted Fixed Support Costs

    Note: Fixed costs are allocated the same way for product costing and performance evaluation.

PLANNING, CONTROL, AND BUDGETS: AN EXAMPLE

I.   **PLANNING (refer to Exhibit 8-1):**

Strategic Plan: To increase the market share by increasing product quality.

Long-Term Objective: Reduce the number of defective units reaching customers to zero.

Short-Term Objective: Reduce the number of defects by 20% for the coming year.

Budgets: To reduce the number of defective units, the expenditures for process control will be increased by 25%. Since this increased expenditure will decrease the number of defects, expenditures for rework and repairs will be reduced by 15%.

II.   CONTROL

Monitoring and Comparison: The actual expenditures for process control was on target; the actual expenditures for rework and repairs were greater than the planned expenditures. The actual defects were greater than the planned amount.

Investigation: Upon investigating, it was discovered that the planned increase in expenditure for process control was not great enough to produce the desired increase in quality.

Corrective Action: By increasing the budget for process control by an additional 15%, the targeted reductions in defects can be achieved.

Feedback: Although the planned reduction in defects was not achieved this year, significant progress was made. The ability to achieve the desired market share within the original time frame is still maintained.

RESPONSIBILITY CENTERS

I. **Responsibility Accounting:** The use of the accounting system to set standards, to measure actual outcomes, and to report the performance of responsibility centers.

II. **Responsibility Center:** A unit within an organization over which a manager is assigned responsibility for a specific activity or sets of activities.

III. Types of responsibility centers:

    A. **Cost Center:** A responsibility center in which a manager is responsible only for incurrence of cost.

    B. **Profit Center:** A responsibility center in which a manager is responsible for both revenues and costs.

    C. **Investment Center:** A responsibility center in which a manager is responsible for revenues, costs, and investments.

KEY FEATURES OF A SOUND BUDGETARY SYSTEM

1. **Frequent feedback on performance.** This allows managers to know how they are doing as the year unfolds and to take corrective action as needed.

2. **Flexible budgeting.** A static budget is for a particular level of activity. It is not reasonable to compare actual costs at one level of activity with budgeted costs for a different level of activity. A flexible budget computes expected costs for any level of activity. This permits comparison of actual costs with expected costs for the SAME level of activity. See Exhibits 8-7 and 8-8.

3. **Monetary and nonmonetary incentives.** Incentives are used to induce a manager to work toward the organization's goals. Incentives can be monetary or nonmonetary or both. Monetary incentives are economic rewards and may not be adequate by themselves to motivate. Nonmonetary incentives appeal to the higher-level psychological needs and consist of such things as job satisfaction, recognition, and increased responsibility.

4. **Participative budgeting.** Allowing managers in the budgetary process tends to increase goal congruence, foster creativity, communicate a sense of self-worth, and use managers' knowledge of local conditions.

5. **Realistic standards.** Budgets should reflect current efficiency levels, seasonal variations, and general economic conditions.

6. **Controllability.** Managers should not be held accountable for costs that they cannot control.

7. **Multiple measures of performance.** Budgets should not be the only measure of managerial performance. If noncontrollable costs are included in a budget they should be labeled and separated from controllable costs.

Translating the concepts of zero-base budgeting into practice requires four steps . . .

1. Identifying decision units.

2. Creating decision packages for each decision unit.

3. Ranking decision units in order of priority.

4. Preparing the budget.

DEVELOPMENT OF STANDARDS

I.   Types of Standards
Ideal standards: Standards that demand maximum efficiency and can be achieved only if everything operates perfectly.
Currently attainable standards: Standards that can be achieved under efficient operating conditions (demanding but achievable).

II. Sources for Quantitative Standards
1.   Historical experience
2.   Engineering studies
3.   Input from operating personnel

III. Factors for Price Standards
<u>Materials</u>
1.   Market forces
2.   Discounts
3.   Freight
4.   Quality
<u>Labor</u>
1.   Market forces
2.   Trade unions
3.   Payroll taxes
4.   Qualifications

VARIANCE ANALYSIS: GENERAL DESCRIPTION

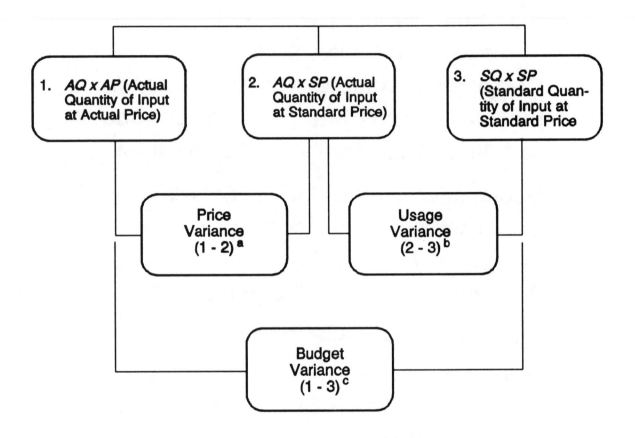

1. *AQ x AP* (Actual Quantity of Input at Actual Price)

2. *AQ x SP* (Actual Quantity of Input at Standard Price)

3. *SQ x SP* (Standard Quantity of Input at Standard Price

Price Variance (1 - 2)[a]

Usage Variance (2 - 3)[b]

Budget Variance (1 - 3)[c]

---

[a] Price Variance = $(AQ \times AP) - (AQ \times SP) = AQ\,(AP - SP)$

[b] Usage Variance = $(AQ \times SP) - (SQ \times SP) = SP\,(AQ - SQ)$

[c] Budget Variance = $(AQ \times AP) - (SQ \times SP)$

VARIANCE INVESTIGATION

I.   The Decision to Investigate

Variances are investigated if two conditions are met:

1. The variance is material
2. The benefits of investigating and taking corrective action are greater than its costs.

II.   Control Limits: Standard ± Allowable Deviation

Investigation occurs for values outside the allowable range.

EXAMPLE: Assume the allowable deviation may be the lesser of $8,000 or 10% of the standard. Suppose the standard is $50,000 and the actual deviation from standard is $6,000. Will the variance be investigated?

ANSWER: Yes. Ten percent of standard is $5,000. Since $6,000 is larger than the allowable deviation, an investigation will take place.

ACTIVITY ANALYSIS

Activity analysis is the process of identifying, describing, and evaluating the activities an organization performs.

Activity analysis produces the following four outcomes:

1. What activities are done.

2. How many people perform the activities.

3. The time and resources required to perform the activities.

4. An assessment of the value of the activities to the organization, including a recommendation to select and keep only those that add value.

DEFINITIONS

Activity-Based Management:	A systemwide, integrated approach that focuses management's attention on activities.
Activity Management:	An assessment of the value of the activities to the organization, including a recommendation to select and keep only those that add value.
Nonvalue-Added Activities:	Activities that are either unnecessary or necessary but inefficient and improvable. These activities cause nonvalue-added costs. Examples: Scheduling, moving, waiting, inspecting, and storing.
Value-Added Activities:	Necessary, perfectly efficient activities. Examples: Direct labor, addition of raw materials, and machining.

COMPUTATIONAL FORMULAS FOR VALUE- AND NONVALUE-ADDED COSTS

Value-added costs = $SQ \times SP$

Nonvalue-added costs = $(AQ - SQ)SP$

where:

SQ =   The value-added output level for an activity

SP =   The standard price per unit of activity output measure

AQ =   The actual quantity of activity output used (if resources are supplied as needed)

or

AQ =   the actual quantity of activity capacity acquired (if resources are supplied in advance of usage)

VALUE- AND NONVALUE-ADDED COST REPORT
For the Year Ended December 31, 1998

Activity	Value Added	Nonvalue Added	Actual
Material usage	$1,600,000	$160,000	$1,760,000
Rework	0	90,000	90,000
Setups	0	360,000	360,000
Inspections	0	60,000	60,000
Total	$1,600,000	$670,000	$2,270,000

TREND REPORT
NONVALUE-ADDED COSTS

Activity	1997	1998	Change	
Material usage	$ 160,000	$100,000	$ 60,000	F
Rework	90,000	50,000	40,000	F
Setups	360,000	160,000	200,000	F
Inspections*	60,000	30,000	30,000	F
Total	$ 670,000	$340,000	$ 330,000	F

*During the year, the supplier evaluation program decreased the number of defective parts to the point where one inspector was reassigned to an open position in the assembly department.

CURRENTLY ATTAINABLE STANDARDS (MODIFIED)

I. Modified currently attainable standards are based on targeted reductions of nonvalue-added costs. These targeted reductions can be motivated internally or externally or both. The main purpose of these standards is to encourage cost reduction and continual improvement.

II. Example: Material handling costs are costing $12 per unit. Currently, the company's product is moved six times, at a cost of $2 per move. Ideally, the number of moves should be reduced to two, with an associated value-added cost of $4.

The marketing department has indicated that if the product's selling price can be reduced by $4, the market share will increase by 20 percent. Management is unwilling, however, to allow a reduction in the profit earned per unit. Identify the standard quantity and material handling cost per unit that would be necessary for the company to achieve the desired increase in market share.

Answer: The nonvalue-added cost per unit for material handling is $8 ($2 x [6 - 2]). The number of moves must be reduced by two to achieve a reduction of $4.

Consequently, *SQ* equal to *4* and *SQ* x *SP* equal to $8 are the currently attainable standard quantity and cost, respectively.

_____

DEFINITIONS

PRODUCT LIFE CYCLE:

The time a product exists from conception to abandonment.

LIFE-CYCLE COSTS:

All costs associated with the product for its entire life cycle.

Three major life-cycle cost elements:

1. Development costs: planning, design, and testing
2. Production costs: conversion activities
3. Logistics support costs: advertising, distribution, warranty, etc.

LIFE-CYCLE COST MANAGEMENT:

Management that focuses on managing value-chain activities so that a long-term competitive advantage is created.

SUMMARY OF OPERATIONAL MEASURES

Quality:
Defects/units
Number of defective units/total units
Percentage of external failures
Pounds of scrap/pounds of materials issued
Purchase orders in error/total purchase orders
Number of errors per purchase order

Carrying Inventory:
Inventory turnover
Days of inventory
Number of inventoried items
Trends in days of inventory

Productivity:
Output/pounds of material
Output/hours of labor
Output/kilowatt hours
Output/persons employed

Time Based:
On-time deliveries/total deliveries
Cycle time
Velocity
MCE

Machine Performance:
Machine availability
Machine utilization

MEASURES OF DELIVERY PERFORMANCE (time based)

I. Definitions

Cycle Time: The time required to produce one unit of product

Velocity: The number of units that can be produced in a given period of time (e.g., units per hours)

Manufacturing
Cycle
Efficiency (MCE) =

$$\frac{\text{Processing time}}{\text{Processing time + Move time + Inspection time + Waiting time}}$$

Note: Processing time is value-added time. The other activities in the denominator are nonvalue-added times.

II.   Example 1

A plant has the theoretical capability of producing 10,000 bikes per quarter. There are 20,000 production hours available each quarter. Compute the theoretical cycle time and velocity.

Cycle time	=	20,000 hrs/10,000 bikes
	=	<u>2</u> hrs per bike
Velocity	=	10,000 bikes/20,000 hours
	=	<u>0.5</u> bikes per hour

III.   Example 2

A product has the following activities and times:

Processing (three departments):	10 hours
Moving (four moves):	3 hours
Waiting (for the second and third processes):	8 hours
Storage (before delivery):	19 hours

<u>Compute MCE</u>.

MCE	=	10/(10 + 3 + 8 + 19)
	=	10/40
	=	<u>0.25</u> or <u>25</u> percent

QUALITY DEFINED

Quality of Design:	The degree of excellence, which is a function of a product's specifications.
Example:	Compare a Cadillac Seville with a Honda Civic. The Seville is a luxury car with specially designed features and the Civic is an economy car with standard features. Both are designed to provide transportation but the design qualities are obviously different.
Quality of Conformance:	The degree of excellence, which is a measure of how well the product meets its requirements or specifications.
Example:	If the Honda Civic does what it is designed to do and does it well, quality exists. For example, if economy cars are designed to provide reliable, low-cost, low-maintenance transportation, the desired quality exists.

ZERO-DEFECT GRAPH

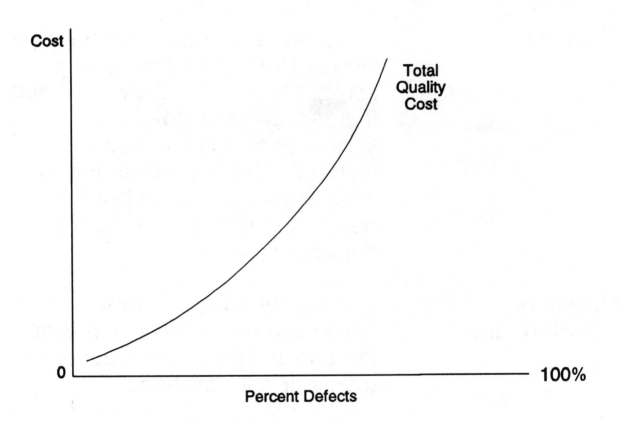

ILLUSTRATION OF PRODUCTIVITY IMPROVEMENT

Technical Efficiency: Condition where no more of any one input is used than necessary to produce a given output.

A. **Technical efficiency improvement:** Using less inputs to produce the same output or producing more output using the same input.

Current productivity:

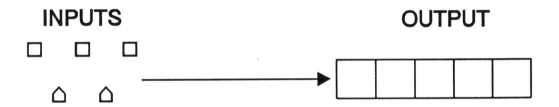

INPUTS   OUTPUT

Same output, fewer inputs:

INPUTS   OUTPUT

More output, same inputs:

INPUTS   OUTPUT

☐   ☐   ☐

   △   △   ⟶

B. **Price efficiency improvement:** Using a less costly input mix to produce the same output.

Combination I: Total cost of inputs = $28

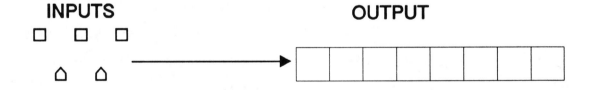

INPUTS   OUTPUT

☐   ☐   ☐

   △   △   ⟶

Combination II: Total cost of inputs = $27

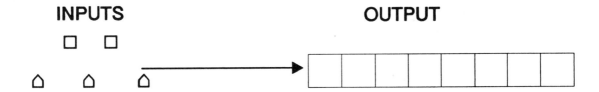

INPUTS   **OUTPUT**

Of the two combinations that produce the same output, the least costly combination would be chosen.

PARTIAL PRODUCTIVITY MEASURES

I.   **Partial Productivity Measurement:** Measuring productivity for one input at a time.

Partial Measure = Output/Input

II.   **Operational Productivity Measure:** Partial measure where both input and output are expressed in physical terms.

III.   Example 1:

In 1996, Tick-Tock Company produced 100 clocks and used 200 direct labor hours and 50 pounds of raw materials. Compute the labor and materials productivity ratios.

Answer:

Labor productivity ratio	=	100 clocks/200 hrs
	=	0.5 clocks per hr
Materials productivity ratio	=	100 clocks/50 lbs
	=	2 clocks per lb

IV.   Example 2:

In 1997, Tick-Tock Company produced 100 clocks and used 175 direct labor hours and 40 pounds of raw materials. Compute the partial productivity ratios. Compared to 1996, has productivity improved?

Answer:

A.   Ratios computed:

Labor productivity ratio   =   100 clocks/175 hrs
                            =   0.57 clocks per hr

Materials productivity ratio   =   100 clocks/40 lbs
                                =   2.5 clocks per lb

B.   Ratios compared:

	1996	1997
Labor	0.50	0.57
Materials	2.00	2.50

Both ratios have improved, so productivity has improved.

PROFIT-LINKED PRODUCTIVITY MEASUREMENT

PROFIT-LINKAGE RULE: For the current period, calculate the cost of the inputs that would have been used in the absence of any productivity change and compare this cost with the cost of the inputs actually used. The difference in costs is the amount by which profits changed because of productivity changes.

To compute the inputs that would have been used (PQ), use the following formula:

PQ = Current Output/Base-Period Productivity Ratio

EXAMPLE: Tick-Tock Company provided the following data for 1996 and 1997:

	1996	1997
Production (no. of clocks)	100	120
Selling price	$500	$500
Materials used (lbs)	50	72
Labor hours used	200	228
Cost per lb of material	$5	$5
Cost per hr. of labor	$10	$10

Compute the profit change attributable to productivity changes.

PQ (materials) = 120/2 = 60 lbs
PQ (labor) = 120/0.5 = 240 hrs

Profit change:

Input	PQ	PQ x P	AQ	AQ x P	(PQ x P) - (AQ x P)
Mat'ls	60	$ 300	72	$ 360	$(60)
Labor	240	2,400	228	2,280	120
		$2,700		$2,640	$ 60

Profits have improved by $60 because of productivity changes.

ENVIRONMENTAL FACTORS AFFECTING PERFORMANCE EVALUATION IN MULTINATIONAL FIRMS

— Economic Factors —

— Political and Legal Factors —

— Educational Factors —

— Social and Cultural Factors —

ENVIRONMENTAL FACTORS AFFECTING PERFORMANCE EVALUATION IN THE MULTINATIONAL FIRM *

Economic factors:

Organization of central banking system
Economic stability
Existence of capital markets
Currency restrictions

Political and legal factors:

Quality, efficiency, and effectiveness of legal structure
Effect of defense policy
Impact of foreign policy
Level of political unrest
Degree of governmental control of business

Educational factors:

Literacy rate
Extent and degree of formal education and training systems
Extent and degree of technical training
Extent and quality of management development programs

Sociological factors:

Social attitude toward industry and business
Cultural attitude toward authority and persons
  in subordinate positions
Cultural attitude toward productivity and achievement (work ethic)
Social attitude toward material gain
Cultural and racial diversity

* Adapted from Wagdy M. Abdallah, "Change the Environment or Change the System," *Management Accounting* (October 1986), pp. 33-36. Used with the permission of the Institute of Management Accountants.

CLASSIFICATION OF COSTS AS PRODUCT OR PERIOD COSTS UNDER ABSORPTION AND VARIABLE COSTING

	Absorption Costing	Variable Costing
Direct Materials	Product	Product
Direct Labor	Product	Product
Variable Overhead	Product	Product
Fixed Overhead	Product *	Period *
Selling Expenses	Period	Period
Administrative Expenses	Period	Period

* Fixed overhead is the only cost that changes classifications between the two methods.

UNIT COSTS COMPARED

Estimated and Actual Costs:

<u>Manufacturing</u>:

Direct materials	$100,000
Direct labor	50,000
Variable overhead	80,000
Fixed overhead	90,000
Total manufacturing cost	$320,000

<u>Nonmanufacturing</u>:

Variable selling	$ 32,000
Fixed selling & administrative	100,000
Total nonmanufacturing	$132,000

Estimated and actual production:	100,000 units
Sales:	80,000 units
Price:	$6.50 per unit
Beginning finished goods:	-0-

<u>Unit Cost</u>:	<u>Variable</u>	<u>Absorption</u>
Direct materials	$1.00	$1.00
Direct labor	0.50	0.50
Variable overhead	0.80	0.80
Fixed overhead	—	0.90
Total	$2.30	$3.20

<u>Value of ending finished goods inventory</u>:

Variable costing:	$2.30 x 20,000	=	$46,000
Absorption costing:	$3.20 x 20,000	=	$64,000

INCOME STATEMENTS: ANALYSIS AND COMPARISON
Using the data from Transparency 14-2

I. ABSORPTION COSTING:

Sales ($6.50 x 80,000)	$520,000
Cost of goods sold: ($3.20 x 80,000)	(256,000)
Gross margin	264,000
Selling and administrative	(132,000)
Net income	$132,000

II. VARIABLE COSTING:

Sales ($6.50 x 80,000)	$520,000
Variable goods sold: ($2.30 x 80,000)	(184,000)
Variable selling	(32,000)
Contribution margin	$304,000
Fixed overhead	(90,000)
Fixed administrative	(100,000)
Net income	$114,000

Difference:

	$132,000
Absorption income	114,000
Variable income	$ 18,000

Explained:

Production	100,000
Sales	80,000
Increase in inventory	0,000
Fixed overhead rate	x $0.90
	$18,000

SOLUTION TO EXERCISE 14-2

1. Fixed OH rate (FOR) = $28,000/10,000

   FOR = $2.80 per unit

The difference is given as follows:

$I_A - I_V$ = (Production - Sales) x FOR
= (10,000 - 8,000) x $3.80
= $7,600

Absorption costing is larger by $7,600.

2a.
Medina, Inc.
Variable-Costing Income Statement
For the Year Ended December 31, 1997

Sales		$232,000
Less variable expenses:		
Variable COGS (8,000 x $14.5)	$16,000	
Variable selling and adm.	28,000	144,000
Contribution margin		$ 88,000
Less fixed expenses:		
Fixed overhead	$38,000	
Fixed selling and adm.	22,000	60,000
Net Income		$ 28,000

2b.
Median, Inc.
Absorption-Costing Income Statement
For the Year Ended December 31, 1997

Sales	$232,000
Less COGS (8,000 x $18.30)	146,400
Gross margin	$ 85,600
Less selling and adm. exp.	50,000
Net Income	$ 35,600

SOLUTION TO EXERCISE 14-3

1.

Ballenger Company
Absorption-Costing Income Statement

Sales	$384,000	$480,000
Less cost of goods sold*	256,000	344,000
Gross margin	$128,000	$136,000
Less selling and adm. exp.	20,000	20,000
Net income	$108,000	$116,000

*Cost of goods sold:

Beginning inventory	$ 0	$ 64,000
Cost of goods manufactured	320,000	280,000
Goods available for sale	$320,000	$344,000
Less ending inventory	(64,000)	0
Cost of good sold	$256,000	$344,000

Firm performance, as measured by income, has increased from year 1 to year 2.

2.

Ballenger Company
Variable-Costing Income Statement

Sales	$ 384,000	$ 480,000
Less variable COGS*	160,000	200,000
Contribution margin	$ 224,000	$ 280,000
Less fixed expenses:		
Fixed overhead	120,000	120,000
Selling and administrative	20,000	20,000
Net income (loss)	$ 84,000	$ 140,000

*Variable cost of goods sold

Beginning inventory	$ 0	$ 40,000
Variable cost of goods manuf.	200,000	160,000
Goods available for sale	$ 200,000	$ 200,000
Less ending inventory	40,000	0
Cost of good sold	$ 160,000	$ 200,000

Firm performance, as measured by income, has improved from year 1 to year 2.

---

3. Since sales have increased with costs remaining the same, one would expect an increase in income. Variable-costing income provides this correspondence whereas absorption costing does not.

SOLUTION TO EXERCISE 14-5

Cocino Company
Income Statement

1.

	Blenders	Coffee Makers	Total
Sales	$2,200,000	$1,125,000	$3,325,000
Less variable COGS	2,000,000	1,075,000	3,075,000
Contribution margin	$ 200,000	$ 50,000	$ 250,000
Less direct fixed costs	90,000	45,000	135,000
Product margin	$ 110,000	$ 5,000	$ 115,000
Less common fixed costs			115,000
Net income (loss)			$ 0

2. If the coffee maker line is dropped, profits will decrease by $5,000 (the product margin). If the blender line is dropped, profits will decrease by $110,000.

3.

	Blenders	Coffee Makers	Total
Sales	$2,420,000	$1,125,000	$3,545,000
Less variable COGS	2,200,000	1,075,000	3,275,000
Contribution margin	$ 220,000	$ 50,000	$ 270,000
Less direct fixed costs	90,000	45,000	135,000
Product margin	$ 130,000	$ 5,000	$ 135,000
Less common fixed costs			115,000
Net income (loss)			$ 20,000

The following list is a sample of the types of questions that can be raised and answered by CVP analysis:

1. How many units must be sold (or how much sales revenue must be generated) in order to break even?
2. How many units must be sold to earn a before-tax profit equal to $60,000? A before-tax profit equal to 15 percent of revenues? An after-tax profit of $48,750?
3. Will total profits increase if the unit price is increased by $2 and units sold decrease 15 percent?
4. What is the effect on total profit if advertising expenditures increase by $8,000 and sales increase from 1,600 to 1,725 units?
5. What is the effect on total profit if the selling price is decreased from $400 to $375 per unit and sales increase from 1,600 units to 1,900 units?
6. What is the effect on total profit if the selling price is decreased from $400 to $375 per unit, advertising expenditures are increased by $8,000, and sales increase from 1,600 units to 2,300 units?
7. What is the effect on total profit if the sales mix is changed?

COST-VOLUME-PROFIT GRAPH

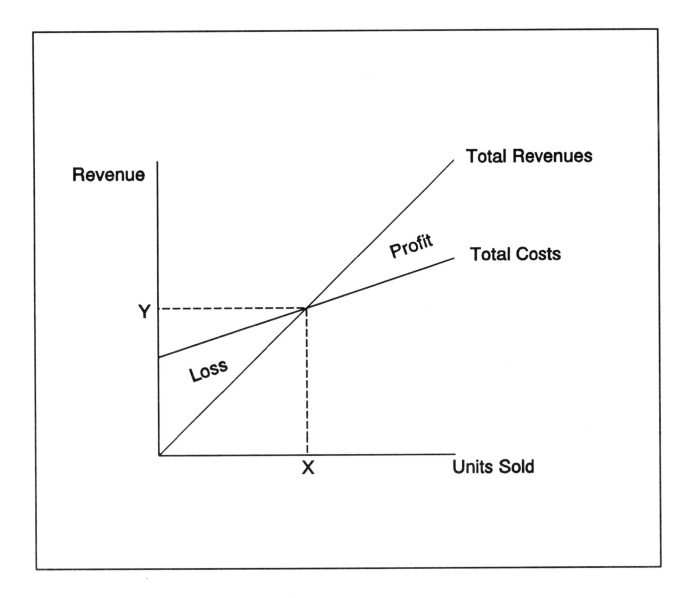

X = Break-even point in units
Y = Break-even point in sales revenues

SIMPLE CVP EXAMPLE

Fixed costs (F)	=	$40,000
Selling price per unit (P)	=	$10
Variable cost per unit (V)	=	$6
Tax rate	=	40%

1. What is the break-even point in units?

2. What is the break-even point in dollars?

Units-Sold Approach

1. Let X = break-even point in units

$$R = TC$$
$$PX = F + VX$$
$$\$10X = \$40,000 + 6X$$
$$\$10X - \$6X = \$40,000$$
$$\$4X = \$40,000$$
$$X = \underline{10,000} \text{ units}$$

2. Break-even point in sales dollars is:

10,000 x $10 or $100,000

This can be shown with a variable-costing income statement. See TTM 15-4.

VARIABLE-COSTING INCOME STATEMENT

Sales (10,000 x $10)	$100,000
Less variable costs (10,000 x $6)	60,000
Contribution margin	$ 40,000
Less fixed costs	40,000
Profit before taxes	$ 0
Less income taxes	0
Profit after taxes	$ 0

Sales Revenue Approach

Alternative approach to solving break-even point in sales dollars:

Let X equal break-even sales in dollars:

$$
\begin{aligned}
R &= TC \\
X &= F + VX \\
X &= \$40,000 + .6X \\
X - .6X &= \$40,000 \\
.4X &= \$40,000 \\
X &= \underline{\$100,000}
\end{aligned}
$$

Note: V is the variable cost percentage which is found by:

$$\frac{\text{Variable Cost per Unit}}{\text{Selling Price per Unit}} = \frac{6}{10} = 60\%$$

What sales in units and dollars are needed to obtain a targeted profit before taxes of $20,000?

Let X = break-even point in units

Sales	$
Less variable costs	_____
Contribution margin	$ 60,000 = $4X
Less fixed costs	40,000
Profit before taxes	$ 20,000

Therefore,

$$\$60{,}000 = \$4X$$
$$\underline{15{,}000} \text{ units} = X$$

Sales in dollars is (15,000 x $10) $\underline{\$150{,}000}$.

Check this by completing the variable-costing income statement.

Sales	$ 150,000	= 15,000 x $10
Less variable costs	90,000	= 15,000 x $6
Contribution margin	$ 60,000	
Less fixed costs	40,000	
Profit before taxes	$ 20,000	

Therefore, it checks!

What sales in units and dollars are needed to obtain a targeted profit after taxes of $24,000?

Let X = break-even point in units

Sales	$
Less variable costs	_____
Contribution margin	$
Less fixed costs	40,000
Profit before taxes	$
Less income taxes	_____
Profit after taxes	$ 24,000

We have the same problem as TTM 15-5 if we knew the profit before taxes.

Trick:

AFTER	=	Profit after taxes
BEFORE	=	Profit before taxes
AFTER	=	(1 - tax rate) x BEFORE
$24,000	=	(1 - .4) x BEFORE
$24,000/.6	=	BEFORE
$40,000	=	BEFORE

Therefore,

Sales	$	=	$10X
Less variable costs	____	=	$6X
Contribution margin	$80,000	=	$4X
Less fixed costs	40,000		
Profit before taxes	$40,000		
Less income taxes	16,000	=	40% ($40,000)
Profit after taxes	$24,000		

$$\$4X = \$80,000$$
$$X = \$80,000/\$4$$
$$X = 20,000 \text{ units}$$

Sales in dollars is (20,000 x $10) $200,000.

The income statement below illustrates that $200,000 in sales will give you an after-tax profit of $24,000.

Sales	$200,000
Less variable costs	120,000
Contribution margin	$ 80,000
Less fixed costs	40,000
Profit before taxes	$ 40,000
Less income taxes	16,000
Profit after taxes	$ 24,000

What sales in dollars is needed to obtain a targeted profit before taxes equal to 20 percent of sales?

Let X = sales in dollars

Sales	$	=	1.0X
Less variable costs	_____	=	.6X
Contribution margin	$40,000 + .2X	=	.4X
Less fixed costs	40,000		
Profit before taxes	.2X		

$$.4X = \$40,000 + .2X$$
$$.2X = \$40,000$$
$$X = \$40,000 \, / \, .2$$
$$X = \$200,000$$

The following variable-costing income statement can be used to check the solution

Sales	$200,000	
Less variable costs	120,000	= .6 ($200,000)
Contribution margin	$ 80,000	= .4 ($200,000)
Less fixed costs	40,000	
Profit before taxes	$ 40,000	

$40,000 is 20% of $200,000. Therefore, it checks!

What sales in dollars is needed to obtain a targeted profit after taxes equal to 6 percent of sales?

Let X = sales in dollars

Sales	$	=	X
Less variable costs	_____	=	.6X
Contribution margin	$	=	.4X
Less fixed costs	40,000		
Profit before taxes	$		
Less income taxes	_____		
Profit after taxes	$___.06X		

Use the trick from TTM 15-6

AFTER = (1 - tax rate) x BEFORE

$$.06X = (1 - .4) \times BEFORE$$
$$.06X/.6 = BEFORE$$
$$\underline{.1X} = BEFORE$$

Therefore,

Sales	$	=	X
Less variable costs	_____	=	.6X
Contribution margin	$40,000+.1X	=	.4X
Less fixed costs	40,000		
Profit before taxes	$ .10X		
Less income taxes	.04X		= 40% (.1X)
Profit after taxes	$ .06X		

$$.4X = 40{,}000 + .1X$$
$$.3X = 40{,}000$$
$$X = \$40{,}000/.3$$
$$x = \underline{\$133{,}333}$$

The following income statement checks the solution:

Sales	$ 133,333	
Less variable costs	80,000	= .6 x $133,333
Contribution margin	53,333	
Less fixed costs	$ 40,000	
Profit before taxes	$ 13,333	
Less income taxes	5,333	= .4 x $13,333
Profit after taxes	$ 8,000	

$8,000 is 6% of $133,333. It checks!

MULTIPLE-PRODUCT ANALYSIS

Product	P	-	V	=	CM	x	Mix	=	Total CM
A	$10	-	$6	=	$4	x	3	=	$12
B	8	-	5	=	3	x	2	=	6
Total CM per package									$18

Total fixed expenses = $180,000

Break-even point:

$$X = F / \text{total CM per package}$$
$$= \$180,000 / \$18$$
$$= \underline{10,000} \text{ packages to break even}$$

Each package contains 3 units of A and 2 units of B. Therefore, to break even, we need to sell the following units of A and B:

A: 3 X 10,000 = 30,000 units
B: 2 X 10,000 = 20,000 units

PROFIT-VOLUME GRAPH

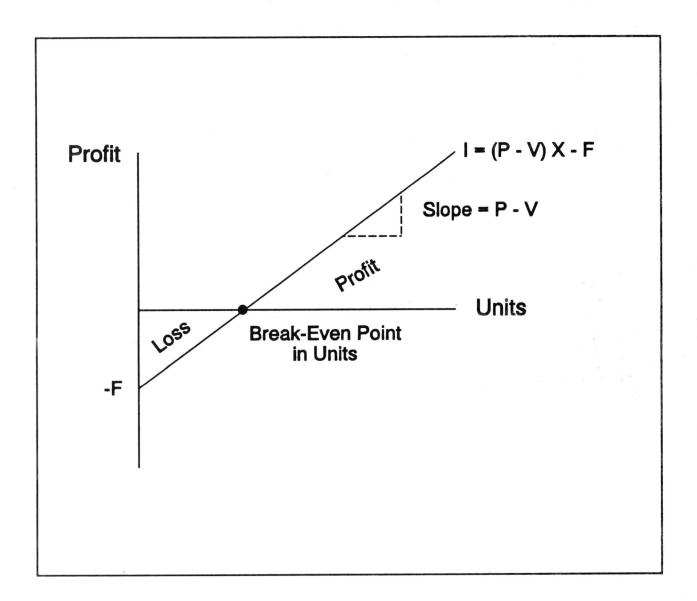

DISCUSS THE LIMITATIONS OF CVP ANALYSIS

A number of limitations are commonly mentioned with respect to CVP analysis:

1. The analysis assumes a linear revenue function and a linear cost function.

2. The analysis assumes that price, total fixed costs, and unit variable costs can be accurately identified, and remain constant over the relevant range.

3. The analysis assumes that what is produced is sold.

4. For multiple-product analysis, the sales mix is assumed to be known.

5. The selling prices and costs are assumed to be known with certainty.

MARGIN OF SAFETY

Assume that a company has the following projected income statement:

Revenues	$100,000
Variable expenses	(60,000)
Contribution margin	$ 40,000
Fixed expenses	(30,000)
Income before taxes	$ 10,000

Break-even point in dollars (R):

R	=	$30,000 / .4	=	$75,000
Safety margin		=	$100,000 - $75,000
Safety margin		=	$25,000

DEGREE OF OPERATING LEVERAGE (DOL)

DOL = $40,000 / $10,000 = 4.0

Now suppose that sales are 25% higher than projected. What is the percentage change in profits?

Percentage change in profits =

DOL x percentage change in sales =

$$4.0 \times 25\% = \underline{100\%}$$

Proof:

Revenues	$125,000
Less variable expenses	(75,000)
Contribution margin	$ 50,000
Less fixed expenses	(30,000)
Income before taxes	$ 20,000

SOLUTION TO EXERCISE 16-3
MAKE-OR-BUY DECISION

1.	Make	Buy
Direct materials	$ 48,000	$ 0
Direct labor	24,000	0
Variable overhead	16,000	0
Fixed overhead	4,800	0
Purchase cost	0	96,000 ($12 x 8,000)
Total relevant costs	$ 92,800	$96,000

Mason should continue manufacturing the part.

2.

Maximum price   = $92,800/8,000

= $11.60 per unit

SOLUTION TO EXERCISE 16-4
KEEP-OR-DROP A SEGMENT DECISION

1. Segmented income statement

	Product A	Product B	Total
Sales	$100,000	$250,000	$350,000
Variable exp.	50,000	145,000	195,000
Contribution margin	$ 50,000	$105,000	$155,000
Direct fixed exp.*	60,000	60,000	120,000
Segment margin	$ (10,000)	$ 45,000	$ 35,000
Common fixed exp.			70,000
Net income (loss)			$ (35,000)

*Product A: 100,000/350,000 x $70,000 = $20,000;
$80,000 - $20,000 = $60,000;

Product B: 250,000/350,000 x $70,000 = $50,000;
$110,000 - $50,000 = $60,000

2. Alternatives	Keep Both	Drop Both	Drop A Keep B	Drop B Keep A
Sales	$350,000	$ 0	$275,000	$150,000
Variable exp.	195,000	0	159,500	75,000
Contribution margin	$155,000	$ 0	$115,500	$ 75,000
Direct fixed exp.	120,000	0	60,000	60,000
Segment margin	$ 35,000	$ 0	$ 55,500	$ 15,000
Common fixed exp.	70,000	70,000	70,000	70,000
Net income (loss)	$ (35,000)	$ (70,000)	$ (14,500)	$ (55,000)

Golding should drop product A unless the common fixed costs can be avoided if both products are dropped.

SOLUTION TO EXERCISE 16-5

1. The company should accept the offer as the additional revenue is greater than the additional costs (assuming fixed overhead is allocated and will not increase with the special order):

Incremental revenue per box	$4.20
Incremental cost per box	3.25
Incremental income per box	$0.95

    Total additional income: $0.95 x 5,000 = 4,750

2. Accepting an order that shows a loss in order to maintain labor stability and community image may be justifiable when the idle capacity is viewed as a temporary state. Qualitative factors often outweigh quantitative (at least in the short run).

    In this case, the possibility of layoffs should be treated as a quantitative, rather than a qualitative factor. There are very real out-of-pocket costs associated with laying off workers. These include the cost of notification, rehiring, retraining, and increased unemployment insurance taxes. The personnel manager should be aware of these costs and have some idea of their magnitude. Of course, these "layoff costs" would be shown in favor of accepting the special order.

SOLUTION TO EXERCISE 16-6

1. Sales $185,000
   Costs   160,000
   Gross profit $ 25,000

	Sell	**Process Further**	**Difference**
2. Revenues	$75,000	$116,000	$ 41,000
Process cost	0	30,150	(30,150)
Gross profit	$75,000	$ 85,850	$ 10,850

The company should process "A" further as gross profit would increase by $10,850. (Note: Joint costs are irrelevant to this decision, as the company will incur them whether or not A is processed further.)

ONE CONSTRAINED RESOURCE

Thurman Company produces two types of disk players: economy and deluxe. The deluxe model has a contribution margin of $40 per unit and the economy model has a unit contribution margin of $25. The components of each model must be assembled manually. Assembly labor available per year is limited to 20,000 hours. The company can sell all that it produces of either model. The assembly time required for the economy model is two hours per unit. Because of the number and complexity of the parts for the deluxe model, the assembly time required is four hours per model. How many of each model should be produced?

Answer:

To maximize total contribution margin, select the product that yields the highest contribution margin per unit of scarce resource:

Deluxe: $40/4 = $10 per hour
Economy: $25/2 = $12.50 per hour

The economy model yields the highest CM/unit of scarce resource. Thus, 20,000/2 = 10,000 units of the economy model should be produced and none of the deluxe.

MULTIPLE CONSTRAINED RESOURCES

To the Thurman Company example for a one constrained resource, add the following additional constraint: the market limits sales of the economy disk player to 3,000 units. Formulate the linear programming problem and solve using the graphical method. Let X_1 = deluxe models and X_2 = economy models.

Formulation: Max CM = $40X_1 + 25X_2$

Subject to: $4X_1 + 2X_2 \leq 20,000$

$X_2 \leq 3,000$

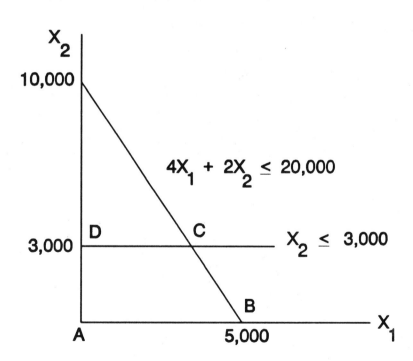

Corner Point	X_1	X_2	CM = $40X_1$ + $25X_2$
A	0	0	0
B	5,000	0	$200,000
C*	3,500	3,000	$215,000
D	0	3,000	$75,000

* Point C is optimal.

The X_1 value of point c is found by substituting the second equation into the first one like so:

$$4X_1 + 2 (3,000) = 20,000$$
$$4X_1 + 6,000 = 20,000$$
$$4X_1 = 14,000$$
$$X_1 = \underline{3,500}$$

CAPITAL BUDGETING

Capital budgeting: The process of making capital investment decisions.

Two types of capital budgeting projects:

Independent projects: Projects that, if accepted or rejected, will not affect the cash flows of another project.

Mutually exclusive projects: Projects that, if accepted, preclude the acceptance of competing projects.

PAYBACK METHOD

Payback Period: The time required to recover a project's original investment.

Example: Investment = $20,000

Cash flow pattern:
Year 1: $ 5,000
2: 10,000
3: 20,000
4: 20,000

Payback = 2.25 yrs.

$5,000 (yr. 1) + $10,000 (yr. 2) + $5,000 (one-fourth of yr. 3).

Possible reasons for use:
1. To help control the risks associated with the uncertainty of future cash flows
2. To help minimize the impact of an investment on a firm's liquidity problems
3. To help control the risk of obsolescence
4. To help control the effect of the investment on performance measures

Major deficiencies:
1. Ignores the time value of money
2. Ignores the performance of the investment beyond the payback period

ACCOUNTING RATE OF RETURN (ARR)

ARR = Average Income/Investment

Average income equals average annual net cash flows, less average depreciation.

Example: Suppose that some new equipment requires an initial outlay of $80,000 and promises total cash flows of $120,000 over the next five years (the life of the machine). What is the ARR?

Answer: The average cash flow is $24,000 ($120,000/5) and the average depreciation is $16,000 ($80,000/5).

$$
\begin{aligned}
ARR \quad &= \quad (\$24,000 - \$16,000)/\$80,000 \\
&= \quad \$8,000/\$80,000 \\
&= \quad 10\%
\end{aligned}
$$

Possible reasons for use:
1. A screening measure to ensure that new investment will not adversely affect net income
2. To ensure a favorable effect on net income so that bonuses can be earned (increased)

Major deficiency: Ignores the time value of money

FUTURE VALUE

Let

F = future value

i = the interest rate

P = the present value or original outlay

n = the number of periods

Future value can be expressed by the following formula:

$$F = P(1 + i)^n$$

Example: Assume the investment is $1,000. The interest rate is 8%. What is the future value if the money is invested for one year? Two? Three?

F = $1,000(1.08) = $1,080.00 (after one year)

F = $1,000(1.08)^2 = $1,166.40 (after two years)

F = $1,000(1.08)^3 = $1259.71 (after three years)

PRESENT VALUE

$$P = \frac{F}{(1 + i)^n}$$

The discount factor, $1/(1 + i)^n$, is computed for various combinations of i and n. See Exhibit 17B-1.

Example: Compute the present value of $300 to be received three years from now. The interest rate is 12%.

Answer: From Exhibit 17b-1, the discount factor is 0.712. Thus, the present value (P) is:

P = F(df)
    = $300 x 0.712
    = <u>$213.60</u>

Example: Calculate the present value of a $100 per year annuity, to be received for the next three years. The interest rate is 12%.

Answer:

Year	Cash	Discount Factor	Present Value
1	$100	0.893	$ 89.30
2	100	0.797	79.70
3	100	0.712	71.20
		2.402*	$240.20

* Notice that it is possible to multiply the sum of the individual discount factors (2.402) by $100 to obtain the same answer. See Exhibit 17B-2 for these sums which can be used as discount factors for uniform series.

NET PRESENT VALUE (NPV)

I. Definition

$$NPV = P - I$$

where:

P   =   the present value of the project's future cash inflows

I   =   the present value of the project's cost (usually the initial outlay)

NPV IS A MEASURE OF THE PROFITABILITY OF AN INVESTMENT, EXPRESSED IN CURRENT DOLLARS.

Example: A project promises to return $10,000 after one year and $20,000 after two years. The project also requires an initial investment of $22,000. Calculate its net present value, assuming a 12% discount rate.

Year	Cash Flow	Discount Factor	Present Value
0	$(22,000)	1.000	$(22,000)
1	10,000	0.893	8,930
2	20,000	0.797	15,940
			$ 2,870

II. Decision Criteria for NPV
A. If the NPV > 0, this indicates:
1. The initial investment has been recovered
2. The cost of capital is recovered
3. A return in excess of the cost of capital has been earned

Thus, the project should be accepted.

B. If NPV = 0, this indicates:
1. The initial investment has been recovered
2. The cost of capital has been recovered

Thus, break even has been achieved and we are indifferent about the project.

C. If NPV < 0, this indicates
1. The initial investment may or may not be recovered
2. The cost of capital has not been recovered

Thus, the project should be rejected.

III. Reinvestment Assumption

The NPV model assumes that all cash flows generated by a project are immediately reinvested to earn the required rate of return throughout the life of the project.

DISCOUNT RATE: THE COST OF CAPITAL

The appropriate discount rate to use for NPV computations is the cost of capital. The COST OF CAPITAL is the weighted average of the returns expected by the different parties contributing funds. The weights are determined by the proportion of funds provided by each source.

Example: A company is planning on financing a project by borrowing $10,000 and by raising $20,000 by issuing capital stock. The net cost of borrowing is 6% per year. The stock carries an expected return of 9%. The sources of capital for this project and their cost are in the same proportion and amounts that the company usually experiences. Calculate the cost of capital.

Source	Amount	Cost	Weight	Cost x Weight
Debt	$10,000	6%	1/3	2%
Stock	20,000	9%	2/3	6%
Weighted-Average Cost of Capital				8%

INTERNAL RATE OF RETURN (IRR)

I. Definition
The internal rate of return is the discount rate that sets the project's NPV at zero. Thus, P = I for the IRR.

Example: A project requires a $10,000 investment and will return $12,000 after one year. What is the IRR?

$$\$12,000 \; / \; (1 + i) \; = \; \$10,000$$
$$1 + i \qquad\qquad = \; 1.2$$
$$i \qquad\qquad\qquad = \; 0.20$$

II. Decision criteria
A. If the IRR > Cost of Capital, the project should be accepted.

B. If the IRR = Cost of Capital, acceptance or rejection is equal.

C. If the IRR < Cost of Capital, the project should be rejected.

III. Reinvestment Assumption
The cash inflows received from the project are immediately reinvested to earn a return equal to the IRR for the remaining life of the project.

NPV vs IRR

There are two major differences between the two approaches:

- NPV assumes cash inflows are reinvested at the cost of capital.

  The IRR method assumes that the inflows are reinvested at the internal rate of return.

- NPV measures the profitability of a project in absolute dollars whereas the IRR method measures it as a percentage.

Conflicting Signals (cost of capital = 10%)

Year	Project A	Project B
0	$(10,000)	$(10,000)
1		6,000
2	13,924	7,200
IRR	18%	20%
NPV	$ 1,501	$ 1,401

Which project should be selected? IRR signals Project B, whereas NPV signals Project A.

The terminal value of Project A is $13,924.

To calculate the future value of B, assume that the $6,000 received at the end of year one is invested at the cost of capital. Thus, the future value of B is $7,200 + (1.1)$6,000 = $13,800.

Project A provides the most wealth and should be selected (AS SIGNALED BY NPV). IRR assumes the $6,000 can be reinvested at 20% when in actuality it is reinvested at 10%.

SENSITIVITY ANALYSIS: AN ILLUSTRATIVE EXAMPLE

Initial Data:

Investment . . . . $(55,000)

Annual cash flow 20,000

Discount rate 12%

Expected life of project . . . . 4 years

NPV Analysis:

Scenario	CF	DF	P	I	NPV
	$20,000	3.037	$60,740	$(55,000)	$5,740
10% less cash	18,000	3.037	54,666	(55,000)	(334)
1 year less	20,000	2.402	48,040	(55,000)	(6,960)
Rate = 14%	20,000	2.914	58,280	(55,000)	3,280
Combination	18,000	2.322	41,796	(55,000)	(13,204)

Before investing, further assessment of the expected life of the project is needed. The likelihood of earning 10% or less of the projected cash flows should also be assessed.

INFLATIONARY ADJUSTMENT: AN ILLUSTRATIVE EXAMPLE

Assume that the rate of inflation is 6% per year.

Analysis Without Inflationary Adjustment (assumes a 12% discount rate)

Year	CF	DF	P
0	$(10,000)	1.000	$ (10,000)
1-2	5,500	1.690	9,295
NPV			$ (705)

Analysis with Inflationary Adjustment

Year	CF	DF	P
0	$(10,000)	1.000	$ (10,000)
1	5,830	* 0.893	5,206
2	6,180	** 0.797	4,925
NPV			$ 131

*   1.06 x $5,500

** 1.06 x 1.06 x $5,500

Notice that adjusting for inflation can affect the decision.

AFTER-TAX OPERATING CASH FLOWS: THE INCOME APPROACH

After-tax cash flow =
   After-tax net income + Noncash expenses

Example:

Revenues	$1,000,000
Less operating expenses*	600,000
Income before taxes	$ 400,000
Less income taxes	136,000
Net income	$ 264,000

* $100,000 is depreciation

After-tax cash flow   = $264,000 + $100,000
                                 = $364,000

AFTER-TAX FLOWS: DECOMPOSITION APPROACH

After-tax cash
  revenues   = (1 - Tax rate) x Cash revenues
After-tax cash
  expense   = (1 - Tax rate) x Cash expenses
Tax savings
  (noncash expenses) = (Tax rate) x Noncash expenses

Total operating cash is equal to the after-tax cash revenues, less the after-tax cash expenses, plus the tax savings on noncash expenses.

Example: Revenues = $1,000,000, cash expenses = $500,000, and depreciation = $100,000. Tax rate = 34%.

After-tax cash revenues	(1 - .34)	($1,000,000)	=	$ 660,000
Less: After-tax cash expense	(1 - .34)	($500,000)	=	(330,000)
Add: Tax savings (noncash exp.)	.34	($100,000)	=	34,000
Total				$ 364,000

DEPRECIATION: TAX-SHIELDING EFFECT

Depreciation is a noncash expense and is not a cash flow. Depreciation, however, SHIELDS revenues from being taxed and, thus, creates a cash inflow equal to the tax savings.

Assume initially that tax laws DO NOT allow depreciation to be deducted to arrive at taxable income. If a company had before-tax operating cash flows of $300,000 and depreciation of $100,000, we have the following statement:

Net operating cash flows	$300,000
Less depreciation	0
Taxable income	$300,000
Less income taxes (@ 34%)	(102,000)
Net income	$198,000

Now assume that the tax laws allow a deduction for depreciation:

Net operating cash flows	$300,000
Less depreciation	100,000
Taxable income	$200,000
Less income taxes (@ 34%)	(68,000)
Net income	$132,000

Notice that the taxes saved are $34,000 ($102,000 - $68,000). Thus, the firm has additional cash available of $34,000.

This savings can be computed by multiplying the tax rate by the amount of depreciation claimed:

.34 x $100,000 = $34,000

TAX LAWS: DEPRECIATION

The tax laws classify most assets into the following three classes (class = allowable years):

Class	Types of Assets
3	Most small tools
5	Cars, light trucks, and computer equip.
7	Most equip, machinery, office equip.

Assets in any of the three classes can be depreciated using either straight line or MACRS (Modified Accelerated Cost Recovery System) with a half-life convention.

Half-life convention: (1) Half the depreciation for the first year can be claimed regardless of when the assets is actually placed in service; (2) the other half year of depreciation is claimed in the year following the end of the asset's class life; (3) if the asset is disposed of before the end of its class life, only half of the depreciation for that year can be claimed.

Example (straight line): A company acquired a five-year property for $100,000:

Year	Depreciation Allowed
1	$10,000
2	20,000
3	20,000
4	20,000
5	20,000
6	10,000

MACRS uses double-declining balance with a half-year convention. This method also switches to straight-line depreciation whenever the straight-line amount exceeds the double-declining balance amount. EXHIBIT 17-8 provides the MACRS depreciation rates for three-, five- and seven-year assets.

Example (MACRS): Assume five-year property costing $100,000:

Year	Depreciation Allowed
1	$20,000
2	32,000
3	19,200
4	11,520
5	11,520
6	5,760

Example: Suppose the asset was disposed of in Year 2. How much depreciation can be claimed?

Answer: Only half for that year:

0.5 x $32,000 = $16,000

CAPITAL RATIONING

$$NPV\ index = \frac{NPV}{Investment}$$

A company has $45,000 of capital available for the following investment opportunities:

Project	Investment	NPV	NPV Index
A	$10,000	$3,000	0.30
B	20,000	4,000	0.20
C	25,000	10,000	0.40
D	15,000	5,000	0.33
	$70,000		

NPV index ranking (greatest to least): C, D, A, B

Investment decision: Invest in C, D, and one-half of A.

CAPITAL BUDGETING: A NEW EMPHASIS

Assume that a company is considering investment in an automated system (estimated life of ten years) that has the following after-tax cash flows:

From tangible benefits	$100,000/year
From intangible benefits	$60,000/year
Salvage value	$150,000
Initial outlay	$1,000,000

The company's cost of capital is 10% but an 18% required rate is used for capital budgeting decisions.

NPV Analysis:

	18% Rate	10% Rate
Tangible only:		
4.494 x $100,000 - $1,000,000	$ (550,600)	
6.145 x $100,000 - $1,000,000		$ (385,500)
Tangible & Intangible:		
4.494 x 160,000 - $1,000,000	(280,960)	
6.145 x 160,000 - $1,000,000		(16,800)
Tangible, Intangible, & Salvage Value:		
(280,960) + (.191 x $150,000)	(252,310)	
(16,800) + (.386 x $150,000)		41,100

Notice how the NPV for the 10% rate eventually becomes positive as all inputs are considered. This emphasizes the importance of using the correct discount rate and the importance of considering all factors that affect cash flows.

INVENTORY COSTS WHEN PURCHASED FROM AN OUTSIDE SUPPLIER

1. **Ordering Costs: The costs of placing and receiving an order**
   Examples: clerical costs, documents, insurance for shipment, and unloading.

2. **Carrying Costs: The costs of keeping inventory**
   Examples: insurance, inventory taxes, obsolescence, opportunity cost of capital tied up in inventory, and storage.

3. **Stockout Costs: The costs of not having sufficient inventory**
   Examples: lost sales, costs of expediting (extra setup, transportation, etc.) and the costs of interrupted production.

4. **Setup Costs: The costs of preparing equipment and facilities so they can be used to produce a particular product or component**
   Examples: setup labor, lost income (from idled facilities), and test runs. When a firm produces the goods internally, ordering costs are replaced by setup costs.

WHY INVENTORY IS NEEDED: TRADITIONAL VIEW

1. To balance ordering or setup costs and carrying costs

2. To satisfy customer demand (e.g., meet delivery dates)

3. To avoid shutting down manufacturing facilities because of:

   a. machine failure

   b. defective parts

   c. unavailable parts

   d. late delivery of parts

4. To buffer against unreliable production processes

5. To take advantage of discounts

6. To hedge against future price increases

INVENTORY COST EQUATION AND THE EOQ

Assuming demand is known with certainty, then the total costs of inventory can be expressed as follows (note wherever ordering cost is used it could be replaced with setup cost)

$$TC = \frac{PD}{Q} + \frac{CQ}{2}$$

$$= \text{Ordering cost} + \text{Carrying cost}$$

where:

TC = the total ordering (or setup) and carrying costs

P = the cost of placing and receiving an order (or the cost of setting up a production run)

D = the known annual demand

C = the cost of carrying one unit of stock for one year.

Q = the number of units ordered each time an order is placed (or the lot size for production)

The order size that minimizes total cost (economic order quantity) is given by the following equation:

$$EOQ = \sqrt{\frac{2DP}{C}}$$

AN ILLUSTRATIVE APPLICATION: EOQ

Assume that Hendrix Company produces a component used in one of its products. The following data pertain to this component:

D	=	1,000 units
Q	=	50 units
P	=	$200/setup
C	=	$40/unit

Required: Calculate the cost of the current lot size being produced. Next calculate the EOQ and determine the savings that will be realized by switching to the optimal lot size.

$$TC = \frac{PD}{Q} + \frac{CQ}{2}$$

$$= \frac{\$200 \times 1,000}{50} + \frac{\$40 \times 50}{2}$$

$$= \$4,000 + \$1,000$$

$$= \underline{\$5,000}$$

$$EOQ = \sqrt{\frac{2DP}{C}}$$

$$= \sqrt{\frac{2 \times 1{,}000 \times \$200}{\$40}}$$

$$= \sqrt{10{,}000}$$

$$= \underline{100} \text{ units}$$

$$TC = \frac{PD}{Q} + \frac{CQ}{2}$$

$$= \frac{\$200 \times 1{,}000}{100} + \frac{\$40 \times 100}{2}$$

$$= \$2{,}000 + \$2{,}000$$

$$= \underline{\$4{,}000}$$

Note that the setup costs = carrying costs for the EOQ.

Savings = $5,000 - $4,000
= $1,000

REORDER POINT

I. When demand is certain

Reorder point   =   Rate of usage x Lead time

Example: Assume that the average rate of usage is 4 units per day for a component. Assume also that the time required to place and receive an order is 10 days. What is the reorder point?

Reorder point   =   4 x 10   =   <u>40</u> units

Thus, an order should be placed when inventory drops to 40 units.

II. When demand is uncertain

Reorder point   =

(Average rate of usage x Lead time) + Safety stock

where:

Safety stock   =

(Maximum usage - Average usage) x Lead time

Example: Suppose that the maximum usage is 6 units per day and the average usage is 4 units per day. The lead time is 10 days. What is the reorder point?

Safety stock   = (6 - 4) x 10

= <u>20</u> units

Reorder point   = (4 x 10) + 20

= <u>60</u> units

THE ORDER POINT DEMAND IS CERTAIN

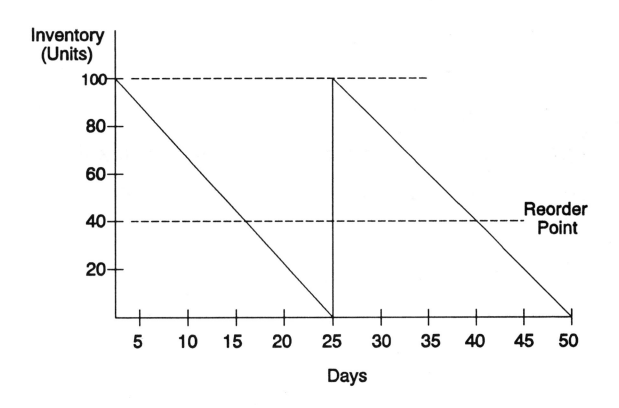

JIT AND INVENTORY MANAGEMENT

1. **Setup and Carrying Costs: The JIT Approach**

    A. JIT reduces the costs of acquiring inventory to insignificant levels by:

        1. Drastically reducing setup time

        2. Using long-term contracts for outside purchases

    B. Carrying costs are reduced to insignificant levels by reducing inventories to insignificant levels.

2. **Due-Date Performance: The JIT Solution**

    A. Lead times are reduced so that the company can meet requested delivery dates and to respond quickly to customer demand.

    B. Lead times are reduced by (1) reducing setup times, (2) improving quality, and (3) using cellular manufacturing.

3. **Avoidance of Shutdown: The JIT Approach**

   A. Total preventive maintenance to reduce machine failures

   B. Total quality control to reduce defective parts

   C. Cultivation of supplier relationships to ensure availability of quality raw materials and subassemblies (the use of the Kanban system is also essential)

4. **Discounts and Price Increases: JIT Purchasing Versus Holding Inventories**

   A. Careful vendor selection

   B. Long-term contracts with vendors

      1. Prices are stipulated (usually producing a significant savings)

      2. Quality is stipulated

      3. The number of orders placed are reduced

COOPERATIVE LEARNING TECHNIQUES

PREFACE

When Neil Davidson, President, gave a keynote address at the 1990 conference of the International Society for the Study of Cooperation in Education, he emphasized that cooperative learning—because of its fulfillment of basic human needs, its growth as a grassroots movement, its solid research base, its endorsement by numerous state and national educational commissions, and its compatibility with virtually every sound pedagogical practice in education—was far from a passing fad.

While we were in agreement with his viewpoint, we certainly did not anticipate the staggering growth of interest in cooperative learning at the postsecondary level within the past three years. Our first attempt at collaboration, a paper on cooperative learning and accounting later published in *Journal of Accounting Education,* also began at that conference. With Barbara's Ph.D. in English literature and background in faculty development and Phil's Ph.D. in accounting and background in college teaching, we made an unlikely pair. On the patio of the Baltimore Convention Center, Barbara painstakingly reshaped Phil's often cumbersome prose and jokingly told him that as a writer, he was a great accountant. Phil, on the other hand, patiently explained terms such as "fixed assets" and "accrual accounting" and dazzled Barbara with his creative accounting applications for cooperative learning. Just as we could not have predicted the surge of interest in cooperative learning, we likewise did not anticipate that our initial collaboration would lead to more co-authored articles, joint workshop presentations, an ongoing friendship between our two families, and finally this book.

This book, carefully tied to Hansen and Mowen's text, *Management Accounting*, fourth edition, represents a fortuitous merging of Barbara's years of experience as a faculty developer dedicated to practical, effective classroom practices and Phil's wealth of experience as a serious-minded professor of accounting. Thus, the book combines both theory and practice and places the concrete examples from the Hansen and Mowen text within a contextual framework. Our *modus operandi* is always good classroom practice. Because of the richness of the material, the earlier chapters in particular provide a variety of documented sources to encourage further reading and reflection.

In the first chapter we place the cooperative learning movement, which is explained in an overview, within the context of the approaches to teaching and learning endorsed by the Accounting Education Change Commission (AECC).

The second chapter addresses the need for change by placing cooperative learning within the broader context of education reform and the factors fueling it, including the changing work place, the changing student populations, and a changing teaching paradigm. The need for change is again tied to the position statements of the AECC. The latter half of the chapter deals with resistances to change by providing answers to key issues such as the "softness" of group work, content coverage, loss of control, student resistance, lack of nontraditional teaching role models, colleague suspicions, evaluation, and the time involved to rework course material.

Because classroom management concerns are critically important in any classroom, but particularly so in one predicated on cooperative teaching and learning, Chapter 3 addresses issues such as the student and teacher roles, course planning, team formation and maintenance, and dysfunctional teams. Chapter 3 also contains a basic cooperative structure, the Cooperative Homework Check.

With Chapter 4, we begin to focus on the day-to-day classroom activities that are easily correlated to the Hansen and Mowen text. We discuss four specific structures—Think-Pair-Share, Value Line, Corners, and Three-Step Interview—explaining how and why they are used and proving specific examples from the textbook. Structures are remarkably versatile, content-free exercises that can be applied to a variety of educational setting and situations. The latter three structures, for example, are useful for group formations.

More advanced structures, predicated on the idea that students will remain in semi-permanent (usually half-a-semester) learning teams, are introduced in Chapter 5. The structures, which are amply illustrated by examples from Hansen and Mowen's text, are divided into three broad categories: (a) structures useful for problem solving, (B) structures useful for brainstorming, and (c) structures useful for reviewing material.

The complex structures, similarly linked to the Hansen and Mowen text, are organized in Chapter 6 by their primary functions: teaching, questioning, and critiquing.

In Chapter 7 we encourage accounting faculty to be both creative and flexible. We also expand the educational horizons by linking cooperative learning to several other sound teaching practices including the use of graphic organizers to focus assignments, case studies, and classroom assessment techniques.

In the final chapter, Chapter 8, we emphasize the value of making a variety of connections: students to students, faculty to students and other faculty, and theory to practice, and finally, through the "Seven Principles for Good Practice In Undergraduate Education," to sound teaching practices.

We are both excited about cooperative learning. We know it results in a number of favorable outcomes in a variety of disciplines. Phil can testify that cooperative learning has transformed his teaching and reinvigorated both him and his students. We sincerely hope you will join the growing number of cooperative learning practitioners at the postsecondary level.

Philip G. Cottell, Jr.
Barbara J. Millis

TABLE OF CONTENTS

CHAPTER 1

COOPERATIVE LEARNING IN ACCOUNTING CLASSES

"Tell me and I'll listen. Show me and I'll understand. Involve me and I'll learn."

Teton Lakota Indians

The stereotype of the bald-headed accountant in a green eye shade poring over a musty ledger in the solitary glare of a swinging light bulb has been replaced by a more realistic picture of serious professionals, both men and women, meeting in board rooms around the world. Unfortunately, the stereotypes in university settings about boring, mind-numbing, overly complex accounting lectures tend to be reinforced by the flickering overheads and silent classrooms prevalent too often in too many accounting departments on too many campuses. This book is about innovation, change, and renewal. It also provides a common-sense, one-step-at-a-time, accounting-based approach to innovation, change, and renewal. Although the general information provided in this book can help accounting instructors transform any class, the examples used here are designed to be used as an instructor's resource guide for *Management Accounting*, fourth edition, by Hansen and Mowen.

Much of the well-intentioned literature on higher education reform tends to be theoretical and exhortative: "Use active learning techniques." "Be responsive in the classroom." "Respect diversity." Equally well-intentioned instructors are often at a loss for practical ways to operationalize these new challenges. Such challenges have come from the accounting profession itself. The Accounting Education Change Commission (AECC) has alerted accounting instructors to the need for new approaches to teaching and learning. Specifically, the Commission endorses active learning, complex problem solving, experiential approaches, group work, and innovative uses of technology. Fortunately, these goals can be realized through a time-tested, increasingly well-known pedagogy called cooperative learning.

UNDERSTANDING COOPERATIVE LEARNING

An Overview of Cooperative Learning

Solidly grounded in theory, research, and practice, cooperative learning provides a pragmatic, practical means to directly increase student mastery and achievement levels. At the same time, this approach fosters a number of other desirable outcomes, such as increasing student self-esteem; building among students mutual respect and liking regardless of ethnic, gender, or cultural considerations; and preparing students to work effectively in a team-oriented work place. Cooperative learning can be regarded as a more structured—and hence more focused and, as practitioners believe, more effective—form of collaborative learning. Collaborative learning advocates have been handicapped by the fact that, like other teaching reform movements, its tenets are often too theoretical for practical applications. Whipple (1987) admits, for example, that collaborative learning embraces an "extraordinarily wide range of programs, projects, pedagogical techniques and classroom strategies" (p. 3); this diffusion too often means that instructors find "the concept ambiguous and too abstract for direct application" (Sheridan, Byrne, & Quina, 1989, p. 49). Because it is under the broad umbrella of collaborative learning, cooperative learning shares with this movement mutual goals, such as promoting active learning, bridging the gulf between students and teachers, creating a sense of community, and ensuring that knowledge is created, not transferred. But, because it is more focused, instructors using the cooperative learning structures described in later chapters can move directly toward successful classroom applications. They must keep in mind, however, the two important principles discussed more fully in this chapter: positive interdependence (students must be motivated, either extrinsically or intrinsically, to work together productively) and individual accountability (students cannot coast on the work of their teammates as happens with undifferentiated group grades for projects or papers, but instead must demonstrate their own content mastery).

What is Cooperative Learning?

Cooperative learning tends to be more carefully structured and delineated than most other forms of small group learning. Cooper and Mueck (1989) describe it as "a structured, systematic instructional strategy in which small groups work together toward a common goal" (p. 1). Most experts agree that several components distinguish cooperative learning from other small group or paired procedures, including collaborative learning, which embraces a wide range of student-student, student-faculty interactions. As indicated earlier, the most important of these cooperative learning elements are positive interdependence and individual accountability. The other three components are appropriate grouping (which usually means heterogeneous grouping), group processing, and team-building social skills.

TWO KEY COMPONENTS

Positive interdependence occurs, according to Kagan (1992), "when gains of individuals or teams are positively correlated" (p. 4:2). The Johnson brothers in numerous publications use the expression "sink or swim together." Johnson, Johnson, and Smith (1991) describe positive interdependence in these words:

> Cooperation results in participants' striving for mutual benefit so that all members of the group benefit from each other's efforts (your success benefits me and my success benefits you), their recognizing that all group members share a common fate (we sink or swim together) and that one's performance depends mutually on oneself and one's colleagues (we cannot do it without you), and their feeling proud and jointly celebrating when a group member is recognized for achievement (you got an A! that's terrific!). (p. 3)

In a traditional educational setting, students tend to work either on their own or in competition with one another. In a cooperative setting, all class members, particularly those grouped in instructor-selected learning teams, contribute to each other's learning. Through careful planning, positive interdependence can be established by having accounting students achieve: (a) mutual goals, such as reaching a consensus on specific accounting problems' solutions or arriving at team-generated solutions for solving, for example, ethical issues in accounting; (b) mutual rewards, such as individually assigned cooperative learning points counting toward a criterion-referenced final grade, points which only help, but never handicap; (c) structured tasks, such as a report or complex accounting problem with sections contributed by each team member; and (d) interdependent roles, such as group members serving as discussion leaders, organizers, recorders, and spokespersons.

Positive interdependence empowers students, including women and diverse students, who might lose their voice in traditional learning situations where the instructor and high-achieving, more vocal students tend to dominate whole-class discussions. Everyone in a well-conducted cooperative learning classroom has an opportunity for equal participation and equal validation.

In cooperative learning, instructors build into their syllabus and class norms the expectation that students will work together. Positive interdependence can be developed in many different ways; many would argue that it can be established most effectively through the design of the assigned activity.

A second component, individual accountability, indicates to students who might be "hitchhikers" (students who do not—for whatever reasons—do a fair share of assigned group work) or "overachievers" or "workhorses" (students who assume a disproportionate amount of the workload) that these roles are unacceptable in a cooperative setting. Such practices are counter-productive in an environment where students, no matter how much mutual support, coaching, and encouragement they receive, are individually responsible for their own academic achievements. Because most accounting students have been acclimated to an academic setting where they compete against fellow classmates, this aspect of cooperative learning is somehow reassuring: their final course grades will be based on their own efforts, uncompromised and uncomplicated by the achievements of others. Instructors also generally applaud this important aspect of cooperative learning. In fact, when their grading systems are fully formulated, students find that their efforts to help others never hurt their own achievements and can, in some cases, actually increase their course grades either directly or indirectly. Research by Webb (1989) indicates that student achievement is directly correlated to the level of elaboration of help that students provide other group members. This finding should come as no surprise to instructors, who already know that those who teach learn the most. Thus, instructors establish for students a "win-win" situation.

Evaluation of students, the area of teaching instructors most often disparage, consumes enormous energy that could be channeled more productively into teaching/learning activities. The question of how to evaluate students engaged in cooperative activities can produce anxiety and uncertainty. There is—unfortunately—no easy solution. Much of the debate centers on the question of whether or not students are intrinsically or extrinsically motivated. Will students work together, helping one another, if there is no direct "pay-off"? The debate is not resolved, but a lot of good arguments on both sides have evolved. Kohn (1986) argues that rewarding students—putting a price tag on efforts—undermines their natural altruistic desire to help others. More emphatically, Kagan suggests that basing even part of student grades on the efforts and achievements of others may be both ethically and legally unwise (private conversation, December 11, 1992).

There is a common misconception that group work automatically entails group grades. Nothing could be further from the truth. Individual accountability precludes this too-often used practice. Undifferentiated group grades for a single project, particularly if the majority of the work is expected out-of-class, invite inequity problems. Too often one student ends up doing the majority of the work. That student often relishes the power associated with this role but resents the lack of input from students who will benefit from the same grade. The students who contribute little receive signals that their efforts are unappreciated or unwanted, and they learn that there is such a thing as a free lunch—they receive a grade they did not earn.

Some accounting professors, like others in preprofessional disciplines, may argue—legitimately, of course—that "real world" preparation should put students in situations where they must negotiate each team member's input and be prepared to accept less-than optimum results, including situations where one team member's performance—or lack of performance—drags down the team grade for all members. Decisions about grading criteria established this way obviously lie with the individual instructor, but most cooperative learning researchers and practitioners do not advocate undifferentiated group grades. Ethical, legal, and morale issues are involved when instructors assign a common grade to all group members for a single project. Arguably, the norms, expectations, and rewards in a university setting—particularly the all-important CPA examination—do not equate to work place realities.

SOME FURTHER ATTRIBUTES OF A COOPERATIVE CLASSROOM

Appropriate grouping is also essential. Researchers such as Kagan (1992) and Johnson, Johnson, Holubec, and Roy (1984) recommend heterogenous teams, reflecting varied learning abilities, ethnic and linguistic diversity, and a mixture of the sexes. In a semester-length academic course, most practitioners recommend instructor-selected learning teams of four. Teams composed of four students work effectively because they are small enough to promote interaction, large enough to tolerate an occasional absence, and balanced enough to permit focused activities in pairs. The teams can be kept in place throughout the semester or, more typically, rearranged at the midsemester point. In briefer situations, a short-term mix of students focusing on specific learning goals is appropriate; depending on the task and the group members these teams can be homogenous. Because most employers value cooperation and teamwork, heterogeneous teams provide opportunities to prepare for or to reinforce practices needed in the work place that accountants will face. The Total Quality Management (TQM) movement, for example, has spread from industry to academe (Marchese, 1991). Instructor-selected teams ensure heterogeneity along a number of lines, including age, ethnicity, and ability. If students are allowed to select their fellow teammates, they tend to seek out friends or students who share similar educational, economic, or ethnic backgrounds. When teams are formed randomly, they may be uneven. It would be counter-productive, for example, for all the high-achievers or all the less academically prepared students to find themselves on one team formed through random grouping.

A fourth component, group processing, helps build team skills, allows students to reflect on the learning process and outcomes, and provides instructors with continuous feedback. Instructors and students monitor group and individual progress. After an assignment or activity, for instance, accounting students could respond to questions such as: "Did all members of the group contribute?" "What could be done next time to make the group function better?" or "What were the most important things I learned today?"

Social skills are also important in cooperative learning. These go beyond mere politeness. Students must recognize the importance of cooperative interaction and mutual respect. Instructors should model appropriate social skills, including ways of providing constructive feedback or eliciting more in-depth responses through probing questions. They should also reinforce these social skills by publicly commenting on ways students use them effectively.

A recent cartoon by Mel Lazarus depicts a swimming coach urging his charges to follow the "buddy system" before leaping into a lake. "Are we here to learn swimming or interpersonal relationships?" demands Ira. The answer, of course, is that collaboration in this situation provides a safe environment where learning can occur. In the college classroom a safe, supportive environment is particularly important with the diverse student population now entering many professions. No one suggests that any students should be "coddled" or that standards should be lowered or altered; however, a positive classroom climate that encourages all students to help one another as they strive for excellence is a worthy goal. Mixing cooperative learning, which offers a strong basis for mutual student support, with traditional delivery methods allows instructors to accommodate special needs or learning styles. Sanford's (1965) early research established the concept that developmental growth is enhanced by a climate of challenge and support. Too much challenge can discourage students, causing drop-outs; too much support results in boredom and loss of interest. Instructors have traditionally focused on covering content, not on uncovering material with students. Those committed to student learning will use a variety of approaches, including cooperative learning, to foster student achievement.

Would-be practitioners are reassured by the fact that cooperative learning techniques rarely replace, *in toto,* traditional approaches to learning such as the lecture or instructor-directed discussion. Cooper (1990) notes that most college and university faculty use cooperative learning techniques only about 15 to 40 percent of the total class time available (p. 2). As Slavin (1989-1990a) cautions, "Successful [cooperative learning] models always include plain old good instruction; the cooperative activities *supplement* but do not replace direct instruction." (p. 3)

The integration of cooperative learning techniques into traditional delivery methods such as lecture does emphasize the facilitative approach most students welcome. Power is shifted from the authority figure of the instructor to the students who then become actively involved in their own learning and in the learning processes of their peers. In informal terms, the instructor becomes not the "sage on the stage," but "the guide on the side." Too often, instructors hoping to improve their teaching focus on "How am I doing? Is my delivery well-paced? Am I covering the content? Do my students like me?" A cooperative learning approach reformulates those questions and asks such things as: "How are my students doing? How can I discover if they are learning the material? Are they relating to me, the other students in class, and the learning experience?" Thus, the cooperative learning approach complements and enhances the movement fostered by Angelo and Cross (1993) toward classroom research. Such research is directed not toward traditional "publish or perish" projects, but to the assessment of what students are learning in an individual classroom. In fact, Cross (1993) postulates that this type of "pedagogical assessment" differs from traditional assessment in that it is tied directly to the teaching and learning process, looking not at "what is," but "what might be." In other words, instructors who introduce activities such as the one-minute-paper into their classroom—an activity that asks students to answer two questions: (a) What was the most useful/meaningful thing you learned during this session? and (b) What question(s) remain uppermost in your mind as we end this session?—can use the data they collect to stimulate informed adjustments in their teaching, but can also share the feedback with students in order to help them improve their learning strategies and study habits. The research—what we already know about student learning—provides a strong incentive, like many others, for innovative changes in the way instructors teach accounting.

The Research Base for Cooperative Learning

Cooperative learning has a long-standing, solid research base. A great deal of the long-term research, augmented by a plethora of recent cooperative learning studies on the postsecondary level, indicates that students involved in structured small group work also develop a liking for the subject matter and a liking and respect for their fellow group members and classmates, regardless of their differing academic, ethnic, gender, or age-related backgrounds.

Cooperative learning is, according to Slavin (1989-1990b), "one of the most thoroughly researched of all instructional methods" (p. 52). Johnson, Johnson, and Smith (1991) conclude:

> During the past 90 years, over 575 experimental and 100 correlational studies have been conducted by a wide variety of researchers in different decades with different age subjects, in different subject areas, and in different settings. . . . Far more is known about the efficacy of cooperative learning than about lecturing, . . . the use of technology, or almost any other facet of education. (p. 28)

Furthermore, although much of the research has been conducted at the K-12 level, Natasi and Clements (1991) conclude that the benefits of cooperative learning, described as "enhance[d] academic achievement and cognitive growth, motivation and positive attitudes toward learning, social competence, and interpersonal relations," seem to be universal. They emphasize that:

> Cognitive-academic and social-emotional benefits have been reported for students from early elementary through college level, from diverse ethnic and cultural backgrounds, and having a wide range of ability levels. . . . Furthermore, cooperative learning has been used effectively across a wide range of content areas, including mathematics, reading, language arts, social studies, and science. (p. 111)

Thus, cooperative learning is also one of the most versatile educational strategies available. It complements virtually every pedagogy or approach known to promote effective teaching and learning: classroom research, the "Seven Principles for Good Practice in Undergraduate Education," stimulus materials, case studies, and problem-based curriculum. (Accountants interested in detailed overviews of the research base for cooperative learning as it applies to higher education should consult Cooper, Prescott, Cook, Smith, Mueck, and Cuseo [1990] or Johnson, Johnson, and Smith [1991]; they should also contact the cooperative learning special interest group [SIG] of the American Educational Research Association.)

SUMMARY

Accounting instructors wishing to respond to the external cries for educational reform (including those initiated within the profession) and their own intrinsic desire to excel will find cooperative learning to be a practical, research-based pedagogy, which will improve teaching and learning in accounting classrooms. The critical attributes of cooperative learning—a more structured form of collaborative learning—are: positive interdependence, individual accountability, appropriate grouping, group processing, and social skills. Cooperative learning techniques supplement rather than replace traditional approaches in the classroom, such as lecture, but their adoption requires a student-centered, noncompetitive approach to learning.

REFERENCES

Angelo, T. A., and K. P. Cross (1993). *Classroom assessment techniques: A handbook for college teachers* (2nd ed.). San Francisco: Jossey Bass.

Cooper, J. (1990, May) "Cooperative learning and college teaching: Tips from the trenches." *The Teaching Professor,* 4(5), 1-2.

Cooper, J. L., and R. Mueck (1989). "Cooperative/collaborative learning: Research and practice (primarily) at the collegiate level." *The Journal of Staff, Program, and Organization Development,* 7(3), 149-151.

Cooper. J., S. Prescott, L. Cook, L. Smith, R. Mueck, and J. Cuseo (1990) *Cooperative learning and college instruction.* Long Beach, CA: The California State University Foundation.

Cross, K. P. (1993, March). *The student side of classroom Research.* Paper presented at the 1993 National Conference on Higher Education, American Association for Higher Education, Washington, D. C.

Johnson, D. W., R. T. Johnson, E. J. Holubec, and P. Roy (1984). *Circles of learning: Cooperation in the classroom.* Alexandria, VA: Association for Supervision and Curriculum Development.

Johnson, D. W., R. T. Johnson, and K. A. Smith (1991). *Cooperative learning: Increasing college faculty instructional productivity.* ASHE-ERIC Higher Education Report No. 4. Washington, D. C.: The George Washington University, School of Education and Human Development.

Kagan, S. (1992). *Cooperative learning.* San Juan Capistrano, CA: Resources for Teachers.

Kohn, A. (1986). *No contest: The case against competition.* Boston: Houghton-Mifflin.

Marchese, Ted. (November 1991). "TQM reaches the academy." *AAHE Bulletin,* 44(3), 3-9.

Natasi, B. K., and D. H. Clements (1991). "Research on cooperative learning: Implications for practice." *School Psychology Review,* 20(1), 110-131.

Sanford. N. (1965). *The American College.* New York: Wiley.

Sheridan, J., A. C. Byrne, and K. Quina (1989). "Collaborative learning: Notes from the field." *College Teaching,* 37(2), 49-53.

Slavin, R. E. (1989-1990a). "Guest editorial: Here to stay—or gone tomorrow?" *Educational Leadership,* 47(4), 3.

Slavin, R. E. (1989-1990b). "Research on cooperative learning: Consensus and controversy." *Educational Leadership,* 47(4), 52-55.

Webb, N. M. (1989). "Peer interaction and learning in small groups." *International Journal of Educational Research,* 13, 21-39.

Whipple, W. R. (1987, October). "Collaborative learning: Recognizing it when we see it." *AAHE Bulletin,* 40(2), 3-7.

CHAPTER 2

WHY CHANGE?

"Nothing ventured, nothing gained."

A Proverb

Innovative teaching methods in accounting courses should be considered within the larger context of teaching in higher education. Issues of quality and accountability have fueled a general movement for educational reform, including a more enlightened view of the research/teaching imbalance in the faculty reward structure (Boyer, 1990). These changing expectations about the need for effective undergraduate education are reinforced by broader societal needs, including the increased use of technology and the short half-life of knowledge in most discipline areas. Life-long learning—including interpersonal and team-building skills—is a virtual necessity for all members of the work force today. The nature of the work force and the diverse student populations that feed it also call for new innovations in the classroom.

FACTORS AFFECTING TEACHING

The Changing Work Place

In the business sector, there is a new emphasis on cooperation and teamwork. The pioneering metaphors of the lone gunman blazing away at clearly defined enemies or the business tycoon rising to the top of the entrepreneurial heap have been replaced by new metaphors of interdependence and cooperation. Many of the leading corporations are moving toward the use of facilitative management practices involving cooperation and teamwork. The movement toward total quality management, for example, incorporates development of cross-functional work teams, quality circles, and a host of other small-group techniques as a means of fostering continuous improvement in quality and timeliness of work. Covey (1989) notes that "cooperation in the workplace is as important to free enterprise as competition in the marketplace" (p. 230). Many factors have fueled this redirection: the increasing turbulence and complexity of the international scene, fast-paced technological change, opening markets accompanied by intense competition, and recessionary trends necessitating quality products at competitive prices.

In recent years many books, such as Kinlow (1990) or Wellins, Byham, and Wilson (1991), have been written about cooperation and teamwork in the business world. The emphasis on teamwork in business and industry parallels the emphasis on cooperation learning in schools, colleges, and continuing education. Students of all levels who are learning skills in interpersonal communication, conflict resolution, group problem solving, and group decision making are being prepared to function in the contemporary business world. Strong arguments can be made for the fact that accounting instructors who neglect these aspects of undergraduate education are doing their students and the profession a disservice.

The Changing Student Populations

Most instructors are aware of the federal Census Bureau's prediction that by the year 2005, 52% of the United States's population will be "minority," if that term still has validity, and one in three students will be of color. Accounting faculty on most campuses are already seeing an influx of women and minority students, many of whom have different educational needs and different approaches to learning than those of traditional students. An increasing number of students are part-timers balancing academic demands with vocational commitments. Ryan (1993) reports that from 1960 to 1990 college enrollments climbed from 3.6 million students to 12.8 million; over five million were part-time: "By 1988 mature students accounted for over 40 percent of all enrolled students, and the proportion of minority students had risen to 18 percent. The proportion of women grew from 37 percent of the undergraduate population in 1960 to 54 percent in 1988." (p. 13)

With this diverse population, Gaff (1992) emphasizes that, "Pedagogical 'business-as-usual' in any pedagogical program—listening to lectures, reading a pre-digested textbook, memorization, and multiple-choice tests—will not allow students to learn what even the most fervently argued courses have to teach." (p. 35) The secret to successful teaching—in accounting as in other disciplines—is a broad, flexible, well-adapted teaching repertoire.

With this new influx of diverse students, learning cannot occur through traditional delivery methods with "authority figures" lecturing to passive adults. In fact, as Giezkowski (1992) points out, the large influx of adult students into colleges and universities—because they are focused and pragmatic and bring with them a wealth of life experiences—has often revitalized the learning environment. Instructors are challenged to juggle the conflicting expectations they may have. As emphasized earlier, versatility is the key. Successful teaching depends on "the flexibility of a college instructor's teaching repertoire and his or her readiness to draw on a range of teaching styles for a variety of ends" (Adams, 1992, p. 15). Varied learning approaches are critically important, Cross (1991) argues, because of what we know of learning:

> What do students already know, and how can new learning be framed to make meaningful connections? The more teachers can develop analogies and metaphors to relate to the backgrounds of students, the more likely new knowledge will become integrated into the schemata or knowledge structure that represents the student's understanding. (p. 28)

Cooperative learning, by allowing time for reflection, rehearsal, and peer teaching, can stimulate all students.

The Changing Teaching Paradigm

As Kuhn (1962) emphasized, breakthroughs in science tend to follow altered ways of thinking or viewing the world. Paradigms frame the way individuals and societies perceive and understand the universe. There is considerable evidence, as several researchers point out (Johnson, Johnson, and Smith, 1991; Boehm, 1992) that a paradigm shift is occurring in teaching. The shift results in a new emphasis on delivery and the role of teaching. As Boehm states, "We are beginning to understand that how we teach is central; it is, in fact, the second content of every course." (p. 37)

This viewpoint has gained enormous credence with the recent publication of Astin's (1993) comprehensive study of the impact colleges and universities have on undergraduate students. In the concluding chapter, "Implications for Educational Theory and Practice," he makes a number of important points. He finds, for example, that "the student's peer group is the single most potent source of influence on growth and development during the undergraduate years" (p. 398); faculty are the second most influential factors on student outcomes. Furthermore, general education curricular structure makes very little difference for most of the 22 outcomes he studied. He concludes: "In short, it appears that how students *approach* general education (and how the faculty actually *deliver* the curriculum) is far more important than the formal curricular content and structure." (p. 425) His research findings suggest that institutions should "put more emphasis on pedagogy and other features of the *delivery system,* as well as on the broader interpersonal and institutional context in which learning takes place" (p. 427).

Because of the effects of the peer group, Astin endorses the use of cooperative learning as an instructional method:

> Under what we have come to call cooperative learning methods, where students work together in small groups, students basically teach each other, and our pedagogical resources are multiplied. Classroom research has consistently shown that cooperative learning approaches produce outcomes that are superior to those obtained through traditional competitive approaches, and it may well be that our findings concerning the power of the peer group offer a possible explanation: cooperative learning may be more potent than traditional methods of pedagogy because it motivates students to become more active and more involved participants in the learning process. This greater involvement could come in at least two different ways. First, students may be motivated to expend more effort if they know their work is going to be scrutinized by peers; and second, students may learn course material in greater depth if they are involved in helping teach it to fellow students. (p. 427)

Astin's work has enormous implications for all disciplines and suggests that faculty and chairs committed to genuine teaching improvement should rethink their curriculum delivery methods.

The Accounting Education Change Commission (AECC) is well aware of these pedagogical needs. This awareness permeates all sections of the AECC's Position Statement No. One, "Objectives of Education for Accountants," including the appendix on "learning to learn." This emphasis on life-long learning introduces these crucial paragraphs on instructional methods:

> Students must be active participants in the learning process, not passive recipients of information. They should identify and solve unstructured problems that require use of multiple information sources. Learning by doing should be emphasized. Working in groups should be encouraged. Creative use of technology is essential.

> Accounting classes should not focus only on accounting knowledge. Teaching methods that expand and reinforce basic communication, intellectual, and interpersonal skills should be used.

Some accounting instructors are just now learning that cooperative learning enhances current teaching practices and enables faculty to fulfill virtually all of the AECC principles advocated above.

Despite these positive results, however, more cautious instructors may be unwilling or unable to consider these significant changes.

Resistances to Change

Any change involves risk-taking, and accounting instructors must be both convinced and confident that the cooperative learning activities they introduce are worthwhile. Their conviction and confidence will go a long way toward convincing students of the value and efficacy of the new approaches.

Because of the risks involved, however, it is easier for instructors—no matter what their discipline—to maintain the status quo, which in most cases means a lecture-centered, instructor-directed classroom. Ekroth (1990) has identified six barriers to instructor change, which have been amplified by Bonwell and Eison (1991, 53-59). One of these barriers is what Ekroth calls "the stability of the situation." On a mundane level, physical settings, seating arrangements, and time schedules rarely vary; more significantly, institutional procedures, the reward system, and the "socialization" that occurs within disciplines—accountants teach as they were taught—argue against innovation. Students, too, reinforce expectations about traditional behaviors: faculty (who contain the knowledge) lecture, and students (who are empty vessels) listen. Furthermore, departures from these traditional roles cause anxiety: "Will this work?" What if students rebel?" "How will my colleagues or chair react?" Thus, if lectures are comfortable for instructors and students, then some instructors have a vested interest in maintaining a pedagogical approach that research clearly shows is less effective than cooperative small groups. Also, many instructors feel comfortable lecturing because they take seriously their expert role or because they enjoy being the center of attention.

Accounting instructors whom we hope are considering adoption of cooperative learning activities may be reassured by the answers to the following concerns:

1. *Group work is "soft." By using it, I will lower my standards and make less rigorous demands on my students.*

As Cross (1986) and many others have emphasized, if we set high expectations for our students, they will rise to meet them. Accounting instructors have an obligation to the profession to produce graduates who are competent in the field. Thus, group work—whatever its other benefits—cannot reduce actual mastery. The good news is that the research consistently shows that structured small group work—group work that builds in positive interdependence and individual accountability—raises student achievement. At the very least, in studies where cooperative learning student achievement does not exceed those in control groups taught by traditional methods, the students learn equally well (Davidson, 1990).

When accounting students are placed in heterogeneous teams and given structured tasks, the teams usually strive for a quality product. Instructors using cooperative learning approaches find that students have three reasons to aspire for quality: (1) their own intrinsic motivation, whether it is stimulated by personal fulfillment/learning or for a targeted grade; (2) their wish to please the instructor, whether it is for affiliative approval or again for a specific grade; and (3) their team commitment, whether their actions are predicated on a desire to "come through" for the team or to avoid the censure of their fellow learners. In a traditional competitive classroom, usually only the first two stimuli are operative; peer pressure, a strong motivating force in structured groups, is not a factor.

Furthermore, in cooperative classrooms, quality is constantly monitored through the group processing discussed in Chapter 1. For example, instructors actively move among groups when they are engaged in structured activities. Thus, they are able to determine and influence the level of learning and to eliminate potential pitfalls, including dysfunctional group interactions that might interfere with mastery of the course content. By listening to the student interactions, they can also identify problem areas in the instruction and can sometimes benefit from hearing students "translate" their lecture material into meaningful language for fellow classmates. Students appreciate their interest and involvement and the opportunity to sit with them, face-to-face, without an intervening podium.

Quality is also reinforced by the insistence in cooperative learning classrooms on individual accountability. Group members, although they coach one another and cooperate on projects, are responsible for their own learning and are tested individually. No one is allowed to coast on the achievements of others, as sometimes happens in less-structured group settings where one or two team members do most of the work on a joint project, but all members receive the same grade.

2. *I can't possibly cover all the content using group work. Lectures are efficient ways to deliver the curriculum needed by students who must take further accounting courses or pass the CPA examination.*

The question of coverage really falls back on the key distinction between teaching and learning. A widely circulated cartoon by Bud Blake shows a young boy declaring of his dog, "I taught Stripe how to whistle." A skeptical friend notes, "But I don't hear him whistling." The boy retorts, "I said I taught him to whistle, I didn't say he learned it." This distinction is critically important. It underscores the need to look beyond content coverage to what students are actually learning.

During course planning, many difficult decisions must be made in terms of curriculum, course requirements, classroom activities, and so forth. It is never possible to fit everything in that one might wish. Thus, when incorporating group work into a syllabus, it may become necessary to cover less, but to cover it in depth, so that students are actually learning the material. Long-time cooperative learning practitioners suggest, however, that through careful structuring, they can actually cover more material than under the traditional lecture-recitation model. The secret lies in developing strategies that encourage out-of-class learning which is then reinforced and validated through in-class activities. In traditional classrooms, many instructors routinely prepare oral presentations to augment each assigned chapter. Too often for too many students, these lectures, however carefully crafted, become rehashes of the textbook material, thus robbing even well-motivated students of any incentive to prepare for class in advance. Carefully structured homework assignments, focused perhaps on supplementary handouts or graphic organizers (discussed in Chapter 7) that clarify course content, can eliminate the need to lecture in detail on the assigned chapters. For example, instructors might use the DEC model described in Chapter 6 where students work in pairs on essays covering the chapter material. Much time can also be saved by focusing homework reviews within groups rather than covering accounting problems with the entire class, as discussed in Chapter 3. Michaelson (1992) describes a variation of cooperative learning called Team Learning (Chapter 6), which uses a series of minitests administered five to seven times a semester, that are given at the beginning of each major unit of instruction. The tests are taken individually and retaken as a group; a group appeals process provides opportunities for immediate, focused feedback and builds group cohesiveness. These minitests enable instructors to "cover" content without lectures, particularly theoretical material, freeing time in class for applied activities such as problem solving. Even if lectures are not as extensive as they might be under a traditional approach, instructors can increase the overall achievement level of students by allowing them time to work directly on content-related problem solving, to explore direct applications, and to undertake guided practice.

3. *If I turn the class over to small groups, I will lose control.*

Professors who assume they are in control of a class simply because they have possession of a lectern will do well to review Boyer's (1987) description of a scene repeated on many campuses where large classes are the norm:

> At a freshman psychology lecture we attended, 300 students were still finding seats when the professor started talking. "Today," he said into the microphone, "we will continue our discussion of learning." He might as well have been addressing a crowd in a Greyhound bus terminal. Like commuters marking time until their next departure, students in this class alternatively read the newspaper, flipped through a paperback novel, or propped their feet on the chairs ahead of them, staring into space. Only when the professor defined a term [that] he said "might appear on an exam" did they look up and start taking notes. (p. 140)

In contrast, in a well-conducted cooperative classroom, despite an elevated noise level, instructors constantly monitor student progress on clearly defined tasks. Each group typically has one student whose specific assignment is to ensure that the group stays on task. The instructor designs the activity and the students carry it out within a specified time frame. Unlike a typical lecture hall, where even seemingly attentive students may be day-dreaming, virtually all students are actively involved in their own learning. Best of all, the students are usually blithely unaware of the degree of "manipulation," and go cheerfully about what they regard as their business.

4. *My students will reject classroom activities they regard as frivolous or irrelevant. Accounting students are often introverted, anyway. They want to learn from an authority figure—me!*

Instructors who convey a lack of confidence in the cooperative learning structures they initiate or who fail to prepare adequately are courting disaster. But thousands of higher-education practitioners can testify that well-designed, well-directed cooperative activities tied to course objectives consistently receive "rave" reviews from students. Johnson, Johnson, and Smith (1991) summarize a wide variety of research findings on cooperative learning. They find that its positive effects on interpersonal relationships have far-reaching results:

> As relationships within the class or college become more positive, absenteeism decreases and students' commitment to learning, feeling of personal responsibility to complete the assigned work, willingness to take on difficult tasks, motivation, and persistence in working on tasks, satisfaction, and morale, willingness to endure pain and frustration to succeed, willingness to defend the col-

lege against external criticism or attack, willingness to listen to and be influenced by peers, commitment to peer's success and growth, and productivity and achievement can be expected to increase. (p. 44)

As emphasized in later chapters, instructors should explain to students exactly what they are doing and why. Dualistic thinkers who assume there are absolute answers to questions (*i.e.,* those in stages one through three in Perry's [1970] scheme or in the early stages of the hierarchy described by Belenky, Clinchy, Goldberger, and Taruk [1986]), may initially reject processes and procedures that cause them to question their entrenched value systems. Talking with students about different learning styles and the desirability of moving toward more sophisticated modes of thinking can help put cooperative learning in a positive perspective. Cooper, Prescott, Cook, Smith, Mueck, and Cuseo (1990) suggest that the cognitive development of beginning college students can be stimulated by exposure to the differing viewpoints of group members.

More importantly, through the structure of the assignments and the group processes, instructors can provide the combination of challenge and support essential for student success (Widick, Knelfelkamp, and Parker, 1975). A challenge is a concept or task, often designed to increase higher-order thinking skills and move students beyond dualistic thinking, that forces students to confront alternate viewpoints and to take demanding intellectual and sometimes personal risks. Supports are the features of the learning situation that minimize the risks and maximize students' likelihood of success.

Cooperative learning, for many reasons, provides both challenge and support. The carefully structured tasks challenge students to move beyond memorization and single-minded viewpoints. The heterogeneity of the groups prompts the exchange of diverse opinions and intellectual stances, plus a thoughtful probing of the team members' reasons for adopting such viewpoints. The groups—because of careful selection, monitoring, and reinforcement of positive interactions—provide a great deal of support for the individual members. In them, students can immerse themselves in hands-on, practical applications and concrete problems where they can begin to understand the more challenging abstractions. Groups also provide a safe environment where students can speak freely about their own fears of mastery or their misgivings about alternate viewpoints that challenge their preconceived notions of reality. This opportunity to verbalize is particularly important for the many dualistic accounting students who enter the profession looking for the "answers."

5. *If I learned accounting the traditional way, then everyone must learn accounting the traditional way: Let the ledgers and students fall where they may. Furthermore, I have no role models. How can I change?*

As mentioned earlier, a paradigm shift has occurred in college teaching, one supported by the Accounting Education Change Commission. Refusing to consider other delivery options simply because of past experiences is a short-sided, counter-productive stance. Certainly, as academics we should be willing to espouse an open viewpoint and approach cooperative learning opportunities with a critical thinking stance. At the very least, a review of some of the cogent literature and discussions with practitioners in accounting or related disciplines will help us make informed choices. Because there is now such widespread interest in cooperative learning, role models are more accessible than they were a few years ago. Interested instructors should join the Cooperative Learning Network in Higher Education by contacting Dr. James Cooper, California State University, Dominguez Hills, HFA-B-316, 1000 E. Victoria Street, Carson CA, 90747. Workshops on cooperative learning are increasingly common on many campuses and at national conferences sponsored by organizations such as the American Association of Higher Education or the Lilly Teaching Conference at Miami of Ohio.

6. *Colleagues, like students, will think I'm not fulfilling my professional obligations if my classroom seems noisy and out-of-control. They won't understand or appreciate these departures from traditional teaching.*

The solution here is simple communication. Instructors should openly discuss their efforts to integrate structured small group work into their courses. They can share with colleagues recent articles on cooperative learning and accounting (Cottell and Millis [1992], Cottell and Millis [1993]). Support from department chairs, discussions at department meetings, and "success stories" will go a long way toward convincing skeptical colleagues that these innovations have merit. Even if a department seems hostile to innovation, Combs (1979) reminds us that "teachers have far more freedom to innovate than they ever use. When the classroom door is closed, nobody, but nobody, knows what is going on in there except the teacher and the students. . . . Teachers may not be able to change the educational system, or their administrator, but the variations possible within an ordinary classroom are almost limitless" (p. 212).

7. *I don't know how to evaluate students who spend so much time focused on group work.*

When instructors are perplexed about whether to assign grades for group activities, they need to put the entire classroom experience into perspective. Do they, for example, assign specific grades to students for their attentiveness during lectures? Similarly, group activities do not have to be graded per se. Students will recognize the value of group activities once they see how the activities relate to their increased learning. As emphasized in Chapter 1, a key component of cooperative learning is individual accountability. Students should take quizzes and examinations individually after they have coached one another through the group activities. To ensure cooperation, however, it is essential that the grading scheme be criterion-referenced, a practice strongly recommended by educational researchers and faculty development experts in any case. Grading on the curve where students are pitted against one another for a finite number of *A*'s will destroy classroom cohesiveness. Many suggest, also, that such practices are inherently unfair because the ability levels of competing students will vary from class to class. Furthermore, the concept of a bell-shaped curve was never intended to apply to atypical populations such as the small percentage of people who attend college or, more significantly, the relatively finite number of undergraduates who select business or accounting as a major.

8. *Introducing cooperative learning activities will take too much time. I already suffer from too many demands; I cannot possibly revise my course syllabus and rework my course content.*

The time factor is a valid concern. Any course revisions take careful preparation and thought. As Cooper (1990) cautions: "The three most important things in setting up a Cooperative Learning classroom are Structure, Structure and Structure." (p. 1) But, as we will repeatedly emphasize, cooperative learning activities complement, rather than replace, entirely more traditional approaches such as the lecture. It is important to begin slowly with some of the more basic structures such as Roundtable, a rapid brainstorming activity, introduced in Chapter 5. Using a course planning sheet (Figure 2-1) may help instructors focus their individual lesson plans. Some instructors, particularly those teaching in three-hour blocks, actually "script" the classroom activities, writing down—with cues—what will happen and how long it will take.

Cooperative Learning Course Planning

Course:

Structure to be introduced:

What will you do?

Why are you doing it?

Questions for Reflection/Discussion

1. How will this activity further your course objectives?
2. How will you introduce this activity to students?
3. How will you form groups?
4. How will positive interdependence be fostered (goal, resource materials, evaluation methods, roles, etc.)?
5. How will you maintain individual accountability?
6. How will you monitor students' interactions and learning?
7. What problems/challenges do you expect?

Figure 2-1

Careful planning will give instructors the self-confidence to introduce activities that will help their students gain academic and interpersonal skills that will enable them to succeed in subsequent accounting courses and in the work place.

Confidence can also be strengthened by initially introducing low-risk cooperative learning strategies. Eison and Bonwell (1988) have conceptualized the degree of risk involved in various classroom techniques by contrasting their various characteristics. (See Figure 2-2.) Thus, to minimize risk, it would seem advisable to begin initially with a relatively short, highly structured activity, such as the Think-Pair-Share structure described in Chapter 4. Plan the activity carefully and choose concrete, noncontroversial subject matter, such as asking paired students to distinguish between the two major subsystems of an organization's accounting information system, after they have had some exposure to the topic. Because a Think-Pair-Share activity is carefully structured and timed, it can be introduced easily even if you and your students have never experienced it before. Bonwell and Eison (1991) caution that student-student interactions involve more risk than student-faculty dialogues but that problems such as off-task

A COMPARISON OF LOW- AND HIGH-RISK ACTIVE LEARNING STRATEGIES

Dimension	Low-Risk Strategies	High-Risk Strategies
Class time required	Relatively short	Relatively long
Degree of structure	More structured	Less structured
Degree of planning	Meticulously planned	Spontaneous
Subject matter	Relatively concrete	Relatively abstract
Potential for controversy	Less controversial	Very controversial
Students' prior knowledge of the subject matter	Better informed	Less informed
Students' prior knowledge of the teaching technique	Familiar	Unfamiliar
Instructor's prior experience with the teaching technique	Considerable	Limited
Pattern of interaction	Between faculty and students	Among students

Figure 2-2*

*This material originally appeared as part of Bonwell, Charles C. and James A. Eison. 1991. *Active learning: Creating excitement in the classroom.* ASHE-ERIC Higher Education Report No. 1. Washington, D.C.: The George Washington University, School of Education and Human Development. This publication in its entirety is available for $17.00 from the ERIC Clearing-house on Higher Education, One Dupont Circle, Suite 630, Washington, DC 20036. (202) 296-2597. Reprinted with permission.

behavior or shy noncontributors will lessen with planning and practice (p. 68). They consider structured small-group discussion, which engenders a high degree of active learning, to be a relatively low risk activity. The payoff is enormous: student-student interactions, as opposed to one-on-one student-faculty exchanges, result in what Kagan (1992) calls the principle of "simultaneity." In a traditional classroom, the instructor calls on students sequentially, a time-consuming, passive activity for all but the targeted student. Even if the instructor encourages student-to-student exchanges, only one person is typically speaking at a time. By initiating paired discussion, on the other hand, the instructor guarantees that virtually half the students in a classroom are actively talking; the other half—those listening—are far more likely to be actively engaged in the learning processing/listening process than often inattentive students involved in a typical whole-class discussion.

SUMMARY

Despite the misgivings of some accounting instructors, there are many compelling reasons to introduce cooperative learning approaches into accounting classrooms. Changing student populations and a changing work place mean that traditional approaches to teaching no longer provide students with the necessary academic and interpersonal skills. In fact, some scholars have suggested that a paradigm shift is occurring in the teaching world, a shift to a more interactive, student-centered classroom. In keeping with this new awareness, the Accounting Education Change Commission advocates more active learning, including group work. Any misgivings can be overcome when instructors begin slowly with low-risk cooperative learning activities.

REFERENCES

Accounting Education Change Commission. (1990, August). "AECC Urges Priority for Teaching in Higher Education." Issues Statement No. 1, Torrance, CA: Accounting Education Change Commission.

Adams, M. (1992). "Cultural inclusion in the American college classroom." In N. V. N. Chism and L. L. B. Border (Eds.), *Teaching for diversity.* New Directions for Teaching and Learning, no. 49. San Francisco: Jossey-Bass.

Astin, A. W. (1993). *What matters in college: Four critical years revisited.* San Francisco: Jossey-Bass.

Belenky, M. F., B. M. Clinchy, N. R. Goldberger, and J. M. Taruk (1986). *Women's ways of knowing: The development of self, voice, and mind.* New York: Basic Books.

Boehm, L. (1992). "In wake of crisis: Reclaiming the heart of teaching and learning." In T. J. Frecka (Ed.), *Critical thinking, interactive learning and technology: Reaching for excellence in business education* (pp. 24-40). Arthur Andersen Foundation.

Bonwell, C. C., and J. A. Eison (1991). *Active learning: Creating excitement in the classroom.* ASHE-ERIC Higher Education Report No. 1. Washington, D. C.: The George Washington University, School of Education and Human Development.

Boyer, E. L. (1987). *College: The undergraduate experience in America.* New York: Harper and Row.

Boyer, E. L. (1990). *Scholarship reconsidered: Priorities of the professoriate.* Princeton, N. J: Carnegie Foundation for the Advancement of Teaching.

Combs, A. W. (1979). *Myths in education: Beliefs that hinder progress and their alternatives.* Boston: Allyn & Bacon.

Cooper, J. (1990, May). "Cooperative learning and college teaching: Tips from the trenches." *The Teaching Professor, 4*(5), 1-2.

Cooper, J., S. Prescott, L. Cook, L. Smith, R. Mueck, and J. Cuseo (1990). *Cooperative learning and college instruction: Effective use of student learning teams.* Long Beach, CA: The California State University Foundation.

Cottell, P., and B. Millis (1992). "Cooperative learning in accounting." *The Journal of Accounting Education, 10,* 95-111.

Cottell, P., and B. Millis (1993). "Cooperative learning structures in the instruction of accounting." *Issues in Accounting Education. 8*(1), 40-59.

Covey, S. R. (1989). *The Seven habits of highly successful people: Restoring the character ethic.* New York: Simon & Schuster.

Cross, K. P. (1986, March). "Taking teaching seriously." Paper presented at the national conference of the American Association for Higher Education, Washington, D. C.

Cross, K. P. (1991, October). "Effective college teaching." *ASEE Prism,* 27-29.

Davidson, N. (1990). "The small-group discovery method in secondary and college-level mathematics." In N. Davidson (Ed.), *Cooperative learning in mathematics: A handbook for teachers* (pp. 335-361). Menlo Park, CA: Addison-Wesley.

Eison, J., and C. Bonwell (1988, March). "Making real the promise of active learning." Paper presented at the national conference of the American Association for Higher Education, Washington, D. C.

Ekroth, L. (1990). "Why professors don't change." In L. Ekroth (Ed.), *Teaching excellence: Toward the best in the academy,* (Winter-Spring). Stillwater, OK: Professional and Organizational Development Network in Higher Education.

Gaff, Jerry. G. (1992) "Beyond politics: The educational issues inherent in multicultural education," *Change: The Magazine of Higher Learning, 24*(1), 31-35.

Giezkowski, W. (1992). "The influx of older students can revitalize college teaching." *The Chronicle of Higher Education,* 38(29), 133-134.

Johnson, D. W., R. T. Johnson, and K. A. Smith (1991) *Cooperative learning: Increasing college faculty instructional productivity.* ASHE-ERIC Higher Education Report No. 4. Washington, D. C: The George Washington University, School of Educational and Human Development.

Kagan, S. (1992). *Cooperative learning.* San Juan Capistrano, CA: Resources for Teachers.

Kinlow, D. (1990). *Developing superior work teams.* New York, NY: Free Press.

Kuhn, T. (1962). *The structure of scientific revolutions.* Chicago: University of Chicago Press.

Michaelson, L. K. (1992). "Team learning: A comprehensive approach for harnessing the power of small groups in higher education." In D. H. Wulff and J. D. Nyquist (Eds.), *To improve the academy: Resources for faculty, instructional, and organizational development, 11* (pp. 107-122). The Professional and Organizational Network in Higher Education, Stillwater, OK: New Forums Press, Inc.

Perry, W. (1970). *Forms of intellectual and ethical development in the college years: A scheme.* New York: Holt, Rinehart and Winston.

Ryan, A. (1993, February 11). Invasion of the mind snatchers. *New York Review of Books, 15*(4), 13-15.

Wellins, R. S., W. C. Byham, and J. M. Wilson (1991). *Empowered teams: Creating self-directed work groups that improve quality, productivity, and participation.* San Francisco: Jossey-Bass.

Widick, C., L. Knelfelkamp, and C. Parker (1975). The counselor as developmental instructor. *Counselor Education and Supervision, 14,* 286-296.

CHAPTER 3

STARTING WITH THE BASICS

"For who hath despised the day of small things?"

Zachariah 4:10

Accounting instructors who wish to introduce structured small group work should keep in mind that underlying cooperative learning is a philosophy predicated on a set of values. An underlying premise of cooperative learning is "a belief in the value and educability of all students and a sense of the mutual responsibility that creates communities" (Sapon-Shevin and Schniedewind, 1989-1990). Cooperative learning thus is not an elitist philosophy; those who consider themselves gatekeepers to the profession who must weed out the unworthy and the unfit will probably find that it does not suit their needs. Instructors should first understand and adopt the philosophy. They can then use appropriate classroom management techniques as they slowly implement structures.

Classroom management strategies help in day-to-day classroom functioning. This chapter focuses on classroom management techniques because they are the grease that keeps the wheels rolling in unison. They guarantee that students and instructors understand and accept their new roles, and they simplify the logistics of classroom maintenance. For instance, many professors—often those with large classes—use team folders to return homework assignments and distribute class materials; later, students put homework and class activities in the folder, often after recording attendance and quiz grades.

The structures themselves, which will be introduced in Chapter 4 and subsequent chapters, provide frameworks for content-centered activities. Structures are the classroom tools that give life to the philosophy. They are essentially content-free procedures, such as a brainstorming technique commonly called Roundtable, which can be used in a number of settings for a variety of purposes. When content is added to a structure—for example, when an accounting instructor asks students to use a Roundtable structure to generate a list of interrelated parts, processes, and objectives of an accounting information system—then it becomes a specific classroom activity. A series of activities becomes a lesson or unit plan. The Roundtable structure might be used later in another activity—perhaps with an entirely different content, such as identifying suitable pizza parlors for an end-of-semester party.

The implementation of cooperative learning structures, discussed in later chapters, can be a rich, life-long experience as instructors grow in their ability to develop increasingly effective lesson plans to promote active learning and team-oriented working relationships among their students. But instructors also need to understand why they are using these structures: this rationale relates directly to the student-centered philosophy of cooperative learning.

COOPERATIVE LEARNING PHILOSOPHY

As Chapter 2 suggests, instructors adopting cooperative learning must understand and embrace the paradigm shift away from competition in the learning environment. Although some might argue that our nation was founded on competition, in reality those assumptions present a distorted view of both history and human nature. Community barn raisings and close-knit pioneer church congregations were far more common than solitary gun slingers. Our educational roots lie in community and peer support: in "little red school houses" across the nation older students helped younger classmates with reading, writing, and arithmetic. Those who might argue for the value of a competitive classroom approach should recognize that competition already permeates our society. Within the last fifty years, American students have been socialized to believe in competition and independent efforts; they have had plenty of opportunities to practice these approaches in classes, on the playing field, and in neighborhood backyards or inner-city alleys. In contrast, in Asia many children typically gather at a classmate's home where, under supervision, they work together on homework assignments. In America, most parents refuse to let little Johnny visit friends until he has finished his homework!

Cooperative learning provides a long overdue balance to the independent and competitive models. Johnson, Johnson, and Smith (1991) applaud the fact that "we are currently leaving an era of competitive and individualistic learning. The 'me' classrooms and 'do your own thing' academic work are fading, and we are entering an era of interdependence and mutuality." (p. 1) In a very real sense, cooperative learning professors form learning communities within their classrooms. In this environment, students view their peers as resources from which to draw inspiration and knowledge rather than as rivals for grades or other rewards, including the instructor's attention. Reciprocal teaching and learning become the hallmark of the cooperative learning class.

As noted earlier, the instructor's role also changes. In a cooperative learning atmosphere a subtle power shift occurs away from the authority figure of the instructor to the students themselves, despite the fact that, as discussed in Chapter 2, the professor—because of the well-organized structures—remains very much in control. The control results from a shift in the classroom that complements a similar shift in the corporate world toward team-centered work place practices. As Michaelson (1992) notes, "the instructor's primary role shifts from dispenser of information to manager of a learning process" (p. 109). A number of desirable outcomes accompany this transfer. As the gap between instructors and students begins to narrow, students and instructors alike find the locus of knowledge in a learning community rather than in one individual. To put it colloquially, "None of us is as smart as all of us." Instructors can feel relaxed in this new role if they think of themselves as expanding their areas of influence rather than as abdicating responsibilities. Instead of narrowly defining themselves only as content or skill experts within a restricted discipline area, they can broaden their perspectives and their effectiveness by adding other roles to their repertoire, such as "facilitator" or "manager." Through this approach they can dissolve what Finkle and Monk (1983) have dubbed "The Atlas Complex," a mind set of teacher-student expectations that keeps instructors firmly in the center of the classroom, bearing on their shoulders the responsibility for all aspects of the course. This new student-centered classroom ensures the creation rather than the transfer of knowledge. Instead of pouring knowledge into the heads of passive students, instructors challenge them to discover, construct, and eventually transform their own knowledge.

As the focus of the classroom changes, student-student interdependence develops. Students become actively involved not only in their own learning, but also in the learning of their peers. They receive from teammates both cognitive support and motivational support. As groups work together on common problems and projects, students benefit from their own verbalization, but they also witness a variety of thinking patterns and strategies such as defining the problem, generalizing, drawing on past experience, or evaluating progress. Additionally, group environments provide an audience's responses to students' beliefs, ideas, and attitudes, an audience that can be taught to skillfully request clarification, elaboration, and justification.

Such settings engender critical thinking because they help students to experience important activities such as identifying and challenging assumptions, and exploring and imagining alternatives (Brookfield, 1987). In fact, research conducted at the National Center for Research to Improve Postsecondary Teaching and Learning (1990) indicates that at least three elements of teaching appear to affect student gains in thinking skills: "(a) Verbalizing methods and strategies to encourage development of learning strategies; (b) Student discussion and interaction; and (c) Explicit emphasis on problem-solving procedures and methods using varied examples." (p. 2) All of these activities routinely occur in well-designed cooperative learning activities.

PLANNING FOR A COOPERATIVE ACCOUNTING CLASSROOM

Making certain that activities are well-designed will enable instructors to avoid the dysfunctional aspects of other group learning strategies. Instructors should, for example, include clear explanations about the nature and purpose of cooperative learning in their course syllabi. Brookfield (1991) cautions: "Being clear about why you teach is crucial, but it is not enough in and of itself; you must also be able to communicate to your students the values, beliefs, and purposes comprising your rationale. You cannot assume that students will understand your rationale or be immediately convinced that your most deeply held convictions have value for them as well." (p. 22)

Instructors should prepare a syllabus which defines cooperative learning, clearly explains the rationale for its use, and explicitly delineates the standard class procedures, including classroom management techniques such as the use of team folders. Direct quotations from the Accounting Education Change Commission will reinforce the importance of active learning, problem solving, and enhanced communication and interpersonal skills. The syllabus should be thoroughly discussed during the first class meeting so that students have an opportunity both to digest and to question classroom approaches that may be new to them. Obviously, the syllabus will contain the usual key components: course information, including how to contact the instructor; required texts and recommended readings; class schedule; course requirements, often linked to the critically important evaluation standards; and class policies, including sections on absenteeism, late assignments, and academic honesty.

Because the syllabus is such an important document, it is wise to pursue the practice of "more is better." A well-constructed, well-thought-out syllabus can not only protect instructors from student complaints or grievances, but can also "promote" them, in the sense that students get an immediate impression of a well-prepared, student-centered instructor. Such impressions—which are the reality also, one assumes!—will help establish credibility if small group work techniques are either new to students or worse, they have been "burned" (a common occurrence) by ill-conceived group implementations in previous classes.

The syllabus, of course, should be free of any classroom practices or course policies, such as grading on the curve, that foster a sense of competition. The evaluation system, as emphasized earlier, should result in individual accountability: students remain responsible for the outcomes of their learning experiences. Most accounting instructors use a criterion-referenced grading scheme based on conventional assignments such as in-class or take-home tests and quizzes, group projects (which in a cooperative classroom assess the value of individual student contributions), and homework. Instructors most comfortable with innovation have moved to completely noncompetitive grading practices such as learning contracts or mastery learning.

In course planning, instructors should also be mindful of the fact that cooperative learning is an in-class pedagogy. Because nontraditional students, such as working adults, are more prevalent on college campuses and because the spiralling costs of education and the recessionary economy have thrust more traditional students into the part-time work force, it may be unreasonable to demand that learning teams meet for extended periods of time outside of class. Students willing to "burn the midnight oil" on independent homework assignments may have difficulty scheduling out-of-class meetings that all four teammates can attend. These scheduling conflicts can cause interpersonal, within-team conflicts; students unable to attend meetings will feel frustration at what they perceive as unfair demands on their time and other teammates will often resent the lack of contributions from the missing students.

This emphasis on in-class learning means that instructors must design classroom activities that maximize the contact time students spend together. First of all, cooperative learning activities must have a clear purpose. Students recognize and resist frivolous activities. Accounting instructors intent on content coverage and student mastery will not, of course, introduce any such frivolous activities, even as "ice breakers," but students must recognize and respect this commitment to course objectives. If they are asked, for example, to generate ideas using a Roundtable, they must see at once the relevance of the activity to accounting content and the course goals.

Assignments must be clearly explained, often augmented by written guidelines or focused work sheets. Too often, students waste critical class time puzzling over unclear directions: "What are we supposed to be doing? What did the teacher tell us to do?" Furthermore, at least initially when students may be skeptical about group work, instructors must explain not only the requirements, but the rationale for each activity or assignment. Attention to these details at the outset ensures that while the learning is student centered, the control of the class remains with the instructor. In fact, instructors using cooperative learning have never been more in control of classes, more aware of barriers affecting student comprehension, or more cognizant of student breakthroughs in learning.

ESTABLISHING STRUCTURED LEARNING TEAMS

The heart of a cooperative classroom lies in structured learning teams. The critically important cooperative learning structures result from interactions within and between these teams. The accounting structures are, in turn, supported by the structures (Figure 3-1). Although some well-known advocates of cooperative learning such as David and Roger Johnson recommend teams of three, university and college-level practitioners prefer heterogeneous groups of four, or "quads." There are several advantages: (a) quads are small enough that group members tend to stay attentive and on task. They can't "hide" or tune-out as might happen, for instance, in a group of eight or, more significantly, in a typical college classroom predicated on whole-class discussion; (b) quads are large enough to function smoothly when a team member is occasionally absent; and (c) quads lend themselves well to pair work, a powerful way to stimulate student achievement and critical thinking skills. If a class divides unevenly, it is easy to add a fifth member to several teams—often a student who may not be as strong as other team members, usually because of absenteeism but sometimes because of weak academic

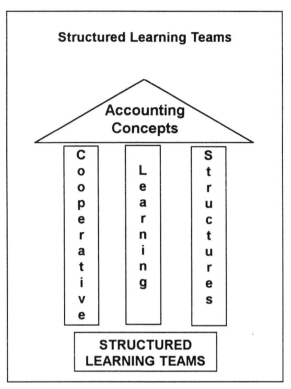

Figure 3-1

preparation. In such teams, of course, the students should never realize who the "add-on" might be.

Probably the easiest way an accounting instructor new to cooperative learning can form heterogeneous teams is through the use of student data sheets. The sheets should be passed out with the syllabus the first class meeting. On them, the students can indicate academic course-related information such as the number of courses taken in the major, relevant outside work experience, and current course and work load. Students willing to share their telephone numbers for distribution in a telephone tree will facilitate out-of-class student contacts. An added benefit of the data sheets is student appreciation for the instructor's interest in their academic and personal lives. This obvious interest helps to build the student-faculty rapport—and trust—needed for a cooperative classroom.

To help with the formation of heterogeneous teams, instructors might want to be certain that they can identify students from diverse backgrounds. If whole-class introductions are made, instructors can jot down tactful descriptions of each student. Some accounting instructors prefer to form teams later in a term after they have gotten a feel for students' abilities and personalities.

In the team formation process, regardless of when it is done, instructors should distribute students from team-to-team based on their academic preparation and ability—particularly in accounting—their gender, their ethnic background, and any other characteristics that might prove useful. The idea is to create teams that will build on students' varied strengths. As Redding (1990) notes, students with different learning styles can, in cooperative learning groups, "teach each other from their special and particular perspectives" (p. 47). This type of heterogeneous grouping also provides opportunities for positive interaction. Slavin (1989-1990) concludes,

"When students of different racial or ethnic backgrounds work together toward a common goal, they gain in liking and respect for one another." (p. 52)

It is important to be able to identify each team member quickly and easily, so that tasks can be delineated and roles assigned. Students can number off within their teams (one, two, three, four), but many instructors prefer to identify teams and team members through the use of playing cards, which can be distributed as the teams are assembled. The playing cards allow the instructor to communicate readily to the students their group assignments (by the rank of the card) and the roles they are to play within that group (by the suit of the card). They also enable instructors to easily keep track of students they have called upon directly—a serious equity concern—by checking off from an ongoing list, for example, the Jack of Hearts or the Two of Clubs. When instructors add extra members, bringing some team totals to five, they can use jokers for the fifth member or can cannibalize a second desk of cards. In the latter case, a team composed of five deuces might contain two "hearts" which can be distinguished by the color of the playing card itself.

The roles assigned within the groups should be rotated frequently to form positive interdependence. This practice discourages domination by one person, a problem common in less-structured group work, and gives all students an opportunity to practice various social, communication, and leadership skills. The following defined roles work well in a cost accounting course:

> **Leader**—keeps the group on the assigned task and ensures that all members of the group have the opportunity to learn, to participate, and to earn the respect of their teammates. Is responsible for seeing that all team members have mastered the learning points in team exercises.

> **Monitor**—acts as the timekeeper for timed exercises. Sees to it that the group's work area is left the way that the group found it. In groups of four assumes the role of any missing group member. During many cooperative learning exercises only one calculator is permitted per team. In such instances the monitor is responsible for the operation of the calculator. In teams of four consults other teams for assistance when the instructor so indicates.

> **Recorder**—keeps records of all group activities including the material contributed by each member for later assessment. (If team folders are used, this person is responsible for recording attendance, homework, and/or quiz scores.) Writes out solutions to accounting problems for groups to use as notes or for submission to the instructor. Prepares transparencies for overhead projection when the group is expected to make a formal oral presentation.

> **Reporter**—summarizes orally the group's activities or conclusions, often based on notes supplied by the recorder. Makes formal oral presentations before the class.

> **Wild Card** (for groups of five)—acts as an assistant to the group leader. Assumes the role of any missing group member in place of the monitor. Consults other teams for assistance when the instructor so indicates.

These assigned roles give all students a sense of importance, raising individual self-esteem while simultaneously building group cohesion. Frequently rotating the roles helps students learn and practice social teamwork skills, including those students needing to cultivate them for the first time. This emphasis on rotating roles prepares all students for success not only in the cooperative learning classroom, but also in the "real world" of business where teamwork is essential.

In addition to the specified roles where various group members assume different responsibilities, groups have regularly assigned tasks such as the Cooperative Homework Check discussed later in this chapter. Instructors can also use the teams as a basis for short-term activities such as the Think-Pair-Share structure discussed more fully in Chapter 4. An instructor, for example, might pose a significant question, such as "What is the relationship between a cost and an asset?" and then allow 30 seconds of wait time before initiating a three-minute discussion. To identify pairs for the discussion, the instructor might ask the heart to pair with the diamond and the club to pair with the person holding the spade. For the final portion of this activity, the instructor might call on a volunteer or two to share the paired conclusions with the entire class or the sharing might be done within the quad.

As indicated in Chapter 1, these heterogeneous learning teams typically remain in place for half a semester. A convenient time to reform these groups is after an hour test or after the midterm, when the achievement levels will be more obvious. Each group should contain a student who performed well on the exam, one who performed poorly, and two or three who performed close to the mean. Once again, additional heterogeneity can be built into the groups by dividing the students as evenly as possible with respect to gender and ethnicity.

Teams will usually find their own working space in the classroom. Students should sit as close together as possible to allow for face-to-face interaction. If possible, the groups should be arranged so that the instructor can circulate among them to monitor team progress and behaviors. This direct student-faculty contact also sends a clear signal that the instructor values student learning. Because the architects who design classrooms often had unenlightened views of learning options, many classrooms are ill-designed for group work, particularly those with seats bolted to the floor in rigid rows. Other than opting for another room, instructors can do little to change these configurations. However, even in an auditorium, through careful planning, instructors can still facilitate planned group activities. A seating chart, such as the one depicted in Figure 3-2, allows students to work within a learning team, including pair work, with a minimum of physical movement.

Establishing a Cooperative Classroom

A culture for cooperative learning must be fostered at the onset. Most students, especially business school students, come from academic backgrounds that reward competitiveness rather than cooperation. In a cooperative learning class, students should understand and follow these fundamental rules: 1) you have the right to ask questions or ask for help in your group, and 2) you have the responsibility to provide assistance in your group. These rules can be extended class-wide, so that students feel free to consult other groups.

Another guideline is important. Most students view instructors as the source of truth and wisdom. They therefore tend to turn immediately to the instructor when a question arises. In order to encourage students to look first to the group for assistance, another class norm should be encouraged: Look first to teammates and classmates for answers; consult the instructor only

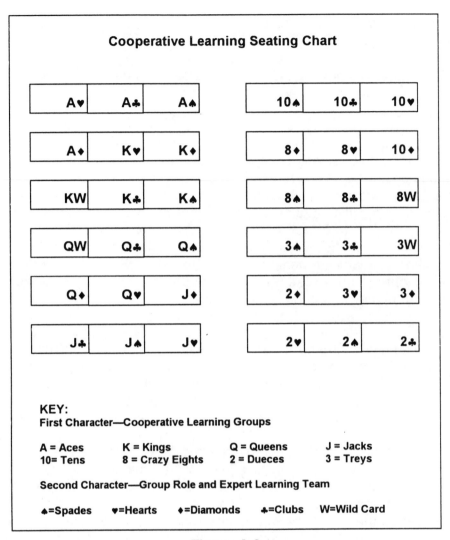

Figure 3-2

when everyone in the group has the same question. Many instructors carry this edict even further and require groups to send the monitor to another team to discover if they know the answer. Students quickly learn that much of the knowledge they seek may be found within the collective wisdom of the group itself. Therefore, a subtle shift occurs, moving the instructor off center stage and into the role of coach or helper.

Because group cohesion is such an important part of successful team learning, many instructors will spend some time on exercises calculated to promote positive relationships. This investment is a judgment call individual instructors must make and will probably depend on their confidence in asking students to do unexpected activities. A decision to deliberately foster team cohesiveness will likely be made only by instructors who are themselves convinced that such activities are not "Mickey Mouse," "grade schoolish," or "hold-me-touch-me-feel-me." But, instructors willing to accept the value of team building and experiment with some specific activities generally find that they encounter fewer student-student problems.

For example, because of the payoffs down the semester, many cooperative learning professors decide to provide ten minutes of class time to determine team names. Although others might regard this exercise as too frivolous or too risky, students tend to bond more quickly when the team name gives them a sense of cohesion. Often the students come up with team names by identifying elements they have in common, a good way to strengthen ties within a heterogeneous group. Teams might, for instance, dub themselves the "No Accounts" if all of them have misgivings about the course challenges, or they might focus on common personal characteristics or hobbies, evidenced by names such as "Four-eyes" or "Travelers." Kagan (1992) recommends exercises such as "uncommon commonalities" where students list things that team members have in common (a close family member who is an accountant, a fear of flying, a love for pistachio ice cream) that distinguishes them from other teams. He also suggests that any team naming project should carry simple rules for the group process, such as: (a) each team member has a voice in the decision, (b) consensus must be reached, (c) consensus does not imply coercion—any team members having serious objections to the group decision should not consent to it (pp. 8:3-8:5). If team folders are used, the teams will often spontaneously decorate the covers based on the team name, an action that aids classroom management because instructors and teams can readily identify the folders.

Establishing group and class norms at the beginning of the semester is also a positive way to build team cohesiveness and head off potential team dysfunctions down the road. Again, many instructors feel that time invested up front in team building—a concept echoed in the corporate world—is time well-spent. Thus, after teams are formed, but before they get down to the serious accounting-related tasks that will be their primary focus as teams for, typically, the next eight weeks, many instructors allow class time to establish group norms. Students identify and establish these guidelines or rules to help their teams function more smoothly.

Solomon, Davidson, and Solomon (Figure 3-3) have developed a work sheet to help students focus on the task of clarifying their own expectations, the expectations they have of their learning team, and finally, the collective expectations they have for their classroom experiences. Team-building exercises such as this help students establish "ownership" of the group process. Every group member initially, as with the team name, must contribute to the group consensus. But perhaps more importantly, because team norms are recorded

(those using team folders usually staple them to the inside cover), they remain a viable reference point for team cohesiveness. A team, for example, might decide that all members should have a voice in decisions. If later a team member suggests that a teammate's input was ignored—perhaps in the heat of discussion—then the group can feel comfortable about turning to that student to be certain they have included his/her alternative viewpoint. Many groups will establish norms such as "We will respect one another's opinions." "We will all contribute our fair share." "We will contact one another if we must be absent." "We will help one another succeed." and "We will all listen attentively." All students should feel—regardless of their previous accounting background—that they are contributing group members. Group norms and expectations establish a climate where students can feel their contributions are heard, and they also motivate students to offer more to the team.

The Quiet Signal

Because structured group work rarely occupies all of the allotted class time, instructors find that a class usually operates between the lecture mode, when the class' attention is focused upon the instructor, and the group mode, when students are actively learning with one another.

**What Behaviors Do You Expect
from Your Teammates?**

Individual Expectations

_____

_____

_____

_____

Paired Expectations

_____

_____

_____

_____

Team Expectations

_____

_____

_____

_____

Figure 3-3*

*Solomon, R., Davidson, N. & Solomon, E. (1993) *The handbook for the
4th R: Relationship activities for cooperative & collegial learning,* Vol. III.
Columbia, MD. National Institute for Relationship Training. Reprinted
with permission.

With well-designed instructions, transfer from the lecture mode to the group mode presents no difficulty. Because students typically become totally absorbed in group activities, however, transfer from the group mode to the lecture mode is not as easy. This desirable outcome of cooperative learning makes it difficult for instructors to regain the class' attention, even when shouting above the din, an undesirable option because of a justified perception of rudeness.

A prearranged quiet signal provides a convenient and uncomplicated solution to this dilemma. Accounting instructors simply explain the need for the signal and then invite students to choose among several options or to identify their own signal. Most often, students will opt for a raised hand. Instructors wishing to capture the class's attention raise their hand. When students notice the signal, they complete any unfinished sentence, raise their own hand, and signal those around them to also raise their hands. Within seconds, this raised hand technique can transform the noisiest classroom to one of attentive silence. Using an auditory signal, such as a tinkling brass bell, can serve as an alternative or a supplement to a raised hand. To provide comic interlude and to prevent students from tuning out a familiar sound, one accounting instructor uses a collection of unusual bells which he alternates throughout the term. The variety of signals keeps student attention from waning. Even flickering lights can prove effective, provided accounting instructors are not in a computer lab!

A timer with a shrill auditory signal serves as a particularly efficient quiet signal because it can, at the same time, allow the instructor to monitor timed tasks. The timer also helps students understand that they must complete tasks within the allotted time. Instructors must be careful, however, that they do not unintentionally annoy or offend students by overuse of this signal.

Group Tasks

Accounting instructors new to cooperative learning should be certain that all exercises related to the structured learning teams (quads) involve students in meaningful activities. A good starting point is to use cooperative learning activities as a stimulating alternative to the ponderous, teacher-dominated task of reviewing assigned homework problems. Students are more likely to work on assigned accounting problems under the cooperative learning method if they know they will let their team down if they are unprepared. Moreover, students appear to learn and retain accounting concepts far better than by their usual passive reception of approved solutions from the front of the room.

The cooperative learning alternative, called a Cooperative Homework Check, has students review homework assignments in their structured learning teams. Class time should be organized so that all groups work on the same problem at once, with groups working faster than others directed to tackle other specified tasks. From time to time, the instructor calls the class together using the quiet signal and asks one or two group reporters to give a presentation on the team's agreed-upon solutions for given problems and the accounting concepts that helped the group reach them.

This cooperative learning structure has an immediate positive effect in a cost accounting class. Because of peer pressure, more students come to class prepared. Also, many more students become more actively involved in the learning process than under traditional methods. Instead of having a handful of students—usually students feeling uncomfortably "on the spot"—respond to instructor questions, all students eagerly share ideas and creative solutions. As a variation on this version of Cooperative Homework Check, instructors may have students routinely cover all their homework responses in a specified amount of time, without necessarily pacing the review so that students are reviewing the same problems at the same time. When there are "bottom line" answers, for example, indicating that students followed all the appropriate steps, students can simply ask all teammates for the answer to the first question. If all agree, then they move rapidly to the second question. If there is again agreement, they move to the next problem. This time, one student may have a divergent answer. At that point, they stop and review that student's work, step by step. They may discover where the student went astray and they have the responsibility to be certain that the student knows why the problem went wrong and how to work it properly. Occasionally, the team may discover that the divergent answer is the correct one.

At the end of the specified time, the homework is slipped into the team folder and the scores recorded on a sheet of paper. Students must be both coached and monitored to be certain that academic dishonesty does not occur. This Cooperative Homework Check replaces the typical homework review where the instructor asks the entire class if anyone had trouble working any of the problems. Often the problem specified and then put on the blackboard is one that many students answered correctly; their time is wasted. Often, too, the slower students will not want to call attention to their deficiencies and will never identify perplexing problems. But the real advantage of reviewing problems within the team is the positive impact of immediate feedback and peer tutoring. Students focus only on those problems that gave them trouble, and they coach on the spot any students needing special attention.

If instructors have opted to use playing cards as a means of team identification, they may introduce additional excitement and a sense of fairness by using a deck of playing cards to provide a random "luck of the draw" when calling upon groups for reports. Students are much more willing to respond when they see a classmate or the instructor draw the card that matches their team identity. After the draw, for example, an instructor might say, "We only have time for three final reports: we'd like to hear from the Hearts who are members of the following teams: Aces, Kings, and Jacks."

An Example

Instructors wishing to use Cooperative Homework Check in their course may do so with the second chapter of the Hansen and Mowen text. The text begins a discussion on the preparation of external financial statements beginning on page 38. The instructor may focus a portion of the day's lecture upon the cost of goods manufactured and the cost of goods sold, giving examples as she normally would. Then the instructor assigns Problem 2-7 as a homework assignment to be discussed during the next class meeting.

When the class reassembles, the instructor directs the cooperative learning groups to check each other's responses to the assigned problem. While the students are engaged in this activity, the instructor moves about the room and occasionally sits in with a group as a listening member. In this manner, the instructor encourages the groups to remain on task and acts as a resource if students are unable to resolve differences.

The instructor will also know when most of the groups have completed the activity. Since groups usually work at different speeds, the instructor should always have a backup activity for the groups who have completed the task. In this case, groups who have completed the main task can begin to complete the requirements of Problem 2-8 as an extension activity.

The phenomenon of varied group pacing gives instructors another opportunity to reinforce the idea that student peers represent a source of knowledge. If some teams have finished but others are still grappling with the problem, the instructor may ask members of the faster groups to serve as temporary peer tutors for the slower groups. Benefits accrue both to the tutoring students who reinforce their understanding of the concept as they teach and to the recipients of the tutoring who receive quality one-on-one instruction in terms they are likely to understand.

Once the instructor senses that most or all of the groups have completed the assigned task, she may use the prearranged quiet signal to regain the students' attention. She may call upon a group in random fashion to provide a report on the solution to the problem. In this case, the instructor may ask the reporter and the recorder to give a joint report with the reporter explaining the solution while the recorder writes it on the blackboard or uses an overhead projector.

Whole-class discussion follows so that student questions can be clarified. The instructor concludes this portion of the class with a summary fortifying the concepts underlying the preparation of financial statements for manufacturing firms.

Hitchhikers

A small number of students in the cooperative learning classroom do not adapt readily to the responsibility of teaching others. A "hitchhiker" is a student who, having been assigned to a structured learning team, contributes little or nothing to it. Needless to say, such students undercut cooperative learning efforts. Instructors can discourage this inappropriate behavior in various ways. Assigning and then rotating group roles in the structured learning teams usually results in equal participation, even by hitchhikers who feel peer pressure to perform in at least a minimal way.

Student assessment of the performance of their group members can also be a powerful tool to encourage cooperation. Completing a form such as the one shown in Figure 3-4 can accomplish this. Students rank the cooperative efforts of their peers using a five-point Likert scale to answer four questions on the form. Students who receive a low peer evaluation often respond to a brief word from the instructor, but their teammates' censure is even more effective. The knowledge of an upcoming peer assessment usually discourages hitchhiking. In fact, the assessment can be done on a trial basis to encourage team discussions (group processing) about the contributions of each member. The point of this early assessment is to change nonproductive behavior, not to punish. Cooperative learning always strives for "win-win" situations.

Another peer assessment technique, which may be offered on a trial basis, consists of assigning students a limited number of points to distribute among their peers. These points may be used as a small component of the students' grade. A peer assessment of this type gives the real-world lesson of dealing with limited resources and making hard personnel decisions.

If the average grade is a high C to low B, twenty-five points work well for a structured learning team of four students. The instructor tells the students that they may not credit any student with more than eleven points. Students also may not split the points. So, if students wish to issue a relatively even split, they would allocate the points among teammates as follows: nine, eight, and eight. A similar plan works for a team of five with thirty-three points and for a team of three with seventeen points. Students do not necessarily have to assign all their allotted points.

Another strategy for dealing with hitchhikers is called the "termination policy." The plan places responsibility upon students for dysfunctional group members. Just as terminations in business organizations require due process, students must have established guidelines—perhaps discussed when they identified team norms— that they are required to follow. If such guidelines are instead instructor generated, they might consist of a verbal warning which cites the specific dysfunctional behavior, including dated concrete examples. These incidents are clearly communicated to the individual and to the instructor.

If the verbal warning does not change the individual's behavior, then students issue a written warning. In this document, students record the date of the verbal warning and the counterproductive actions since that time. Students give a copy to the individual and to the instructor.

Cooperative Learning Peer Evaluation

The following peer evaluation of your cooperative learning group members is a tool to help enhance your expereience with cooperative learning. Its purpose is to determine those who have been active and cooperative members as well as to identify those who did not participate. Be consistent when evaluating each group member's performance using the guidelines given below.

1-NEVER	2-RARELY	3-SOMETIMES	4-USUALLY	5-ALWAYS

**Has the student attended your Coopera-
tive Learning Group on a regular basis?** 1 2 3 4 5

**Has the student made an effort at
assigned work?** 1 2 3 4 5

**Does the student attempt to make con-
tributions and/or seek help within the
group when he/she needs it?** 1 2 3 4 5

**Does the student cooperate with group
effort?** 1 2 3 4 5

Name of the student being evaluated: _____

Group name or number (i.e., tens, aces, twos): _____

Figure 3-4

The third stage of the termination process may consist of a meeting with all group members and the instructor. If the individual still is unwilling to become a productive member of the group, then termination or removal from the structured learning team occurs, perhaps with an accompanying penalty.

If possible, the instructor should avoid assuming the unpleasant role of referee. If teammates have assigned roles, then the instructor may quietly remind the group leader that one of her responsibilities is to ensure responsible and equitable participation. In more extreme cases, the instructor may encourage elected team representatives, members of the Quality Circle discussed in Chapter 7, to try to correct hitchhiker or other dysfunctional problems. Because the instructor is actively involved with the teams on a day-to-day basis, he or she can often become aware of potential problems before they escalate.

Active Instructor Participation

As indicated earlier, cooperative learning instructors must be actively involved in the assigned group activities. Instructors who systematically rotate among groups for short periods of time discover at least five desirable outcomes. First, they become more aware of the kind of learning that is going on. They can, for example, determine through observation which students are struggling and make certain that they receive whatever support might be useful. More broadly, by listening to explanations couched in peer terminology as opposed to "professorese," instructors learn the source of student confusion and can work on ways to alleviate it, particularly if the confusion highlights problems common to most students perplexed by difficult accounting concepts. When recognizing this situation, instructors may reinforce the value of student input by gaining the class's attention with a quiet signal and then by asking a student—one they know through group monitoring can respond effectively—to clarify the issue.

Second, the instructor's presence suggests to students that she cares about them and about their learning. This result should not be underestimated. Research on student motivation consistently indicates that students regard instructor concern and personal attention as a critical element in their desire to persevere.

Third, when students know that the instructor will be an occasional group member, they are more likely to prepare in advance. Students cannot hide their lack of preparation when instructors are sitting next to their blank sheets of paper.

Fourth, instructors have far more opportunity to interact with students—and hence get to know them in a positive setting—than with the "see me after class" approach. Students feel more comfortable about instructors, and instructors quickly learn that the "sea of faces" they glimpse from the podium is really composed of unique individuals. In this way, cooperative learning helps establish the interpersonal rapport needed for effective teaching.

A final outcome comes from the information instructors gather about each group's interactions; this information helps them later with the group processing so important to effective cooperative learning. As a group participant, instructors are able to look for the rare signs of group dysfunction, such as students with poorly developed social and interaction skills, or students who are "mentally drifting" rather than contributing. The group leader then becomes a means to bring these students more actively into the learning process. A gentle reminder to the leader of her group role usually solves these problems.

When sitting with a group, instructors will find it vital to enforce from the start the rule about questions. Initially, students will turn to the instructor for the solution to a perplexing point or for reassurance that the answer is right. Tactful but firmly directed questions to the group encourage students to rely upon one another.

Instructors listening to group discussions will discover unique student approaches to problem solving, a positive result of the cooperative approach. Or, they may overhear a student practicing a social skill which is particularly important, such as asking a classmate to elaborate on a statement about the reporting phase of the accounting information system. Both learning and group interactive processes can be reinforced and enhanced if the instructor publicly calls attention to student contributions, whether they are a novel approach to an accounting problem or a probing question that helped a fellow classmate clarify his thoughts in a way that was meaningful and productive for teammates as well. Such activity bolsters student confidence that they too can be a source of knowledge and support.

Instructors should become aware of one other caveat. At some institutions, solutions manuals may be available to students because of departmental policies or for other reasons. Students may attempt to bring photocopied pages of these manuals into their structured learning teams. These pages quickly become a new authority and hamper active learning. If possible, instructors should encourage students to establish their own learning norms to preclude use of these crutches.

SUMMARY

Accounting instructors wishing to improve the effectiveness of the teaching and learning processes have taken positive steps by choosing to initiate cooperative learning along with the Hansen and Mowen text. For success, instructors must have made a philosophical commitment to cooperative learning's key principles, particularly to positive interdependence and individual accountability. This commitment and enthusiasm must be clearly communicated to students and must be expressed in all classroom elements, including the course objectives and the syllabus. Careful planning is essential. Practical classroom management logistics, such as group formation and duration, the role of students, and the role of the instructor, make for a smooth-running class. It is also essential to establish a quiet signal that will quickly regain students' attention. Some accounting instructors feel that team-building activities help establish faster group cohesiveness and that team norms or guidelines provide parameters for expected behavior. These guidelines, as well as other approaches, can discourage inappropriate behavior, such as hitchhiking. Once the climate is set for a cooperative classroom, accounting instructors can use the structures—the tools to implement cooperative learning—described in the following chapters.

REFERENCES

Brookfield, S. D. (1987). Developing critical thinkers: Challenging adults to explore alternative ways of thinking and acting. San Francisco: Jossey-Bass.

Brookfield, S. D. (1991). The skillful teacher: On technique, trust, and responsiveness in the classroom. San Francisco: Jossey-Bass.

Finkle, D. L. and G. S. Monk (1983). "Teachers and learning groups: Dissolution of the Atlas complex." In C. Bouton and R. Y. Garth (Eds.), Learning in groups. New Directions for Teaching and Learning, No. 14 (pp. 83-97). San Francisco: Jossey-Bass.

Johnson, D. W., R. T. Johnson, and K. A. Smith (1991) Cooperative learning: Increasing College Faculty Instructional Productivity. ASHE-ERIC Higher Education Report No. 4 Washington, D. C.: The George Washington University, School of Education and Human Development.

Kagan, S. (1992). Cooperative learning. San Juan Capistrano, CA: Resources for Teachers, Inc.

Michaelson, L. K. (1992). "Team learning: A comprehensive approach for harnessing the power of small groups in higher education." In D. H. Wulff and J. D. Nyquist (Eds.), To improve the academy: Resources for faculty, instructional, and organizational development, Vol. 11 (pp. 107-122). Stillwater, OK: The Professional and Organizational Development Network in Higher Education.

National Center for Research To Improve Postsecondary Teaching and Learning. (1990). "Teaching thinking in college." Accent on Improving College Teaching and Learning, No. 7. Ann Arbor, Michigan: NCRIPTAL.

Redding, N. (1990). "The empowering learners project." Educational Leadership, 47(5), 46-48.

Sapon-Shevin, M. & Schniedewind, N. (1989-1990). "Selling cooperative learning without selling it short." Educational Leadership, 47(5), 46-48.

Slavin, R. E. (1989-1990). "Research on cooperative learning: Consensus and controversy." Educational Leadership, 47(4), 52-55.

Solomon, R., N. Davidson, and E. Solomon (1993). The handbook for the 4th R: Relationship activities for cooperative and collegial learning, Vol. III. Columbia, MD: National Institute for Relationship Training.

CHAPTER 4

PUTTING STRUCTURE INTO YOUR STRUCTURES

"If you don't know where you are going, you will probably end up somewhere else."

Laurence J. Peter and Raymond Hull

A number of cooperative learning structures offer accounting instructors good starting points for use in the instruction of accounting concepts. As emphasized earlier, structures are the content-free building blocks, or tools, of cooperative learning. Instructors add their own content-specific information to create a classroom activity tied to course objectives. Many structures used by a wide variety of instructors at all levels of education are effective in accounting courses. Because much of the early work on cooperative learning was done at the K-12 level, the nomenclature, unfortunately, does not always suggest the rigor associated with postsecondary accounting courses. Instructors committed to the principles of cooperative learning and the positive effects it will have on student achievement and affective behaviors must simply remain open-minded and ignore the sometimes "cutesy" terminology. The point is: cooperative learning works, call it what one will.

The cooperative learning structures discussed in this and subsequent chapters are powerful tools to achieve specific classroom objectives. Obviously they can remain nameless or can be renamed, but best of all, structures can be modified—or new structures invented—to serve specific accounting needs. This chapter concentrates on basic or introductory cooperative learning structures that may be easily implemented into the cost accounting course.

Your chosen text, *Management Accounting*, fourth edition, by Hansen and Mowen, is well suited to the implementation of cooperative learning because its underlying foundation rests on solid teaching principles. Instructors who have adopted this text and who undertake cooperative learning will have made important strides toward implementing the recommendations of the Accounting Education Change Commission.

The five structures discussed in this chapter—Think-Pair-Share, Roundtable, Value Line, Corners, and Three-Step Interview—are relatively simple to implement and the final three are useful for group formation exercises. All of these structures, however, need to be carefully planned.

STRUCTURE/STRUCTURE/STRUCTURE

Structure is essential to the cooperative learning environment. The more organization built into classes—through focused structures and through the classroom management techniques discussed in Chapter 3—the more meaningful active learning becomes. When structure is lacking or haphazard, which has occurred too often in students' previous group work experiences, students wander off task. Uncommitted learners revel in the opportunity to "blow it off," as more serious students chafe at the wasted time and question the validity of small group work.

Therefore, besides initially "selling" students on the value of group work in theory, particularly by emphasizing that it develops the teamwork skills needed in the corporate world, instructors should gradually acquaint students with some of the structures outlined in this and subsequent chapters. The instructions for each activity, as emphasized earlier, must be clearly articulated and preferably put in writing. Work sheets or graphic organizers (discussed in Chapter 7), particularly if used one-per-team, focus group work and also emphasize the importance of positive interdependence. Using a variety of cooperative learning structures prevents boredom and provides varied learning opportunities. To eliminate the problem of off-task students, instructors should build into every activity an extra topic, assignment, problem, or step for groups that work more rapidly than others.

THINK-PAIR-SHARE

Think-Pair-Share is probably the best-known and most widely used cooperative learning structure. Many people use it without, in fact, connecting it to cooperative learning or realizing that a single man, Frank Lyman (1981), was responsible for its creation and dissemination. Because of its simplicity and versatility, Think-Pair-Share offers an entry point for accounting instructors new to cooperative learning. It is a relatively low-risk activity.

In Think-Pair-Share, a cooperative learning structure encouraging increased student participation and higher-order thinking skills, students learn a new response cycle to accounting questions, one based on student interaction and hence, active learning. This easy-to-use technique has wide applications, even in large lecture classes.

To initiate a Think-Pair-Share activity, the accounting instructor poses a question which cannot be answered facilely with a response based on rote memorization; often the question is a probing one without a single definitive answer. Students are given time, usually less than a minute, to *think* of a response. The importance of this "think time" cannot be overemphasized. Instructors new to cooperative learning may find that moments of silence in a class seem overly long. They must resist, however, the temptation to hurry the process, since these moments cause students to more fully develop higher-order thinking skills.

An instructor may prefer that this "think" period be used to allow students to write their responses, a practice ensuring that most students are on task. This practice also helps instructors fulfill calls for writing across the curriculum. These individual responses can be collected at the conclusion of the class, if desired.

Next, students *pair* with another classmate, often a member of their structured learning team, to discuss their response to the question. This phase of Think-Pair-Share reinforces the principle of simultaneity in the accounting classroom. In the lecture and recitation technique only two people, the instructor and a designated student, interact. Other students may or may not be attentively listening or actively mulling over their own responses. In Think-Pair-Share, all persons are simultaneously involved in paired discussion, and fifty percent of a class are vocal.

In the third phase, the instructor invites students to *share* their responses. If the sharing is done with the class as a whole, instructors will find that students whose ideas have been reinforced, refined, or challenged through discussion with a peer will be eager to volunteer. Instructors will no longer face a paucity of student participants but will have the "problem" of which of many respondents to recognize. Furthermore, the level of responses is far more intellectually rich than responses typically coming from a situation where an instructor merely tosses off a question and waits for the hands of the most assertive students to shoot skyward. As a general rule, it is wise to limit a whole-class follow-up to four to six responses in order to avoid repetition, particularly if the question encourages complex answers.

Responses during the share period do not necessarily need to involve the whole class, particularly if instructors have formed students into ongoing structured learning teams. Because much of the benefit from this activity comes from the reflection and subsequent verbalization, instructors can simply ask that students share their paired discussions within the small but safe framework of their ongoing structured learning team.

Although a Think-Pair-Share activity can be initiated quickly and easily—sometimes spontaneously during a lecture with random pairs when an instructor senses a need for students to "process" or reflect on the material—instructors who are committed to the formation of structured learning teams might consider pairing stronger and weaker students by assigning the former to major suits (hearts and spades) and the latter to minor suits (diamonds and clubs). Suit colors may then be used as the basis for pairs or dyads called "suit partners." For example, within the structured learning team, the club would have been assigned to the student who had performed poorly and the spade to the student who had performed well. These students would form one dyad while the students who had performed about the mean, holding diamonds and hearts, would form the other dyad. In groups of five the wild card would replace any missing group member or join with the black suits to form a triad. Students, of course, should not be aware of these instructor-designed internal structures. These stronger-weaker designations also prove useful with other structures, such as Jigsaw, discussed in Chapter 6.

Other sharing alternatives for Think-Pair-Share enhance its flexibility. One option is to eliminate the final share phase, having accomplished the most important elements of the activity by having students reflect and then verbalize their responses. Too often instructors assume that students expect every contribution to be acknowledged and validated publicly. These whole-class sharings are often unnecessary and time-consuming. Thus, the Think-Pair-Share activity can be initiated without structured learning teams in virtually any setting where people are seated together. In fact, many public speakers have used its power to generate active audience engagement.

Even in its simplest form, Think-Pair-Share offers benefits to students and instructors alike. At a minimum, students have valuable wait time to think through questions before any discussion begins. Moreover, students have an opportunity to rehearse responses mentally and orally with a peer before being asked to share publicly. This process enhances oral communication skills and confidence. All students have an opportunity to share their thinking with at least one other person, thereby increasing their sense of involvement.

Instructors also benefit, since students spend more time actively learning accounting. Students who might have "tuned out" during a traditional lecture and recitation presentation actively listen to each other during Think-Pair-Share activities. After rehearsing in pairs, they are more capable of volunteering well-thought-out responses. Instructors also have more in-class time to think themselves. They can concentrate on asking higher-order questions, observing reactions, and listening to responses. Think-Pair-Share is easy to learn, easy to use, and easily creates a more relaxed atmosphere than calling on individual (and often ill-prepared) students.

The Think-Pair-Share structure, a powerful learning tool, can also be used for complex, extended student exchanges. It can be used, for example, to reach consensus by asking students to agree upon a single solution for an accounting problem or issue. For issues, students can conversely be asked to play devil's advocate with their partner and draw out deeper informed responses by carefully phrased probing questions that might be expected from an opposing viewpoint. The Think-Pair-Share structure is particularly powerful when used for reciprocal teaching, an approach receiving increasing attention in higher education. McKeachie, Pintrich, Lin, and Smith (1986), for instance, conclude: "The best answer to the question, 'What is the most effective method of teaching?' is that it depends on the goal, the student, the content, and the teacher. But the next best answer is, 'Students teaching other students.'" (p. 63)

On a basic level, reciprocal teaching can be used efficiently when a vast body of information, such as accounting concepts and terminology, needs to be committed to long-term memory. Students study the body of material independently, but to ensure mastery some in-class time is permitted for paired coaching. Students prepare flashcards for pre-test coaching with the word to be defined on the front of the card and the answer on the back. Working in pairs or dyads, one student assumes the role of tutor, holding up the cards with the definitions in rapid succession. If the "tutee" gives an accurate definition, he or she receives the card. If the answer is incorrect or partially correct, the tutor shows the flip side of the card and allows time for study and reflection. The two might discuss ways to master the elusive definition, such as through a pneumonic device. The card is then placed at the back of the deck for a subsequent response. When the tutee has earned all of the cards through correct responses, the roles are reversed until both partners have mastered the material. Reciprocal teaching is also useful for material requiring higher-order thinking skills. In Chapter 6, for example, we introduce the idea of paired essays, an efficient way to "front load" course material, so that class time can be used effectively for processing what students have already learned during independent study.

Think-Pair-Share also can build accounting skills through paired problem solving. A problem-solving period can be extended by asking students to solve accounting exercises using a variation of this structure. Accounting exercises developed in Think-Pair-Share sessions replace the more traditional, but less effective, practice of placing a numerical example on the blackboard or on an overhead for students to mechanically duplicate in their notes. Because in Think-Pair-Share students actively derive solutions and their underlying concepts, rather than copy them, they feel ownership and are more likely to retain the knowledge.

An Accounting Concept Example

An objective suggested in Hansen and Mowen's second chapter reads, "Explain the differences between traditional and contemporary management accounting systems." During a lecture, the instructor may explain the concept of a system and how a cost management system fits into this concept. Then the instructor poses a question to the class in this manner: "The text mentioned two major cost management systems. Take thirty seconds to consider how these two systems differ."

After a timed thirty seconds of silence, the instructor says, "Now share your response with your suit partner." He gives the students one minute to share their responses in dyads and then calls the class back into the lecture mode with the quiet signal. As the final segment of Think-Pair-Share, the instructor calls for volunteer responses until he gets an exemplary one, usually with the first student, due to the reflection and rehearsal time.

Another Think-Pair-Share structure may immediately follow with the question, "What are the benefits of a contemporary management accounting system?" The same Think-Pair Share procedure would follow this question. If the instructor desires, a whole-class discussion or some reinforcing comments may follow these two Think-Pair-Share activities.

An Accounting Exercise Example

Learning Objective 3 for Hansen and Mowen's fourth chapter calls for students to be able to describe traditional costing approaches. During the course of her lecture on this topic the instructor can utilize a series of Think-Pair-Shares to reinforce student understanding of and ability to calculate overhead rates and use them to assign overhead to product. The instructor may use an example with two departments, one of which is labor intensive while the other is machine intensive. The instructor asks students to individually compute a plant-wide overhead rate and use that rate to assign overhead to product for both departments in the example. After the allotted time they verify their responses in pairs. The "share" portion occurs when the instructor asks for a volunteer to respond before the whole class.

As the next step the instructor asks students to individually calculate a departmental overhead rate for each department and to use those rates to assign overhead to product. She repeats the process of verification and calls for a volunteer.

As a final Think-Pair-Share, the instructor asks students to consider silently which of these systems is better for assigning overhead to product and why. After the think time the students pair to exchange their thoughts on this question. The instructor then may call upon several volunteers to respond before the class and let this process flow naturally into a whole-class discussion.

Roundtable

Roundtable, a cooperative learning structure useful for brainstorming, reviewing, or practicing a skill, uses a single sheet of paper and pen for each cooperative learning group. Students in the group respond in turn to a question or problem by stating their ideas aloud as they write them on the paper. It is important that the ideas be vocalized for several reasons: (a) silence in a setting like this is boring, rather than golden; (b) other team members need be reflecting on the proffered thoughts; (c) variety is encouraged, because teammates learn immediately if someone has come up with a similar idea and they will not repeat it when their turn comes; and (d) hearing the responses said aloud means that students do not have to waste valuable brainstorming time by reading the previous ideas on the page.

Team members are encouraged not to skip turns, but if their thoughts are at a standstill they are allowed to say "Pass" rather than turn the brainstorm into a brain drizzle. Thus, there is almost universal participation in Roundtable. As the paper circulates clockwise, team members are encouraged to record ideas as rapidly as possible, resulting in the quick generation of a number of ideas.

As a variation of Roundtable, instructors can substitute a piece of acetate and a transparency pen. Students rapidly record responses on the acetate using the same Roundtable procedure. To provide summary, the instructor asks one or two designated reporters to share their groups' results with the entire class, using an overhead projector. In another variation, called Gallery Tour, students stand over a desk and brainstorm in Roundtable fashion, recording their ideas with markers on a large piece of flip chart paper. The sheets can remain in place or be posted. The instructor then gives students a few minutes to tour the room, reviewing the ideas brainstormed by other groups. This activity, if used at all, should be reserved for late in the semester when students are accustomed to small group learning and more willing to accept novel approaches.

Many creative uses can be made of the ideas generated, depending on their nature. For example, using a Roundtable students could identify the most important ethical issues facing accountants. A composite of all the ideas could be compiled and used later in a problem-solving activity called Send-a-Problem, discussed in Chapter 6. Ideas for paper topics could be generated, compiled, and circulated to all students.

In Roundtable, the multiple answers encourage creativity and deeper thinking. Thus, students familiar with the concepts will still find the group exploration challenging. The organizational format of Roundtable—one piece of paper and one pen per group—reinforces the concept of positive interdependence and also serves as a team-building exercise because group members feel a sense of accomplishment when reviewing their team-generated list. Instructors looking for good question prompts will find that the end of chapter material in Hansen and Mowen's text contains many exercises, problems, and cases which require multiple responses.

An Example

As their second learning objective for Chapter 7 of the text, Hansen and Mowen state that students should be able to explain reasons why support costs may be assigned to producing departments. Roundtable provides a cooperative learning structure in which students may develop and reinforce the objectives for allocation of support department costs.

In cases where structured learning teams have not been formed, students may gather into groups of four or five with those seated around them. The instructor gives them directions to use only one pen and one sheet of paper for this exercise. She also relates the rules of roundtable: only the student with the paper and pen speaks, the paper and pen circulate clockwise, a student may pass, the idea must be spoken as well as written, and so forth. Instructors will find a brief review of the Roundtable procedures, whereby students respond to prompting questions about the rules, will cause the structure to run more smoothly.

The instructor announces that the objective of the closed-book exercise is for each group to derive reasons why firms allocate support-department costs to producing departments. The instructor challenges them to generate as many reasons as possible within a five-minute period. Once all instructions have been issued, she signals for the students to begin. During the course of this activity the instructor should remember to actively circulate among the groups to ensure that they are on task.

After five minutes have elapsed, the instructor gains student attention with the prearranged quiet signal. She then directs student attention to the IMA objectives listed on pages 246–247 of the text and tells them to compare and contrast their reasons with the those objectives. A whole-class discussion about the theory for allocation of support department costs will flow naturally after conducting this structure.

USING COOPERATIVE LEARNING STRUCTURES FOR GROUP FORMATION

Once the stage is set, careful team formation can ensure the success of small groups. As discussed earlier, cooperative learning advocates agree that heterogeneity enhances the effectiveness of structured group work. To the greatest extent possible, groups should be composed of high, low, and middle achievers of both genders and various ethnic and cultural backgrounds and ages. Three cooperative learning structures—Value Line, Corners, and Three-Step Interview—can help instructors rapidly and meaningfully create heterogeneous teams.

These teams may or may not become the semi-permanent structured learning teams which form the heart of the cooperative classroom. For the sake of variety and the opportunity for students to meet other classmates, instructors may create temporary teams for brief in-class assignments and interactions. These three structures lend themselves well to rapid, varied team formation.

Value Line

A Value Line ascertains students' opinions in a quick and visual way by asking them to line up according to how strongly they agree or disagree with a statement or proposition. In an undergraduate accounting course, for example, instructors may ask students to respond to the following statements:

> The plus/minus grading system should be instituted at our university.

> Business majors should be required to take more liberal arts courses.

> My primary reason for choosing my major was career enhancement.

Clear instructions reinforced by visual aids are particularly important for implementation because many students are unaccustomed to active learning that involves active movement. To initiate the structure, instructors should briefly give students arguments for or against the proposition and show them a five-point Likert scale on an overhead. Instructors ask students, after a moment of "think time," to choose the number that best describes their position on the issue. To avoid indecisiveness, it is a good idea to have the students jot down their number before the next step. Instructors next ask students who have chosen "1" to stand at a designated point along the wall of the room. The students who have chosen "2" follow them, and so forth until all students are lined up. It is important to stretch the line sufficiently so that students are not bunched together in large clumps.

After the students have formed a continuous line based on their own opinions, instructors must identify the midpoint. The easiest way to do this is to ask students to ignore the original number they selected as the basis for their location in the line and instead to count-off sequentially, calling out numbers from one end of the line to the other so that each student now has a unique identifying number. The instructor finds the median student by dividing the last number by two.

The next steps are critically important. The instructor forms the first group of four students by taking one from each extreme of the line and two from its midpoint. To ensure the rapid and accurate identification of these four students, it is helpful to use an overhead allowing the instructor to draw lines through the numbers who have been assigned to teams. A simple numerical grid (Figure 4-1) works well. In a class of 30, for example, the instructor would call the numbers 1, 30, 14, and 15, striking over them on the grid. For the next team, she would call 2, 29, 13, and 16, again striking over the numbers on the grid. For additional clarity, if the group is large, instructors can ask a student from the first group formed to record on the blackboard or a flip chart the four numbers as they are called out for each team. When their numbers are called, students approach the instructor—or in a large class, a designated student—and each of the four team members receives a playing card of the same rank but of a different suit (*e.g.,* Team one would be composed of four aces: heart, diamond, spade, and club; the second team would be composed of four deuces: heart, diamond, spade, and club, etc.).

Once teams are formed, they should be instructed to sit closely together. If the instructor wishes to assign seats, she will have placed cards identical to those distributed at student desks using the cooperative learning seating chart discussed in Chapter 3 as a guide. Students quickly find their seats by locating the card identical to the one they hold.

Instructors continue to form groups with this procedure until all students have been assigned to a group and have found their designated seats. Any students left over join a group as a fifth member. The teams thus formed will have a constructive variety of students, particularly the earliest ones which have the greatest range, with students holding opposing viewpoints mixed with those identifying with more moderate stances. Figure 4-2 depicts the Value Line structure visually.

A Value Line also lends itself well to paired discussion. To form pairs or dyads where students can exchange viewpoints on various topics, instructors have the students line up as before based on their stance on a controversial issue. This time, instead of pulling four students from the ends and midpoints to form a quad, the instructor breaks the line at the midpoint and literally doubles it back around so that the two students at each end are paired, and so on (*e.g.,* 1 and 30 pair; 2 and 29 pair; 3 and 28 pair, etc.). Pairing students of opposing viewpoints allows them to stretch their perspectives and to learn to examine at least two sides of an issue. These monitored exchanges promote critical thinking skills by helping students to recognize the validity of alternate viewpoints and to identify and question their own assumptions before exploring alternative patterns of thought.

Instructors may wish to form new groups at various times during the semester for short-term or long-term projects or assignments. When such groupings are not made on the basis of issues or values but on the basis of a neutral topic such as birthdays, they are simply called Line-Ups rather than Value Lines. A convenient time for regrouping students occurs after examinations. At this point a nonactive modification of Value Line or Line-Up can create heterogeneity with respect to achievement level. Here, instead of a student line-up, instructors privately rank the students by their performance on the exam and group students as they did in Value Line by continually drawing students from the two end points and the middle. The instructor can announce new group assignments on the day the exam is returned. Forming a private line-up using test scores ensures that each group will have a strong performer, a weak performer, and two or three students who performed near the mean. Cooperative learning advocates agree that heterogeneity with respect to ability enhances the learning of all group members. Clipping a playing card to the returned examination facilitates the reassignment procedure.

Creating new groups after an exam also gives everyone in the class a fresh start. Students may not want to leave their old groups, but reformation gives everyone the opportunity to work

1	2	3	4	5	6	7	8	9	10
11	12	13	14	15	16	17	18	19	20
21	22	23	24	25	26	27	28	29	30
31	32	33	34	35	36	37	38	39	40
41	42	43	44	45	46	47	48	49	50
51	52	53	54	55	56	57	58	59	60
61	62	63	64	65	66	67	68	69	70

Figure 4-1

with more and more diverse people. Moreover, periodic reorganization of the class eliminates the occasional dysfunctional group.

Corners

To initiate Corners, instructors ask students to join a group—often the four choices are designated by a specific corner of the room—based on a mutual interest, preference, or question solution. These groups are thus homogeneous based on the selection criteria. In an undergraduate accounting class, for example, students could select a group based on career objectives. As an alternative, students could select a group based on their agreement with one of four responses to a statement such as: "The greatest value of college life comes from: (a) academic subjects studied, (b) social skills acquired, (c) networks formed with peers and professors, and (d) the opportunity to interact with people of differing backgrounds, cultures, and views."

Instructors first announce the four options, making certain that students clearly understand them. An overhead transparency often clarifies the four choices. In addition, a visual aid, such as a sign posted in each corner or area of the room, helps students know exactly where they should move. As in the Value Line formation, the instructor first provides "think time" before asking students to choose a corner at a given signal. While in their corners, students might briefly discuss the topic which generated the group formation. For example, students could talk about the perceived benefits of their particular major.

After each group reaches consensus or finishes sharing relevant ideas within an allotted time span, the instructor can ask that representatives from each corner share the group's best ideas with the rest of the class. If desired, the instructor can mix students from each corner group to form the semi-permanent structured learning teams where students will study designated

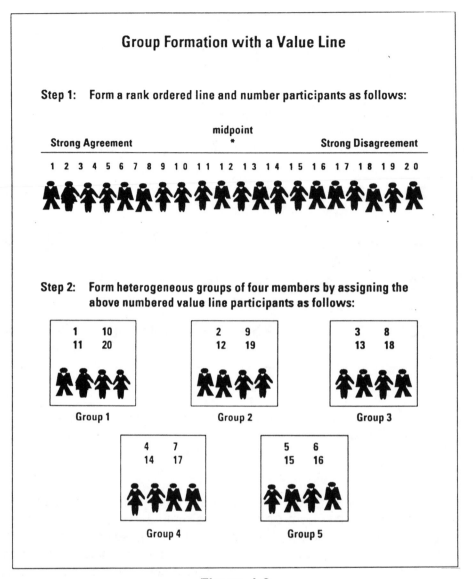

Figure 4-2

course material. These newly formed teams welcome problem-solving activities that will capitalize on each student's area of expertise or opinion. For example, teams composed of students with different career objectives can determine the types of accounting information needed by managers, financial analysts, and government regulators.

Three-Step Interview

A structure called the Three-Step Interview guides students into student-selected heterogeneous groups. Three-Step Interview builds from pairs (dyads) into groups of four. It is an excellent "ice breaker" for an initial class meeting provided that the students perceive interview questions as interesting and course-related. Instructors ask students to find partners whom they don't know well, preferably someone of the opposite sex, someone who does not look like them. After finding a partner, they sit down, so that the instructor can help any stray class members locate partners. If there is an uneven number of students the instructor can suggest that three students work as a triad. The students decide who will be the initial interviewer or the instructor can designate that person by a joke such as, "Okay, I want the person with the shortest hair to begin the interview." Students interview their partners for a specified number of minutes—often two or three—depending on the complexity of the interview questions. Besides ascertaining some introductory background information, such as name, hometown, and intended major, the interviewer asks for opinions on class-related topics. In a management accounting class the designated question might be, "What accounting information not found in published financial statements might managers find useful?"

At the prearranged quiet signal, the two switch roles and the other person is interviewed for the same number of minutes. The instructor then asks each dyad to join another dyad to form a set of four, or quad. For the next four minutes, the members of these newly formed groups introduce their partners to the other group members, succinctly sharing their ideas. If the class paired evenly but the third step will result in an unintegrated pair, it may be necessary to split this dyad—with apologies—so that each of these two students can be added as a fifth member of another group. It is advisable to foresee this problem as soon as the pairs are formed so that instructors can identify the two students to be "ripped asunder" and alert them early in the process that they will need to be reassigned because of the unequal breakdown of students. If a triad is already in place, then there is no need to break up the odd-pair: they simply join the threesome to form a group of five.

The interview topic, usually opinion or evaluative questions, should allow each student to contribute to the discussion; that is, the initially interviewed student cannot give the definitive answer. Additional topics useful for a management accounting course could be to ascertain student speculation on one of the learning objectives of the first chapter of the Hansen and Mowen text before they have read the chapter. For example:

> In what ways do you suppose financial accounting and management accounting are similar?

> In what ways do you suppose financial accounting and management accounting are different?

> What roles do you suppose a management accountant might play in an organization?

It is important in this activity, as in others, to provide what is often called a "sponge" or an "extension." This is an extra question, problem, or activity to be completed by groups working more rapidly than others. The knowledge that there is an expectation of on-task behavior and added responsibilities keeps students from rushing through tasks in order to "goof off." Thus, in Three-Step Interview, it is important to add an extra question or two for those who finish early. If the Three-Step Interview is used during the semester rather than at the beginning, more complex interview questions can help students process the course material.

The Three-Step Interview is fairly versatile, meshing well with other structures. For example, after students have formed groups by means of either Value Line or Corners, the formal interview structure allows them to get to know the other group members and to discuss the issue posed in Value Line or the topic used in Corners. If used within the context of the semi-permanent structured learning team when playing cards are involved, students pair with their suit partner (by color of suit), and the major suits (hearts and spades) spend several minutes soliciting involved responses on the designated discussion questions from their partners.

At the quiet signal, the two switch roles and the minor suits (diamonds and clubs) do the interviewing. Finally, the structured learning team reconvenes and each person summarizes the information gathered during the interviewing process with his or her suit partner. At that point, depending on the nature of the questions, the team may or may not want to work for either consensus or a delineation of the various divergent viewpoints.

The Three-Step Interview serves a number of functions. Besides its value as an ice-breaker, it can be used at any point in a term to help students process course material. Students can interview one another, for example, about the salient points of a key chapter. As an added benefit, this structure provides an excellent opportunity to practice and reinforce effective listening skills. If students have to summarize information provided by their partners, they are more likely to attend and also to be certain that they understand the viewpoint. During the interview process, instructors should also be listening so that they can compliment and therefore reinforce effective teamwork skills such as asking probing questions or providing positive reinforcement. They will also want to be certain that students are sharing relevant, accurate information. The structure promotes team bonding as students share ideas and experiences. And finally, the Three-Step Interview focuses attention on important accounting topics by allowing students to "connect" with the material in a personal way.

SUMMARY

Accounting instructors who are committed to the philosophical basis of cooperative learning and are willing to invest in the planning to manage a student-centered classroom must now begin gradually to introduce some of the tools—the structures—that help students to master their complex subject matter.

Perhaps the most basic, most low-risk cooperative learning structure is Think-Pair-Share: instructors pose a question and allow about 30 seconds of "wait time" for reflection or a few minutes of focused writing (Think). They then ask students to turn to a partner and verbalize their thoughts on the designated question (Pair). Finally, if desired, instructors have students share their thoughts during a rapid whole-class discussion or within their structured learning team (Share).

In Roundtable, an extremely versatile structure, students brainstorm ideas which may be shared or applied in a number of ways. Students not only receive the benefits derived from thinking and talking about accounting concepts, but they also learn the importance of alternating speaking and listening in a small group situation.

Three other structures, all of them useful for team formation, are relatively easy to implement: Value Line, Corners, and Three-Step Interview. Value Line, probably the most logistically difficult to manage with large classes, results in a human Likert scale after students are asked to take a position based on their stand on a particular topic or issue. To form pairs, the line is broken in the middle and folded back so that students are paired with those having opinions unlike their own. Or, instructors can form heterogeneous quads by calling two students from each extreme of the line and two from the midpoint until all students have been assigned to a team. In Corners, students go to a designated area to discuss a topic with like-minded colleagues. The instructor can then pull students from each of the four corners to form a heterogeneous quad. Three-Step Interview, which is useful for team formation, can also be used within a semi-permanent structured learning team to discuss key content questions.

Regardless of the structure chosen, the secret to a successful cooperative learning classroom is careful planning and organization. All of the activities must be carefully explained to students and clearly tied to course objectives. The classroom techniques discussed in Chapter 3 will assure smooth implementation of the structures discussed in this chapter.

REFERENCES

Lyman, F. (1981). "The responsive classroom discussion." In A. S. Anderson (Ed.) *Mainstreaming Digest.* College Park, MD: University of Maryland College of Education.

McKeachie, W. J., P. R. Pintrich, Y. Lin, and D. A. Smith (1986). *Teaching and learning in the college classroom: A review of the research literature.* Ann Arbor: The University of Michigan.

CHAPTER 5

TAKING A BIGGER BITE

"What I hear, I forget; what I see, I remember; what I do, I understand."

Chinese Proverb

Although we have entitled this chapter "taking a bigger bite," we recommend that instructors take small steps in implementing additional cooperative learning. Too often, swept away by enlightened enthusiasm, instructors will launch into a new pedagogy without sufficient preparation. When the results are less than optimal, some instructors react by retreating: "Oh, I've made a good faith effort to try small group learning, and it just doesn't work." Such well-intentioned efforts are counter-productive for both students and instructors. It is far better to become familiar with the theory and practice of cooperative learning by reading materials such as this text and by talking with colleagues, and then introducing gradually some of the more basic structures. The decision to place students in structured learning teams, for instance, is a crucial step for building a cooperative classroom, but it so significant that it should not be undertaken without preparation and support. Instructors may initially want to introduce relatively low-risk cooperative learning structures gradually over a semester in their cost accounting course. As instructors gain experience, they may then more quickly adopt more cooperative learning structures.

We hope you have reflected on the basic components and rationale for cooperative learning discussed in the first three chapters and that you have implemented some introductory structures outlined in Chapter 3 (Cooperative Homework Check) and Chapter 4 (Think-Pair-Share, Roundtable, Value Line, Corners, and Three-Step Interview). If you have, you are ready to plan your next accounting course using the Hansen and Mowen text in conjunction with structured learning teams kept in place throughout a semester or half a semester. Once instructors have established structured learning teams, they can consider more advanced cooperative learning structures. In this chapter these advanced cooperative learning structures are divided into three categories: (a) structures useful in building accounting problem-solving skills, (b) structures useful for controlled discussions, and (c) structures useful for reviewing material. Because of their versatility, however, virtually all these structures serve multiple purposes.

STRUCTURES USEFUL IN BUILDING ACCOUNTING PROBLEM-SOLVING SKILLS

The Accounting Education Change Commission has endorsed instructional methods that enable students to identify and solve unstructured problems. Cooperative learning is ideally suited for building problem-solving skills. The advanced structures discussed in this chapter enhance student learning as students strengthen their understanding of accounting concepts and tone their problem-solving skills.

Structured Problem Solving

Within the structured learning teams that form the basis of a cooperative classroom many activities promote problem-solving ability. Effective use of these teams depends in part on the assignment of numbers, playing card suits, or some other designator to identify group members quickly and relatively anonymously. Kagan (1992) has named the structure we describe Numbered Heads Together, terminology which may be a turn-off for college-level students. The Johnson, Johnson, and Smith (1991) term for the structure, Problem Solving Lesson, again smacks too much of the primary or secondary level. We prefer to call this multi-purpose structure Structured Problem Solving.

Although we have included Structured Problem Solving under advanced structures because its use is facilitated by the implementation of structured learning teams, in reality this is a fairly easy structure to initiate. Students within quads have assigned identities achieved by numbering off (1, 2, 3, 4 with a fifth member replacing an absent classmate or responding in tandem with the student designated as a 4) or by some other method such as playing card suits. The instructor poses a question or problem(s) and announces a time limit. The question is often posed as a directive because the power of Structured Problem Solving lies in the peer coaching that occurs within the team. Instead of asking, for instance, "What is a prime cost? What is a conversion cost?" the instructor might say, "Be certain that everyone on the team knows the components of prime cost and conversion cost and how they relate to product." It is useful to build in, as in Think-Pair-Share, a few seconds of reflective time, allowing students to collect their thoughts or to think more deeply. The students then work together for the specified amount of time. This time can be brief or extended depending on the complexity of the questions (high or low consensus) or problems to be mastered. At the end of the time period, the instructor calls a number or a playing card suit and those designated students must respond on the group's behalf.

The responses can take several variations. For example, the instructor might ask that the students holding clubs raise their hands if the team can provide an answer. If a limited number of hands go up, then it is useful to provide a few additional minutes of teamwork with the admonition, "Be certain that the club on your team can represent your viewpoint." Then the instructor can call on four to six people—depending on the complexity of the question or problem—to respond before the class as a whole. In other cases, those designated might go to the blackboard to work through the accounting problem.

Students also welcome an alternative to the whole-class sharing, one that augments simultaneous learning, class building, and inter-team connections. Instructors identify by number or suit the students who will be the team spokesperson and send them to another team where they share their group's ideas. All the twos or all the hearts, for example, might rotate clockwise to the next team. This fresh approach results in the active involvement of one quarter of a classroom, and yet the activity takes the same amount of time as a traditional whole-class discussion response where only one student is active.

Another sharing approach works well if the responses are brief but multiple, such as a list of items generated through a Roundtable brainstorming session. Instructors then have the designated students stand up and call out one response from the team's list in turn, rotating about the room. To avoid repetition, the students keep track of the other responses and sit down when their team's list has been exhausted. If the question generates many responses—such as a question relating to management decision options—then several rounds of energetic answers result.

Structured Problem Solving has many benefits. For instance, it encourages full and even participation because the instructor can keep track of the students called upon rather handily by noting the suit called upon and the specified team responding during a whole-class share. More importantly, however, it shifts the focus in a classroom to a cooperative rather than a competitive mode. In a typical whole-class discussion, the instructor poses a question and waits—sometimes for an uncomfortably long period of time—for hands to shoot upward. Usually, only a handful of students will be energetically competing for the instructor's attention. The rest may simply tune out. When one student is selected, the others in competition for the instructor's attention are often secretly thinking, "I hope he botches it, so that I can share my ideas." This kind of negative scenario does not occur with Structured Problem Solving. Instead, all students prepare their team response together, resulting in a more sophisticated caliber of responses. Instead of individuals competing for the instructor's attention, there is an expectation that everyone is potentially able to respond to the question. Because the response is a team-generated one, students designated as the team spokespersons find their role far less threatening than when they are called upon for individual responses. Students who normally do not participate feel far more comfortable speaking up under this structure. It is also less threatening to hear an instructor call for responses from the diamonds, for instance, than to be singled out by name. Because team members are responsible for the learning of others—no one knows whom the instructor will select as spokesperson and everyone wants the team to perform well publicly—positive interdependence is sustained. Furthermore, students are likely to remain attentive if they know they may be the team spokesperson. Because students will be individually tested—if appropriate—over the material covered, individual accountability is still fostered.

Structured Problem Solving at first glance seems to be sabotaged by the use of predesignated team roles discussed in Chapter 3. For example, at the beginning of each class period the instructor may routinely signal the roles for the day by writing them on the board next to the suits of cards as below:

> Spades—Monitor
>
> Hearts—Leader
>
> Diamonds—Reporter
>
> Clubs—Recorder

Or roles may routinely rotate in a given order from student to student. Upon entering class, students know in which capacity they must act for the day, thus potentially eliminating the element of positive interdependence in Structured Problem Solving because the reporters will already have been identified. The solution here is to tell students that for this activity, their usual roles are no longer operative. Group reporters or spokespersons will be chosen at random, perhaps by drawing a card from another deck. The role of leader is particularly important in Structured Problem Solving because that individual is responsible for checking to see that all group members understand and can summarize the discussion points and/or problem solutions. The instructor may wish to assign that role in advance with the understanding that any team member, including the leader, may be the reporter.

Structured Problem Solving may be used to augment lectures in much the same way as Think-Pair-Share. The chief difference lies in the nature and complexity of the learning objectives. For example, if the questions, tasks, or problems are complicated enough to warrant input from more than two individuals, particularly if one student is less academically prepared, then it is clearly advantageous to use Structured Problem Solving.

It works, for instance, whenever the instructor, as part of her lecture, has formerly placed a numerical example on the board or on an overhead. To ensure both mastery and transferability of knowledge, instructors can ask students within their structured learning teams to work out solutions to problems using the concepts they have just heard in the lecture. The numerous problems in the Hansen and Mowen text provide many numerical examples effectively used with Structured Problem Solving.

An Example

In Hansen and Mowen's Chapter 7, Learning Objective 4 combined with Problem 7-2 works well with Structured Problem Solving. The instructor will have given the class an overview of cost allocation and its objectives. The students will also have familiarity with allocation of a single support department's cost to several producing departments.

At this time the instructor introduces the possibility of more than one support department and the complication that they provide service to each other. The instructor tells the students that one solution to this problem is the direct method. For visual learners, he may want to diagram the direct method in a similar manner to Exhibit 7-6 of the text. Then, instead of "spoon feeding" the students a numerical example, he directs them to the first requirement of Problem 7-2 and asks them to solve it in their structured learning teams.

After the elapse of a preannounced time, the instructor reassembles the class using the quiet signal. A reporter from a randomly selected group gives the group response to the questions and perhaps describes how the group reached its conclusion. The instructor then encourages questions from the class, which are first directed to the responding group.

Resuming a lecture stance, the instructor now introduces a second method for allocating the support department costs, the sequential method. The instructor explains why this is considered superior to the direct method and diagrams the procedure in similar manner to Exhibit 7-9. Redirecting student attention to Problem 7-2, the instructor asks the students to work the second requirement as a numerical example. After the time has elapsed, the instructor calls upon a different group to provide a report. Whole-class discussion may follow to reinforce the concepts and clear up grey areas.

Finally, the instructor turns to the reciprocal method. Here students are given not only a diagram, but also a formula, again without a numerical example. The students get the numerical example by working the third requirement in their structured learning teams. Throughout the three phases of this structure, the instructor should be actively participating by rotating among the groups and helping those who become confused or frustrated.

This Structured Problem Solving ends with a final group report and whole-class discussion. Accounting students, like others, are often hungry for closure. Particularly early in a semester, they may not trust the group process entirely and hence feel frustrated if the instructor—the authority figure—does not validate or reinforce their group learning through summary lectures or concluding whole-group discussions. Students will want to know that their notes are accurate for future study. The instructor will want to reinforce positive interdependence by fostering the notion that peer students constitute a source for correct solutions.

Whole-class discussion should reach beyond simply the right answer. To enhance higher-order thinking skills, the instructor should encourage students to be able to compare and contrast the three methods. Moreover, they should be able to enunciate why one method may be superior to another.

Discovery Method

Davidson (1990), a mathematician, has described what he calls the Discovery Method in detail. He found that calculus students placed in structured learning teams, can, with initial guidance and an adequate foundation, derive complex theorems and proofs on their own without having seen the instructor demonstrate them. He also discovered that students participating in this kind of learning situation retain far more than students taught through traditional mathematical methods.

Accounting students, like calculus students, can benefit from the Discovery Method. As in the example cited earlier, students given a few fundamental principles can discover an accounting method, model, or system on their own.

Besides aiding in mastery of specific course material, the Discovery Method, because the process of working through steps provides experiential learning which transfers into long-term memory, results in greater retention than under traditional lecture or discussion methods. Self-esteem rises because students assume ownership of the concept or method that they have discovered. Furthermore, because they can attribute their success to mutual effort, students increase their sense of competency and control. This process of working with unstructured accounting problems and cases fulfills key objectives of the Accounting Education Change Commission. Perhaps most important, the Discovery Method is both challenging and fun for students.

An Example

Instructors may use the Discovery Method to enhance student learning early in the course. Learning Objective 2 for Chapter 4 of the Hansen and Mowen text provides an excellent opportunity. The Discovery Method should be initiated in class before instructors assign the fourth chapter for out-of-class reading. During an introductory mini-lecture, the instructor briefly describes a manufacturing environment and its likely components.

As a closed-book exercise, the instructor then asks the students to design a system that could capture the cost of making a product. After they have worked on this question on the conceptual level, the instructor hands the students data similar to that found in Exercise 4-1. However, because the students have had no class exposure to product costing the problem requirements are modified. The instructor asks the students to use the system they have designed to assign a cost to product.

After the prearranged time has elapsed, the instructor returns to the lecture mode with the quiet signal and randomly calls for two or three group reports. The instructor then leads a whole-class discussion, pointing out the similarities and differences of the methods the students have "discovered." Finally, the instructor introduces product costing procedures to the students, emphasizing the similarities between the methods "discovered" by the students and the conventional methods used in management accounting.

Think-Pair-Square

A modification of Think-Pair-Share, Think-Pair-Square (Lyman, 1981) provides accounting in-structors with a useful structure when they desire group interaction but not a whole-class dis-cussion. Instructors will find Think-Pair-Square particularly useful for simple accounting prob-lems where the answer is either right or wrong. It can be used successfully, however, with more complex problems as well.

In Think-Pair-Square students still are given time to consider a response and to share it with a partner. The two may also work together on paired problem solving. If playing cards are used, the suit partners described earlier work well here. The difference between Think-Pair-Share and Think-Pair-Square occurs in the last phase where students share each other's responses in their structured learning teams instead of in front of the whole class, a less time-consuming, often more focused activity.

This within-team sharing is important to be certain that the pairs have solved the problem(s) correctly. Think-Pair-Square is a more advanced structure than Think-Pair-Share because of its reliance on structured learning teams. Whereas a Think-Pair-Share activity can be con-ducted spontaneously with partners who have not previously been acquainted and then brought to closure through anonymous whole-class sharing, Think-Pair-Square relies upon student familiarity with a predesignated partner within a structured learning team. Thus, in Think-Pair-Square greater responsibility for learning is assumed by the students.

An Example

Instructors may wish to use Think-Pair-Square in conjunction with Learning Objectives 1 and 2 of Chapter 15 in the Hansen and Mowen text. The instructor conducts her lecture on CVP analysis as she would normally until she comes to the place where a numerical example is ap-propriate. The instructor places the responsibility for the example on the students' shoulders. Thus, after describing the operating-income approach for calculating the breakeven point, the instructor directs student attention to the data of Problem 15-1. She tells students to individu-ally calculate the breakeven point, to verify the answer with a suit partner, and finally to ensure the recurrence of the answer within the structured learning team. No time consuming whole-class report need be given. In the unlikely event that a structured learning team cannot arrive at consensus, the group monitor seeks help from a neighboring group.

The instructor proceeds to the next aspect of CVP analysis, the contribution-margin approach. Having explained this aspect she uses another Think-Pair-Square from the same problem to create a numerical example. The instructor thus rapidly progresses through increasingly com-plex aspects of CVP analysis with a series of Think-Pair-Squares. Students eventually gain confidence in their ability to grasp concepts and to rely upon their peers. The positive interde-pendence and group processing aspects of cooperative learning are thus reinforced.

STRUCTURES FOR CONTROLLED DISCUSSION AND BRAINSTORMING

By participating in small group discussions, students learn to interact positively while mastering accounting concepts and methods. Occasionally, however, structured learning teams will con-tain people who do not function easily within a group setting. Such people might range from those with overbearing personalities to those who are quiet or painfully shy. In these cases the former may dominate group discussion, creating a stressful environment and compromising the learning of others. Quiet or shy students may remain withdrawn, thereby depriving their teammates of the unique insights they might have. As indicated in Chapter 3, many of these problems can be eliminated or diminished by taking the time to allow team building and the establishment of group and class norms and expectations. Assigning and rotating specific group roles, particularly the leader and monitor, also helps groups with such members function more smoothly.

Some cooperative learning structures can minimize such dysfunctional behavior in accounting courses. Three structures—Talking Chips, Concept Formation, and Cooperative Learning Case Study—give all team members an opportunity to contribute, afford equal learning opportunities for all, and ensure that each contributor receives respect as an individual. Moreover, these structures directly increase student interpersonal skills and communication ability. Instructors will therefore want to use these structures to guide students into more controlled discussions of accounting issues.

Talking Chips

Talking Chips encourages full and even participation from members of cooperative learning groups, particularly when the issue is controversial. In this structure each group member has a token, the "talking chip," although accounting instructors may feel more comfortable with different nomenclature. A pen or paper clip or even the playing card identifying group membership works well as a talking chip. The chip—whatever object all group members elect to use— serves as a ticket giving its holder permission to share information, contribute to the discussion, or make debating points. After having contributed, the student must surrender the talking chip by laying it down in full view of the other team members until all students in the group have participated. After all students have spoken in random order and four (or five) chips have been laid down, they all retrieve their talking chips, and the next round of discussion ensues. Once students are accustomed to this somewhat artificial but highly effective structure, the conversation flows freely but evenly as students quickly relinquish their chips, wait until others have contributed, and then make their next point.

Talking Chips builds listening, communication, and interpersonal proficiency. Group members, especially those who tend to "spout off," consider more carefully what they have to say before speaking, since they surrender the right to talk afterwards. Reticent students, because they understand the ground rules, participate in a safe environment where they are encouraged to contribute. If discussion is delayed because they are not comfortable responding, they may pass, but team members, particularly the leader, should ask direct but gentle questions to draw the person into the discussion. Many accounting issues, including discussion of ethical vignettes or the issues surrounding financial reporting, are appropriate for Talking Chips. Instructors will find an abundant range of cases and problems with controversial issues at the end of each chapter in the Hansen and Mowen text.

Instructors need not confine their use of Talking Chips to controversial issues. This structure can be used at any time equitable discussions are desired. Student team members, too, may request the use of Talking Chips during any group activity, including Structured Problem Solving. Instructors should encourage the leaders, who are responsible for keeping the teams on task and for ensuring learning opportunities for all group members, to use this option.

The use of Talking Chips helps students learn the importance and mechanics of an equitable discussion. Once students have mastered these skills, Talking Chips may no longer be necessary.

An Example

Instructors may use Talking Chips to heighten student understanding of management accounting information systems (Learning Objective 1 of Chapter 1). From the Hansen and Mowen text or the instructor's lecture, students will know the three broad objectives of these systems. The instructor, having explained the Talking Chips procedure and its purpose, directs the students within structured learning teams to derive a list of information requirements for a cost management information system. As each student suggests an item of information, she links it to one or more of the three broad objectives. After the preannounced time has elapsed, the instructor uses the quiet signal to reassemble the class, calls for one or more group reports, and leads a whole-class discussion.

Concept Formation

Mauro and Cohen (1992) suggest a syntax for concept formation and cooperative learning. In Concept Formation students attain understanding of an accounting concept by actively proceeding through the specific to the general during group discussion in four phases. In the first phase the instructor asks the students a question that generates a list of objects or ideas. Students create this list in structured learning teams. To maximize participation, the instructor may direct the students to perform this task by using a specific structure such as Roundtable, discussed in Chapter 3.

During the second phase the instructor asks the students to group their objects or ideas into classes. To add interest to this phase, students may design a diagram, called a web map, with the category placed in the middle and the individual ideas placed around it. A spoke connects the centered category or class to the surrounding ideas.

The third phase consists of the students labeling the various categories they have generated. In the final phase, called processing, students analyze the criteria they used for listing the items.

An Example

Learning Objective 4 of Hansen and Mowen's Chapter 16 calls for students to be able to explain the basic concepts of constrained optimization. Concept Formation gives the instructor an excellent structure to accomplish this goal.

The instructor begins by asking the class what prevents a firm from producing and selling an infinite amount of each of its products. A minute or so of think time benefits students at this point. The instructor directs the students to gather into their structured learning teams and generate a list of their ideas. Depending on the social skills level of the group, the instructor may wish to add the constraint of using a Roundtable for this purpose.

Once a preannounced time limit has elapsed, the instructor tells the students to identify ideas which have commonality and to cluster them. The instructor may choose to introduce students to the web map at this point with an example containing ideas with which they are already familiar (*e.g.,* depreciation expense and amortization expense are both noncash). The instructor also gives the students a time limit for this portion.

As the third portion of the class, the instructor tells the students to label the clusters or classes they have formed. At this point some whole-class discussion will benefit students. The instructor may wish to randomly call for two or three group reports.

Next, the instructor directs the structured learning teams to discuss how each particular idea fell into a particular cluster. Students may wish to alter the clusters they have formed during this processing phase. Finally, the instructor reassembles the class with the quiet signal and leads a whole-class discussion about different kinds of constraints. After the students have engaged in this activity, an instructor lecture on the technical aspects of linear programming will hold more meaning for the students.

Cooperative Learning Case Study

Most instructors typically conduct case study discussions through animated whole-class discussions. Unfortunately, unless the instructor singles out individuals for responses, rather than waiting for volunteers—a challenging practice causing considerable stress—rarely will all students participate. Instead of using the traditional whole-class discussion of cases, instructors can allow students to wrestle with cases in their structured learning teams where active learning occurs simultaneously. For example, teams can be given several of the same questions to answer, but each individual team will have one or two specifically focused questions or issues to work through. If a group finishes early, they turn to the specific questions assigned to another team as a sponge activity. Clearly defined preassigned group roles are useful in this situation so that discussion time is not wasted in determining, for instance, who will lead the group discussion, record the results, or present the results. The instructor actively monitors the groups by rotating among them to ascertain the depth and level of student understanding. After the allotted time elapses, assuming that groups have completed the assigned tasks, the instructor initiates the report-outs after the quiet signal has brought everyone to attention. Because each group wrestled with different focus questions, students are more likely to attend to the report-outs than if the same material were simply rehashed. If the case lends itself to closure, the instructor might summarize the student discoveries or ask a particularly capable student to do so.

An Example

The Hansen and Mowen text contains several cases at the end of each chapter which can be adapted for Cooperative Learning Case Study. Case 6-1 provides an opportunity using an ethical vignette. The problem presents a conversation in which a management accountant is asked to engage in questionable behavior. All of the structured learning teams would consider this portion of the problem.

The problem next gives four independent requirements, each of which could be analyzed by a different structured learning team. Each team discusses and analyzes its assigned portion and prepares a formal report to be presented before the class by the reporter, giving students practice with oral communication. The report should be supported by overhead transparencies prepared by the group's recorder. Not all teams will necessarily report, particularly if more than one team has worked on the same portion. The other teams, however, should be given the opportunity to add any comments after the reporting team has concluded their presentation.

After four presentations have been made, the instructor may initiate a whole-class discussion to compare and contrast the different ethical aspects of the problem. Alternatively, further discussion and summarization may take place in the structured learning teams, perhaps using a Talking Chips structure.

STRUCTURES FOR REVIEWING MATERIAL

By reviewing material, instructors reinforce and—one hopes—augment student learning. Unfortunately, many students, perhaps because traditional review sessions often are uninspired rehashes of familiar material, do not respond enthusiastically to this vital step in the learning cycle. Instructors may become frustrated at this lack of student interest. Instructors using cooperative learning will find that two specific structures—Cooperative Learning Review and Stand Up and Share—will increase student involvement and interest in review sessions.

Cooperative Learning Review

A Cooperative Learning Review can replace the traditional review used by many accounting instructors. In the traditional review, students are supposed to come to the sessions with questions about the course material. Sometimes, instructors prepare outlines of key concepts which the class has covered during previous sessions. Too often students arrive with a single question, "What is on the exam?" Too often instructors end up doing the bulk of the work.

In a Cooperative Learning Review, each student brings to class a question about the course material but, unlike the traditional review, this time the structured learning team members provide the answers. In order to maximize participation, instructors ask students without course material questions to compose an accounting problem for their group members to solve.

The more pre-review planning for a Cooperative Learning Review, the more student participation and learning will occur. Instructors tell students that they must hand in at the beginning of the class the question they pose or the problem they write. This fosters positive interdependence. Instructors also caution the monitors in the structured learning teams to strictly watch the time so that all students have the opportunity to have their questions answered or their problems worked by the group.

Because students know the instructor will review the questions they pose, they formulate challenging ones that reinforce concepts and principles. Students writing accounting problems discover first-hand the kinds of information needed in problem-solving conditions. Learning about the questions their peers have generated reinforces the group processing component of cooperative learning. As the students actually wrestle with the questions and problems in a safe environment, their knowledge of accounting principles is reinforced and enriched.

During the last fifteen minutes of the review session, reporters should summarize the activities and findings of their team for the entire class. Instructors need to ascertain that all major exam topics have been addressed and quickly address any gaps. A Cooperative Learning Review, properly conducted, will result in unprecedented active learning for instructors and students alike.

Stand Up and Share

During a Cooperative Learning Review a Stand Up and Share structure can ensure that all students are exposed to all key material. Each group develops a list of the accounting topics it has discussed during the Cooperative Learning Review. The group then assigns one topic to each student. At a cue from the instructor, all students stand up. The instructor randomly calls on students to share their assigned topic and perhaps say a few words about it. As the student shares, the instructor writes the accounting topic on the board. After each student shares, he or she sits down, and anyone who has the same or a similar review point also sits down. This sharing and recording of review topics continues until all students are seated.

The Stand Up and Share accomplishes three important objectives. First, team building and positive interdependence are emphasized as students make sure that all group members have something to contribute. Second, the whole-class effort extends the sense of cooperation beyond the individual structured learning teams. Third, the list of review topics generated by the sharing portion constitutes a guide for student exam preparation.

SUMMARY

Instructors who have read this chapter are primed to use several advanced cooperative learning structures in combination with the Hansen and Mowen text. Because the Hansen and Mowen text builds upon accounting concepts rather than only on techniques, these advanced structures help instructors enhance student learning at a more meaningful level.

If instructors are willing and able to take the important step of implementing semi-permanent structured learning teams, they will find these structures fairly easy to initiate. They can be used for a variety of purposes, including problem solving, discussion and brainstorming of topics, and reviewing material.

Structured Problem Solving, for example, is ideal for mutual problem solving. At the same time it fosters peer teaching, greater student involvement, and positive interdependence leading to greater team rapport. The Discovery Method, another problem-solving structure, leads to greater student mastery and retention. Think-Pair-Square promotes team unity and ensures mastery by allowing students to quickly verify solutions reached in pairs within the structured learning team.

Three structures can be used in accounting courses to generate discussion of accounting-related issues. With Talking Chips, students contribute viewpoints equitably through the relinquishment of a "chip" of some sort. Concept Formation affords students the opportunity to uncover an accounting concept by moving from a specific list of ideas to an overriding concept. Cooperative Learning Case Study allows students to learn through the proven case study method in an environment less stressful to students and instructors alike than traditional case studies.

To review accounting topics, two structures, Cooperative Learning Review and Stand Up and Share, are complementary. Both of them rely on student, rather than instructor, input for meaningful review of material.

Accounting instructors who are considering cooperative learning structures to supplement their traditional presentations need to realize that these structures, although proven to be effective, take careful planning and are enhanced by the use of ongoing structured learning teams rather than random reformation of teams whenever an activity seems desirable. Once instructors are both committed and comfortable with cooperative learning techniques, they will never go back to their earlier methods of teaching.

REFERENCES

Davidson, N. (ed.) (1990). Cooperative learning in mathematics: A handbook for teachers. Reading, MA: Addison-Wesley.

Johnson, D. W., R. T. Johnson, and K. Smith (1991). Active learning: Cooperation in the college classroom. Edina, MN: Interaction Book Company.

Kagan, S. (1992). Cooperative learning. San Juan Capistrano, CA: Resources for Teachers, Inc.

Lyman, F. (1981). "The responsive class discussion." In A. S. Anderson (Ed.), Mainstreaming Digest. College Park, MD: University of Maryland College of Education.

Mauro, L. H., and L. J. Cohen (1992). "Cooperating for concept development." In N. Davidson and T. Worsham (Eds.), Enhancing thinking through cooperative learning (pp. 151-168). New York: Teachers College Press.

CHAPTER 6

SWALLOWING HOOK, LINE, AND SINKER

"If you would thoroughly know anything, teach it to others."

Tryon Edwards

In this chapter we turn to more complex cooperative learning structures. Instructors who have succeeded with some of the basic and advanced cooperative learning structures discussed in the previous chapters will find that adding complex structures to their teaching repertoire creates variety and adds interest to the classroom dynamic for students and for themselves as well. To use the structures covered in this chapter, instructors will need to carefully plan each classroom activity. This planning will pay rich rewards in terms of deeper student comprehension of accounting principles and appreciation of the learning process. When instructors share with students their methods and motives, they help them develop lifelong skills of "learning how to learn."

Students actively involved with complex cooperative learning structures enhance their learning skills as they themselves take more responsibility for understanding the material. Instructors who use these structures prompt their students to teach, to question, and to evaluate the learning of their peers. Each of these activities results in greater student understanding. Each also promotes the two key elements of cooperative learning: positive interdependence and individual accountability. Although each of these complex structures stimulates multiple cognitive and affective outcomes—and that is their value—we divide them here according to their primary functions: teaching, questioning, and critiquing.

STRUCTURES FOR STUDENT TEACHING

Virtually every instructor recognizes that by teaching they have learned more deeply the content and concepts of their discipline. This sentiment is expressed by the quotation that heads this chapter. Ironically, under a strict lecture format, conscientious instructors polishing and updating their presentations continue to add to their growing knowledge. The students, on the other hand, may or may not come close to mastering the same body of material or developing the same analytical skills. In the cooperative learning structures discussed in this section, instructors give their students the rich opportunity to learn by teaching.

Jigsaw

Accountants often confront complex, challenging problems involving multiple pieces of information necessary for a final, overall solution. Such problems are ideally suited for the cooperative learning structure Jigsaw. In this structure, each member of the structured learning team assumes responsibility for a specific part of a problem. They are responsible not just for mastering or knowing their part; they must also be able to teach the material to their fellow teammates. Thus, working together, the group merges the various portions to solve the "puzzle."

In Jigsaw, students temporarily leave their structured learning teams to form expert learning teams which may be organized, for example, on the suits of the playing cards. The student holding the heart from each of the groups meets with all the other hearts in the accounting classroom. Those holding spades, diamonds, and clubs form similar expert teams. Figure 6-1 illustrates how an accounting class of twenty can be quickly transformed from five structured learning teams into four expert learning teams with five members, one from each of the original groups. If classes are larger students can form two or more expert teams on the same piece of the puzzle. If the original structured team consists of five members rather than four, then two students pair and work as a unit in their expert team and when they return to their original team.

In expert learning teams, students master or solve their part of the accounting problem. They also discuss and develop strategies to teach the solution—and the process of deriving it—to the other members of their structured learning teams once they have rejoined them. Students must recognize that for Jigsaw to succeed, no one should leave his or her expert team without the ability to explain clearly—to teach—the accounting process and procedures just developed. Instructors will be moving among the various expert teams monitoring their progress and checking to see that all students are involved. After the prescribed time, the students return to their structured learning teams where each expert student in turn teaches his or her respective piece of the accounting puzzle.

Instructors must work hard to structure the team activities, the physical logistics, and the time frame of a Jigsaw. This is not a structure that should be attempted by relative newcomers to cooperative learning, particularly if large classes are involved. Students, too, must be coached to understand both the mechanics and the value of Jigsaw. Instructors must guard, for example, against student tendencies to get off task. Instructors must clearly communicate to students that more is at stake than finding "the right answer." The ability to teach fellow teammates—and hence master and retain important materials and develop analytical skills—lies at the crux of Jigsaw. Thus, a properly executed Jigsaw provides benefits that far outweigh its costs in terms of time and effort.

Like most complex structures, Jigsaw reinforces the most basic tenets of cooperative learning. Positive interdependence is fostered by the fact that students must work together and teach one another in order to get the "big picture," all of the information and skills they will need as accountants. At the same time, individual accountability is reinforced by the fact that students must learn all the information, not just their own portion, because they are tested individually. The fact that students interact within two different groups reinforces the idea of heterogeneity as a way to bring multiple perspectives to a given problem. The positive interactions that result from these brief but intense encounters in the expert groups help to develop the skills accountants will need in the "real world." The fact that expert teams have the responsibility of making certain that all members can successfully teach the materials/conclusions also reinforces the important concept of group processing and accountability.

An Example

Jigsaw works effectively with a number of accounting topics. Instructors will find an excellent application opportunity with Problem 14-13 in the Hansen and Mowen text. Learning Objective 1 of Chapter 14 of the text calls for students to be able to calculate measures of profit using absorption and variable costing while Learning Objective 3 has as its goal the ability to deter-

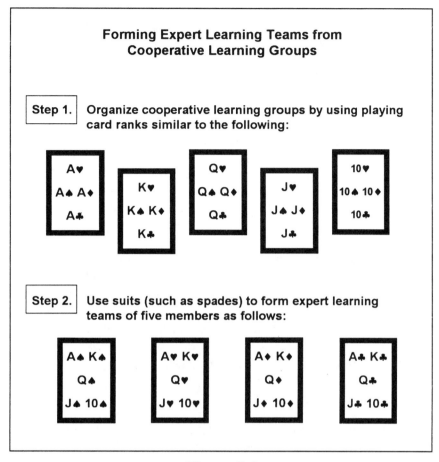

Figure 6-1

mine the profitability of segments. This problem focuses upon these two Learning Objectives in particular.

Following a brief expository lecture, instructors divide the class into expert learning teams, one for each card suit in the structured learning teams. When teams have a fifth member, identified in some cases with a "wild card," that student joins the clubs in their expert learning team as an equal working partner. Instructors indicate the classroom space to be occupied by each of the expert learning teams and give the students the following instructions:

Spades—Work the first requirement of Problem 14-13.

Hearts—Work the second requirement of Problem 14-13.

Diamonds—Work the third requirement of Problem 14-13.

Clubs—Work the fourth requirement of Problem 14-13.

Instructors specify the amount of time students will need to complete the exercise, providing, if possible, extra task-related discussion questions to serve as relevant "extension activities" for groups working faster than others. They should remind students that they should be considering their upcoming teaching responsibilities. Next, after using the quiet signal, the instructor explains to the students the teaching task they face, encouraging them to plan with care the teaching strategies they will use to enable their teammates to achieve similar mastery. Students should be encouraged to think creatively about their approach by rehearsing their presentation and by designing visual aids or study sheets. If necessary the instructor should give the students additional time to be certain that all expert learning team members understand how they will teach their original teammates to work the problem and how they will explain the concept it exemplifies.

Jigsaw takes careful monitoring. Since these expert teams do not have the defined roles identified in the structured learning teams, students do not always function as efficiently in these new, temporary teams. Instructors must ensure that students remain focused on both the Learning Objectives—working the exercise and identifying the respective concept—and on the subsequent teaching task. Clearly, too, they must be certain that students are producing valid responses.

Once satisfied that the students are ready, the instructor once again gains control of the class with the quiet signal and tells the students to return to their structured learning teams. The instructor urges the team monitor to confirm that each student in the group understands their problem and its underlying concept and is sufficiently prepared to teach their teammates. Then the students, rotating in turn, teach their respective parts of the overall accounting task. After sufficient time has elapsed, the instructor may conclude the class with a brief summary of both the accounting concepts and the purpose of Jigsaw itself.

Within-Team Jigsaw

In Within-Team Jigsaw, expert learning teams consist of a pair formed within the structured learning team. Any fifth member (sometimes identified with a wild card or joker) joins a pair to form a triad. If instructors are using playing cards to identify team roles, the suits can be used for pairing, black suits forming one pair and red suits the other. These suit partners function as smaller expert learning teams, similar to their larger counterparts formed in Jigsaw.

Instructors who use Think-Pair-Square should explain the difference between that structure and Within-Team Jigsaw. In Think-Pair-Square, students simultaneously work on the same task and verify their answers in the structured learning team. In the more complex Within-Team Jigsaw, suit partners work on two distinct parts of an accounting "puzzle." Their task in the structured learning team is to put together the pieces to arrive at a solution and to teach other members of the structured learning team their portion of the problem.

Within-Team Jigsaw is easier to implement than Jigsaw. Its disadvantage lies in the fact that the "puzzle" can have only two pieces. In Jigsaw the number of pieces is limited only by the imagination of the instructor and the number of students in the class. Within-Team Jigsaw, however, can be a creative, efficient way to ensure content mastery.

An Example

Instructors will find Within-Team Jigsaw has many applications in the management accounting course. For example, Learning Objective 1 of Chapter 14 of Hansen and Mowen's book provides an opportunity for this structure. The instructor wants students to be able to explain the differences between variable and absorption costing. Problem 14-1 furnishes data from which students can make calculations from a variable-costing standpoint and from the absorption-costing view. The instructor tells students holding spades and clubs to complete requirement 1—the absorption-costing approach—while students holding the hearts and diamonds simultaneously complete requirement 2—the variable-costing approach.

The instructor alerts students that they will be responsible not only for calculating the correct figures, but also for explaining to the other pair or triad how to accomplish the calculation. Each pair must therefore spend a portion of their time with their suit partner devising a teaching strategy.

When the quiet signal signifies the conclusion of the specified work time, the students regroup in their structured learning teams. There they teach one another their portion of the problem. They are also asked to complete the third requirement of the problem. This final requirement will cause students to delve deeply into the impact of variable costing, which is a focus of the Learning Objective.

Team Learning

Team Learning, a challenging teaching method closely related to cooperative learning, was developed by Michaelsen (1983; 1992) as a way of coping with large classes. It places much of the responsibility upon students for their own learning and enables instructors to focus less class time on basic concepts and more on higher-order applications. Team Learning departs from one cooperative learning principle in that a large component of the students' grade is group based, a practice not recommended by cooperative learning researchers such as Spencer Kagan. On the other hand, Team Learning reinforces the group processing function of cooperative learning by highlighting the benefits of working together in a practical way. Team Learning relies on structured learning teams kept in place throughout the term.

Team Learning occurs in four phases. First, students study an assignment, such as a chapter of the Hansen and Mowen text, prior to coming to class. The second phase occurs during class when the instructor administers a short closed-book quiz, which students take individually. The third phase ensues after students have finished the individual quiz. The instructor administers an identical quiz, which the students now complete as a closed-book group test within their structured learning teams.

During this third phase, students must come to consensus, since only one quiz is completed for the group. Much teaching occurs as students attempt to maximize their group score; the individual quiz and the group quiz weigh equally in the determination of their final course grade. Since the group grades are almost without exception higher than the individual scores, students quickly learn to value their peers as sources of learning and knowledge.

In the fourth and final phase, the students may open their books. The instructor announces the suggested correct answers for the quiz and gives the students an opportunity to appeal, using a form such as the one shown in Figure 6-2. The appeal process prompts students to delve deeply and energetically into their texts, focusing on the most relevant quiz-related material. Learning occurs and is reinforced during this phase. Therefore, instructors should be quite liberal in granting appeals. They may even wish to announce occasionally that because of the number and caliber of the appeals, an incorrect answer will receive credit. Credit is given, however, only to teams that appeal or challenge, thereby motivating students to work actively with their structured learning teams to pour over the text to verify or refute the announced answers. Students cannot rely upon the work accomplished by other groups.

Test and Quiz Appeal _____

Group _____

Question Chapter _____

Question Number _____

Proposed Correct Answer

Rationale for Your Appeal:

Supporting Evidence:

Instructor Decision:

Figure 6-2

Instructors should count the individual quizzes and group quizzes heavily in the determination of the course grade in order to maximize the utility of Team Learning. The remainder of the course grade may rest on traditional assessment measures such as midterm exams, papers, projects and/or final exams.

Team Learning quizzes are not given every class period. In fact, the value of team learning lies in the fact that the process, like the DEC process described later, ensures that students learn the foundational material. Having mastered the "basics," students may then move on to higher-order skills such as structured problem solving. The instructor no longer has the responsibility to get the students "up to speed" by way of a lecture or class discussion. Students now shoulder that responsibility. Experienced cooperative learning instructors are able to "front load" much of the student learning, thereby freeing class time for student information processing activities rather than instructor-dominated information giving.

During class periods following Team Learning activities, instructors can focus on problem-solving skills, challenging students to tackle problems not previously assigned. They will have sufficient class time to include case study instruction through activities focused by the Structured Problem Solving described in Chapter 5, to provide in-class meetings for long-term team projects, or to devote to any other activities promoting higher-order critical thinking.

STRUCTURES FOR STUDENT QUESTIONING

As mentioned in Chapter 2, dualistic thinkers who assume there are absolute answers to questions need to be encouraged to move beyond these simplistic levels. Often instructors will assume that animated whole-class discussions will lead students to reflect on multiple viewpoints and discard outmoded ways of thinking. Such discussions provide useful class interactions when used occasionally, but, for many reasons, they cannot be the sole vehicle for challenging student assumptions and encouraging higher-order thinking skills. For one thing, whole-class discussions are unpredictable. Successful discussions depend on many variables: the instructor's experience and skill in managing such exchanges, the constellation of personalities enrolled in the class and their reactions to instructor or student contributions, the academic preparation and "real-life" experiences of the participants, and the nature of the topic itself. Furthermore, within a whole-class exchange, many students are able to hide as nonparticipants, behavior promoted by innate shyness, by lack of comfort or confidence with confrontations before large audiences, by lack of preparation, or by simple apathy. Cooperative learning structures enable instructors to help students learn to question the truth of assumptions or propositions, but they do so within a highly structured environment with far fewer variables and hence less unpredictability. A supportive but cooperative learning setting contrasts sharply, for example, with a classroom arena where the instructor relies on the stimulating Socratic method of challenging students with a series of thought-provoking questions. Both techniques are valuable; savvy accounting instructors use both. But the value of cooperative learning questioning lies not only in the comfortable climate which encourages participation, but more importantly in the fact that often the students, not the instructors, pose the challenging questions. Structured Controversy and Guided Reciprocal Peer Questioning are stimulating ways to develop higher-order thinking skills within a supportive environment.

Structured Controversy

Structured Controversy, sometimes called academic controversy (Johnson, Johnson, and Smith, 1991; and Johnson and Johnson, 1987), develops critical thinking skills by compelling students to examine accounting issues for which there are no "right answers."

As in Within-Team Jigsaw, students initially work with partners in their structured learning teams, such as suit partners if playing cards are used. In preparation for the activity, instructors identify a controversial topic that lends itself well to two opposing viewpoints and gather material, such as articles, monographs, or book chapters, that support either or both sides. Designated chapters from the Hansen and Mowen text, for example, could be used as resources. (If this structure is to be used for a long-range project, then the students themselves—with coaching—can identify and accumulate the material.) Each pair or dyad within the structured learning teams takes one side of the controversial issue. In the first of five phases of Structured Controversy, students research and review the instructor-provided materials and discuss their side of the issue. They synthesize and organize their findings and prepare to advocate and defend their positions.

In the second phase, the two pairs alternatively present their side of the issue, giving full rationales and explanations for their stance. The other pair listens attentively, keeping in mind that during the next phase they will be challenging the points they hear and also defending their own positions.

In the third phase, during a general discussion, all four students seek to become fully informed about both sides of the issue and begin to weigh critical arguments in favor of both. Instructors should stress that the students' purpose should be to become more informed about the issue rather than to win debates. They should use skillful questioning techniques to draw out their fellow teammates and to encourage everyone to examine deeply all sides of the issue. The result of the discussion, which must be conducted and carefully monitored according to any established group or class norms for productive behavior and interaction, is often intellectual disequilibrium and uncertainty. This phase of the activity is particularly important because Brookfield (1987) and others have emphasized that critical thinking depends on identifying and challenging assumptions and subsequently exploring and conceptualizing alternatives. Curiosity prompted by this discussion often leads to a search for additional information.

If the process is carried through its full five phases, then during the next step students reverse their positions and each pair argues forcefully for the opposing viewpoint. Building on what they have heard earlier and what they have come to learn through their own research and the subsequent team discussion, each pair or dyad should present the best possible case.

In the fifth and final phase, the team works together to synthesize their findings and prepare a group report. This final review should reflect the best information and critical reasoning from both sides. To ensure individual accountability, the instructor may wish to administer an examination over the issue that students will take independently.

An Example

Learning Objective 4 of Chapter 7 in Hansen and Mowen offers instructors an opportunity to use Structured Controversy. This structure should follow student mastery of the technical aspects of allocating support-department costs using the direct, sequential, and reciprocal methods. The instructor may ask the students holding the black suits to develop arguments favoring use of the direct method and/or the sequential method. Simultaneously, students holding the red suits do the same with respect to the reciprocal method. After going through the five phases described above, skipping perhaps the fourth step where pairs reverse roles, the students develop a fuller picture of the considerations a businessperson must make when deciding how to allocate support-department costs. The discussion also enhances student ability to appreciate that diverse solutions may exist for a business problem.

Guided Reciprocal Peer Questioning

Instructors wishing to encourage critical thinking skills and relativistic conceptualizing will find Guided Reciprocal Peer Questioning a particularly apt structure. Developed and researched by King (1992; 1990), this structure helps students to generate task-specific questions which can then be answered within the structured learning team.

To initiate this activity, instructors conduct a short lecture on an accounting topic. Following the lecture, instructors provide students with a set of generic question stems to use as a guide for formulating their own specific questions about the lecture content. Figure 6-3 provides a list of

---

General Questions

What is the main idea of ... ?

What if ... ?

How does ... affect ... ?

What is the meaning of ... ?

What is a new example of ... ?

Explain why ...

Explain how ...

How does this relate to what I've learned before?

What conclusions can I draw about ... ?

What is the difference between ... and ... ?

How are ... and ... similar?

How would I use ... to ... ?

What are the strengths and weaknesses of ... ?

What is the best ... and why?

Figure 6-3*

*This figure appears in *Critical thinking, interactive learning and technology* by Alison King, page 162. Arthur Andersen and Co., 1992. Reprinted with permission from Arthur Andersen and Co.

generic questions. This list contains some questions more appropriate and challenging to dualistic thinkers, such as "What is the difference between...and...?" Other questions are more appropriate for the more advanced relativistic thinkers, such as "What are the strengths and weaknesses of...?"

Instructors provide students with the time to write individually two or three specific, thought-provoking questions, using the generic stems, on the lecture they have just heard. Students do not need to be able to answer the questions they formulate; their purpose is to generate discussion. This self-questioning step encourages students to identify the relevant lecture concepts, to elaborate on those ideas in their minds, and to think about how the ideas are connected to each other and to their own prior knowledge and experiences.

After the allotted time has elapsed, the students put these questions to use in their structured learning teams. Here the leader poses one of the specific questions he or she has written to which the other team members respond. Since the questions do not have a single right answer, reflective discussion follows. Each student in turn offers a question for the team to discuss. Everyone should have an opportunity to pose at least one question. The leader should be careful that there is equitable participation both in the discussion and in the questions shared.

In designing a Guided Reciprocal Peer Questioning activity, instructors should schedule the time elements carefully. Time should be allotted, for example, for whole-class discussion at the end of the exercise. Here the students can share insights, concrete examples, and particularly cogent explanations that arose in their group work. The instructor, who will have moved among the groups during their discussion period, also has an opportunity to elaborate on any cloudy points or to clear up any misconceptions about the accounting topic under study.

An Example

Hansen and Mowen provide a good topic for Guided Reciprocal Peer Questioning with Learning Objective 2 of Chapter 18 in the text. The instructor begins the activity with a short lecture on the basic features of JIT purchasing and manufacturing. After the lecture, instructors, using an overhead projector or handouts, give the students the list of generic question stems in Figure 6-3. They tell students that their task is to write, using the stems, two specific questions about the effects that JIT may have on a company's results. The first time this structure is used, instructors should provide specific examples to help students understand the process of generating effective questions. Students then have several minutes to review their lecture notes, to rehash the key points and their relevance to other knowledge or first-hand experiences, and to formulate their specific questions.

Following the period for individual work, the instructor signals the students and explains the guidelines for the discussion portion of the activity. Leaders, for example, are asked to ensure that the discussion stays on topic and that all students are included. The instructor specifies the time constraints and encourages all students to be certain that each teammate has an opportunity to pose at least one question. The students then begin a structured yet animated discussion about the JIT environment and its effect on manufacturing throughout the industrialized world. Both the instructor and the leader should attend carefully to the group dynamics so that all students have an opportunity to offer their questions and their responses to those posed by their teammates.

Because students often welcome closure and worry that their team discussion may not have covered all the salient points, a whole-class discussion is useful. The instructor, based on team observations, can provide a succinct summary, inviting contributions, or she might ask a particular team to summarize.

STRUCTURES FOR STUDENT CRITIQUING

The structures in this section, like the ones presented earlier in this chapter, contain rich learning opportunities for students. In each case, students formulate questions, suggest answers to the questions of others, and evaluate the responses generated by peers. Students therefore learn not only about accounting concepts, but also about the learning and teaching process itself.

Three-Stay One-Stray

Instructors new to cooperative learning sometimes express concerns about time constraints. As students experience more depth of understanding of course material, breath of coverage of new material may diminish. However, instructors can limit this decrease with careful planning and structuring.

One time-consuming part of many cooperative learning structures is the report-out to the whole class. Three-Stay One-Stray is a structure that simultaneously omits the report-out and places more responsibility for learning on the students themselves. The structure not only enhances student understanding of accounting topics, but also teaches students to question and critique the solutions of others, a critical skill for the accounting professional. Moreover, it is more efficient than the whole-class report-out for student closure and reinforces to students that the source of solutions lies within the learning community rather than the authority-figure instructor.

Instructors initiate this structure as an addendum to another structure, such as Structured Problem Solving or Talking Chips. A student, usually the monitor, is designated as the one who will stray. That is, the student leaves the structured learning team and rotates to another group. Thus all structured learning teams contain three or four of the original members plus a visitor. In these modified groups the solutions to an accounting problem or the lists generated in controlled discussion are compared and contrasted. During the ensuing discussion students reach closure as to the best resolution to the issue at hand. Active instructor involvement is crucial in this structure to guide students in their efforts.

Send-a-Problem

The Send-a-Problem structure gives students the opportunity to identify or focus on their own issues or problems and to observe the problem-solving process in the context of community. The exact source of this structure is unclear, but a version of it was generated by the Howard County, Maryland Staff Development Center in 1989, inspired by Kagan's (1989) high consensus oriented Send-a-Problem structure using rotating flashcards for content review.

The steps in Send-a-Problem, once each team identifies the issue or problem it will address, are fairly straightforward: (a) Each team discusses its particular problem and generates within the given time frame as many solutions as possible; the solutions, recorded on a sheet of paper, are placed in a folder (an envelope will also work well) on which is written the problem addressed. (b) The folders are passed clockwise to another team who does not open the folder. That team, seeing only the problem identification but not the solutions generated by the previous team, follows an identical procedure and brainstorms solutions, placing their recorded conclusions in the folder or envelope. (c) The folders are passed a third time, but in this case, the team opens the folder and reviews the ideas/solutions generated by the other two teams. They are able to add additional ideas of their own, but their primary task is to identify the two most viable solutions to the given problem or issue. Instructors may want them to use a star or a check to identify these solutions.

To strengthen the sense of interconnectedness within the class and to reinforce team cohesiveness, instructors can ask the recorders to write their team names at the top of the solution page. During the final report-out, teams can thus receive public acknowledgement if their solutions are selected.

To initiate Send-a-Problem, instructors must have at hand a list of problems or issues for which the structured learning teams can generate solutions. These issues can be identified by the instructor, but students have far more "investment" in the activity if they have generated the possible topics themselves. To do this, instructors can use the Roundtable structure discussed in Chapter 4 to compile a lengthy list of possible topics, or they can leave the activity less structured and simply ask each structured learning team to generate the list using a Structured Problem Solving approach. It may be useful to have each team rank order the problems in the order of their importance. The issues typically are discussed at the same class meeting, but an alternative particularly attractive for instructors teaching 50-minute classes is to have students generate the problem topics during one session and then to pose them for discussion at the ensuing session.

To begin the problem-solving segment of Send-a-Problem, the instructor, with file folders or envelopes in hand (or alternatively, in the hands of the structured learning teams if team folders are used to set up the class), announces the activity and its time limits. Each team chooses a single problem to focus upon initially. If time permits, the instructor can ask each structured learning team to reach a consensus on the problems they would like to address, rank ordering their choices. The options, if generated within class, can be listed on flip chart paper or on the blackboard so that the instructor or the teams can not only identify their preferences, but can cross off topics as they are selected. If the topics have been generated at a previous class meeting or are instructor-selected, the instructor can use an overhead projector and/or handouts to alert students to their choices and to help them realize that topics have been selected by other teams. If time is limited, instructors might arbitrarily call on one team member (identified by a number or playing card, as in Structured Problem Solving) to make the selection for their team. When flip chart paper is used, these specified team members rush to the posted sheets and cross off the issue their team will address.

Once each team has a specific problem to focus upon, the activity proceeds in the highly structured manner outlined earlier. Teams are given a specified number of minutes for each step. Instructors need to make judgment calls about the time allotment for this activity. It can be used successfully as a brainstorming activity with each team "blitzing" through as many solutions as possible within a narrow time limit such as three minutes per step. Most often, however, the structure is used as a vehicle for meaningful discussion, thoughtful synthesis, and creative problem solving.

Group reports can provide useful closure. The reporters announce the issue their quad discussed, the two solutions they have chosen, and, if desired, the team that suggested them. The creativity and multiplicity of solutions reinforces the value of structured teamwork.

Instructors will find Send-a-Problem useful for reviews, particularly prior to the final examination. To initiate a review, the instructor brings to class old quiz problems or exercises attached to folders or envelopes. The quiz problems, obviously, reflect topics that have been covered during the semester that may appear on the final examination. Each structured learning team receives one of the envelopes.

The instructor tells the students that their team will have ten minutes to solve the quiz problem as a closed-book exercise. When time has expired, the students put their solution inside the envelope and pass the packet clockwise to the neighboring team. Students in the next group solve the same problem without looking into the envelope and add their solution at the end of ten minutes. Depending on the length of the class period, this procedure may be repeated up to five times so that each group solves five problems.

On the final pass, the instructor tells the students to retrieve all the solutions in the envelope and select the best solution, taking into account not only the "right answer" but also the neatness of form and presentation. Group reporters in turn designate the problem, briefly explain the best approach to solving it, and identify, if desired, the group that presented it.

An Example

Send-a-Problem is a good structure to accomplish Hansen and Mowen's Learning Objective 5 in Chapter 16, which calls for students to be able to discuss the impact of cost, including the legal system and ethics, on pricing. The instructor begins the session by giving students think time to consider pricing practices which they believe may be unethical. Volunteers call out these practices as the instructor writes them on the outside of separate large envelopes while a student assistant lists them on the board.

The instructor directs students in their structured learning teams to choose the two or three practices they would best like to discuss. Then he gives each team leader the opportunity to call out the issue. As she does so, the instructor hands her the envelope corresponding to this issue, and the student assistant strikes the issue from the list on the board.

Once each structured learning team has an issue, the instructor tells students to discuss the ethics and legality of the issue and write a conclusion within the specified time. After time has elapsed, the instructor directs the students to place their conclusion in the envelope and to pass it to the group to the right where the process is repeated. The instructor admonishes students not to look at the solution inside the envelope.

After as many iterations as time permits, the instructor announces on the final pass that students should take the other groups' solutions out of the envelope and choose the one they believe to be the best write-up. Reporters may be asked to summarize the conclusion chosen before the class with an opportunity for an accompanying whole-class discussion.

Dyadic Essay Confrontations (DEC)

In addition to building student understanding of accounting concepts and the learning process, DEC (Dyadic Essay Confrontations), developed by Sherman (1991), allows instructors to incorporate meaningful writing assignments in their courses. Instructors will find DEC particularly valuable for students more advanced in the learning process. Probably its most important use is to ensure that students read and understand the assigned reading material, thereby freeing class time for mastery and processing activities.

In DEC, the instructor assigns readings, such as a chapter from the Hansen and Mowen text, or a chapter complemented by a primary source or other selected readings. Students are responsible outside of class for the following: (a) reading and reflecting on the assigned material, (b) formulating an integrative essay question, one which encourages comparisons between the current material and material previously covered, (c) preparing a model response to their own question which is no longer than one-page, single-spaced, and (d) bringing to class a copy of their essay question and on a separate page their model answer.

During class time, students are responsible for the following: (a) exchanging essay questions with a student with whom they are randomly paired, (b) writing a spontaneous essay in response to the question they receive from their partner, (c) reading and commenting on both the model answer to the question they received and on the spontaneous answer provided by a classmate to the essay question they formulated, looking in each case for divergent and convergent ideas, and (d) participating—if time permits—in a general discussion of the topic.

Dyadic Essay Confrontation—Form One

Name: _____   Team: _____

Assigned Reading: _____

Your Question:

_____

Your proposed answer to the question (limited to space on this page):

Figure 6-4

Instructors will find the DEC forms shown as Figures 6-4, 6-5, and 6-6 useful in the implementation of DEC. Students prepare their question and suggested response during the out-of-class phase on DEC Form 1. They also record their question on DEC Form 2 which is given to the random partner as the in-class writing assignment. DEC Form 3 serves instructors and students alike as a guide for assigning a grade to the entire DEC.

The essays over the assigned material—both the out-of-class open-book paper and the in-class closed-book spontaneous essay—are evaluated, but their weight depends on the overall grading criteria. To lighten the paper grading load, the essays, if they are of sufficient quality, may be assigned points counting toward the final grade rather than assigned a specific letter grade. DEC can be used as an ongoing assignment over the course of a semester to ensure mastery of the Hansen and Mowen text. Students who have read and written two essays over a series of chapters will retain far more material than those who have merely heard a lecturer expound on them.

Dyadic Essay Confrontation—Form Two

Name: _____ Team: _____

Assigned Reading: _____

Your Question:

_____

Name of Peer Partner: _____ Team: _____

Space for peer partner to answer.

(Answer limited to space provided on this page plus the back.)

Figure 6-5

As should be obvious, a complex and yet highly focused structure such as DEC has enormous value for university teaching and learning. With the virtue of versatility, it can promote higher-order thinking skills; focus students on outside assignments so that time is available for interactive group work rather than for lectures designed to cover the content; foster student-student interdependence, resulting in respect for diverse opinions; and reinforce the value of peer learning. It also complements writing across the curriculum efforts.

As a modification of DEC, instructors may have the students compose an accounting problem and a suggested solution. Students participating in the problem-writing portion of this structure glean a greater understanding of the underlying accounting concepts than they do by working problems from a book. Moreover, students find that discussions of their own solutions to the problems they have posed is more meaningful to them than discussion of solutions asked by unknown textbook or case authors.

Dyadic Essay Confrontation—Form Three

Your Name: _____ Your Team: _____

Name of Peer Partner: _____ Team: _____

Student Evaluation of Peer Partner

Evaluate your peer partner on the three attributes in the table below. Use the following guidelines: Exceptional - 10; Good - 9; Competent - 8; Deficient - 7; Failure - 6.

Quality of question posed	
Quality of proposed answer to posed question	
Quality of in-class response to your questions	

Instructor's Evaluation of Peer Partner

Quality of question posed	
Quality of proposed answer to posed question	
Quality of in-class response to peer's question	
Overall writing ability	
Ability to evaluate another student's work	

Grade for the DEC: _____

Figure 6-6

DEC Examples

Learning Objective 1 in Chapter 1 of Hansen and Mowen provides a good choice for a DEC activity. The instructor assigns the chapter and one or more related articles for student reading. Students, after reading the chapter and the assigned article(s), prepare an essay question that they believe would test another student's knowledge of management accounting information systems. Students write this question on DEC Forms 1 and 2; on DEC Form 1 they write their own essay responding to the question they have posed.

In class, the students are randomly paired, and they exchange DEC Forms 2. Each responds to their partner's question. After time has expired for the in-class writing phase, they exchange DEC Forms 1 and compare and contrast their respective answers. A whole-class discussion may follow. Instructors may ask students to grade both questions and answers on DEC Form 3 and they might choose to ask students to hand in all material for credit.

As an accounting problem application for DEC, instructors may choose any of the text's Learning Objectives which are problem oriented. Instructors direct the students to write their own accounting problem which would test whether or not a peer student had mastered the learning objective. They also provide an answer key to the problem posed. In class, the students work each others' problems, discuss their two responses, and evaluate them as if they were grading an accounting test. Writing and evaluating accounting problems in this manner heightens student awareness of information that must be available to solve real-world accounting problems.

SUMMARY

The complex cooperative learning structures described in this chapter enrich students' understanding of both accounting and their own learning processes. Such structures are amazingly versatile and can be used for a variety of purposes. Jigsaw and Within-Team Jigsaw, for example, can be used to encourage student teaching, an important way to master material. Team Learning, a variation of cooperative learning, relies heavily on teaching within the team as students prepare elaborate appeals on quizzes they have taken both individually and collectively.

Developing focused questions can be a powerful way to synthesize material and challenge fellow classmates. Two structures, Structured Controversy and Guided Reciprocal Peer Questioning, emphasize the value of this technique. Finally, to help students learn to critique and analyze problems and their solutions, instructors can use Three-Stay One-Stray, Send-a-Problem, and DEC. All these structures promote higher-order thinking and build other skills necessary for the work place, including the ability to work constructively with others during tension-filled intellectual probing.

Instructors should experiment slowly with these structures. They cannot be implemented facilely. They take more thoughtful preparation than the basic and advanced cooperative learning structures. But, once instructors and students understand the underlying concepts and the implementation logistics, they prove to be stimulating tools to help students come to terms with the rich variety of information and the challenging skills that comprise the accounting profession.

REFERENCES

Brookfield, S. D. (1987). Developing critical thinkers: Challenging adults to explore alternative ways of thinking and acting. San Francisco: Jossey-Bass.

Johnson, D. W.; and R. T. Johnson (1987) Creative conflict. Edina, MN: Interaction Book Company.

Johnson, D. W., R. T. Johnson, and K. Smith (1991). Active learning: Cooperation in the college classroom. Edina, MN: Interaction Book Company.

Kagan, S. (1989). Cooperative learning resources for teachers. San Capistrano, CA: Resources for Teachers, Inc.

King, A. (1990). "Enhancing peer interaction and learning in the classroom through reciprocal questioning." American Educational Research Journal, 27(4), 664-687.

King, A. (1992). "Promoting active learning and collaborative learning in business administration classes." In T. J. Frecka (Ed.), Critical thinking, interactive learning and technology: Reaching for excellence in business education (pp. 158-173). Arthur Andersen Foundation.

Michaelsen, L. K. (1983). "Team learning in large classes." In C. Bouton and R. Y. Garth (Eds.), Learning in Groups (pp. 13 - 22). New Directions for Teaching and Learning, No. 14. San Francisco: Jossey-Bass.

Michaelsen, L. K. (1992). "Team learning: A comprehensive approach for harnessing the power of small groups in higher education." In D. H. Wulff and J. D Nyquist (Eds.), To improve the academy: Resources for faculty, instructional, and organizational development, 11 (pp. 107-122). The Professional and Organizational Network in Higher Education, Stillwater, OK: New Forums Press, Inc.

Sherman, L. W. (April, 1991). "Cooperative learning in post secondary education: Implications from social psychology for active learning experiences." Presentation at the American Educational Research Association, Chicago, IL.

CHAPTER 7

CONTINUING TO GROW

"Of all the responsibilities that a teacher has, none is more important than communication with students. Of all the functions that a teacher performs, none is more complex."

James S. O'Rourke, IV

Accounting instructors who have successfully integrated cooperative learning structures into their classrooms will, by the nature of the student and pedagogical challenges, keep their teaching skills dynamic. They will continue to grow professionally as they move from the old paradigms of teaching toward more student-centered views supporting an atmosphere of community and cooperation. In this chapter we explore topics which augment and enhance cooperative learning structures and create a better learning environment for accounting students and instructors alike. Instructors will learn how an open mind and creative flexibility enable them to combine cooperative learning structures with other good teaching methods such as using graphic organizers. Finally, we discuss classroom assessment, a communication tool enabling instructors to test the pulse and climate of the learning communities they create.

REMAINING FLEXIBLE

Student excitement about learning can dull with repetitive teaching methods, even cooperative learning structures. Students become restive when they come to class knowing exactly what to expect. Instructors should set a goal that students will come to class curious as to what learning adventure lies ahead. Instructors may meet this objective by mixing, matching, and combining cooperative learning structures within their repertoire, and by combining cooperative learning with other pedagogies with which they are comfortable.

Mix—Match—Combine

Accounting instructors may teach the material presented in Hansen and Mowen's text with varying or alternating cooperative learning structures. For example, in one class session a series of Think-Pair-Squares may be useful to reinforce student understanding of several learning objectives. In another class session, these same objectives might best be examined with a Jigsaw, where students have greater responsibility for the teaching.

Cooperative learning structures may also be progressive. A Think-Pair-Share may be modified by having students engage in the "think" and "pair" parts, but in place of whole-class sharing, they immediately use a Roundtable within their structured learning teams to generate a list of ideas. These two structures may be further enhanced by a homework assignment which leads to a Dyadic Essay Confrontation (DEC) in the following class session.

The DEC structure may be modified and strengthened by augmentation with question stems from Guided Reciprocal Peer Questioning (GRPQ), discussed and illustrated in Chapter 6. Because most students have not experienced opportunities to write questions as required by DEC, the question stems normally associated with GRPQ provide a good starting point to ask questions that probe higher-order thinking and learning. Instructors simply give students a handout listing the question stems (Figure 6-3) and explain their use. Instructors who use DEC as a graded exercise can assess the quality of the question posed as well as the written essays.

Examples

Hansen and Mowen's Learning Objective 3 in Chapter 12 states that students should be able to compute and explain return on investment (ROI) and residual income (RI). Instructors can use cooperative structures on various levels to meet this objective. Those who wish to remain at the basic level may use lecture combined with as many as eight Think-Pair-Shares: (1) What characteristics should a performance measure have? (2) Write three formulae for ROI. (3) How do we determine operating assets? (4) What is margin? (5) What is turnover? (6) What advantage is gained by decomposing ROI into margin and turnover? (7) Write the formula for RI.

At the advanced level, the instructor uses data from Exercise 12-2 and has students provide their own numerical example in a series of Think-Pair-Square structures. These may be combined with the Think-Pair-Shares during the instructor's lecture. Following these activities, the instructor reinforces student learning by employing Structured Problem Solving to have students fulfill the requirements of Exercises 12-3, 12-4, and/or 12-8.

Instructors with multiple learning objectives in mind may choose to use complex cooperative learning structures for teaching performance measures. For example, a Structured Controversy enables students to practice questioning techniques while developing critical thinking skills. In this instance, instructors give students holding black suits the assignment to develop arguments favoring use of ROI while students holding red suits simultaneously develop arguments in favor of using RI. As students proceed through all the steps of Structured Controversy, they will not only learn the details of computation and use of the two performance measures, but also an appreciation of the strengths and weaknesses of each.

In another approach, instructors may develop student writing and questioning skills and at the same time front load the material with DEC. Instructors assign the article cited in footnote 1 of the chapter as outside reading. Students write an essay question and response based upon this reading. In class they exchange questions with a random partner and respond using a DEC. This DEC may be followed by higher-order application and discussion of performance measures.

Hansen and Mowen's Learning Objective 3 for Chapter 8 furnishes an occasion to use progressive cooperative learning structures. Here the objective states that students should be able to identify and discuss the key features that a budgetary system should have to encourage managers to engage in goal-congruent behavior. Instructors may use a brief lecture combined with Think-Pair-Share to introduce the subject. The Think-Pair-Share topics might include the following: (1) What is a static budget? (2) What is a flexible budget? (3) What is goal congruence? (4) What is dysfunctional behavior? (5) Contrast participative budgeting with traditional budgeting. (6) What should be the relationship between responsibility and accounting in controlling costs? (7) What is myopic behavior?

Following the lecture, students use a Talking Chips structure to fulfill the requirements of Problem 8-3. During this activity students may utilize the concepts drawn out during lecture and Think-Pair-Share. To further reinforce the learning objective the instructor follows by showing a list of generic question stems and asks students to formulate questions about budgeting and goal congruence. Students discuss these questions in turn in their structured learning teams.

Accommodating Other Teaching Methods

Cooperative learning, as mentioned earlier, is rarely used one hundred percent of the time. In fact, most faculty in higher education use structured small group work only about 15 to 40 percent of class time (Cooper, 1990). Accordingly, converts to cooperative learning continue to use teaching methods they may have employed in the past. Usually these methods consist of lecture, lecture and recitation, class discussion, and/or traditional case studies. However, some accounting instructors using more non-traditional methods have been able to incorporate cooperative learning into their styles with great success.

Cooperative learning's flexible attributes permit instructors to alter the structures without disrupting methods already in place. One accounting instructor, for example, successfully integrated cooperative learning structures with collaborative learning, a less structured form of small group work where much of the student interaction is out-of-class.

The instructor was already comfortable with student groups of three who were expected to meet out of class to prepare presentations on accounting topics which were subsequently made in class. He felt three to be the optimal size for these presentation groups and did not wish to increase the group size to accommodate cooperative learning structures based on quads. He thus continued to use three-person structured learning teams, a practice advocated in any case by Johnson, Johnson, and Smith (1991). This practice had no adverse effects on cooperative structures where whole groups were involved. However, structures such as Think-Pair-Share, Think-Pair-Square, and Within-Team Jigsaw, which depend upon paired activity, become awkward with groups of three.

To overcome this handicap, the instructor developed a 3 X 3 team concept. Each student was a member of a three-member structured learning team with rotating group roles. However, the student's suit partners were not in the same team but were instead in a neighboring, identically configured structured learning team. When the instructor wanted to use paired work, students simply joined their suit partner in the neighboring team.

TEACHING ENHANCEMENT TECHNIQUES

Instructors may enhance cooperative learning in many creative ways. Stimulus materials, for example, are sound pedagogical tools. Stimulus materials can be anything that triggers or focuses creative student thinking. They can be a film, a case study, a quotation, or even a cartoon. Graphic organizers, a visual stimulus providing an alternative or a supplement to a formal outline, help students come to terms with complex materials. They are an effective way to stimulate student thinking because they focus tasks and also appeal to learners who respond to visual cues. Case studies, discussed in Chapter 6, stimulate active learning and higher-order thinking skills including analysis, synthesis, and application.

Graphic Organizers

Graphic organizers are handouts which help students organize information and ideas by providing a practical frame for given tasks. They furnish a visual, holistic representation of facts and their relationships. When one handout is used in each structured learning team, they also reinforce the value of positive interdependence. Accounting instructors wishing to view many practical examples of graphic organizers should consult McTighe (1992).

Graphic organizers enhance student learning in cooperative learning settings by providing a focal point for discussion in the structured learning teams. They offer a common frame of reference for thinking. After using the graphic organizer, members of the structured learning teams have a tangible product of the group's discussion which can provide a basis for further reflection and thinking. This aspect aids the group processing component of cooperative learning.

Graphic organizers are also useful for whole-class sharing. Each team can be given, for instance, a transparency acetate for a report-out using an overhead projector. Students working with graphic organizers within their structured learning teams expand their critical thinking skills because they consider the viewpoints of others. Graphic organizers, like team webbing activities where students jointly prepare a visual depiction of an abstract concept, help students become more aware of the creative, logical links between ideas because this normally invisible part of the thinking process becomes perceivable.

An Example

Instructors wishing their students to focus upon effects of transfer pricing in a decentralized firm (Hansen and Mowen's Learning Objective 5 in Chapter 12) may design a graphic organizer. This graphic organizer might consist of a matrix with five rows for the transfer pricing methods—market, negotiated, full cost, full cost plus markup, and variable cost plus fixed fee—and two columns corresponding to the advantages and disadvantages of each method.

Instructors may use this graphic organizer in conjunction with either a Structured Problem Solving, Roundtable, or Talking Chips structure. Students work in their structured learning teams to fill in the organizer. The instructor may enhance the session by reproducing the graphic organizer on transparency acetate so that the recorders can fill in the team's conclusions for a whole-class report to be given by the reporter.

CLASSROOM ASSESSMENT TECHNIQUES

Classroom Assessment Techniques (Angelo and Cross, 1993) provide instructors with a simple, refreshing way to find out if and how well students are learning. As Angelo (1994, p. 5) notes, "As teachers committed to improving student learning—each of us needs ways to find out how well CL [cooperative learning] works for the particular students in our classes." By using such focused feedback, instructors can make mid-course adjustments in their teaching to help students learn better. Classroom Assessment Techniques (CATs) give instructors a particularly useful way to ascertain the effectiveness of new teaching methods, such as cooperative learning, with which they are experimenting.

The use of Classroom Assessment offers at least three benefits to students and instructors. First, when instructors use Classroom Assessment to monitor teaching effectiveness and make mid-course corrections, they actively involve students in assessing their own learning. This active involvement fosters metacognition and builds upon the group processing function of cooperative learning. Second, because these techniques encourage instructors to experiment with and vary their teaching techniques, students tend to enjoy the learning experience more. And third, instructors receive richer personal rewards by turning teaching into a dynamic and intellectually stimulating activity in its own right.

To use Classroom Assessment most successfully, instructors must keep in mind that the primary purpose of conducting these techniques is to find out how well students are learning and, based on this information, to make mid-course adjustments in teaching to improve their learning. Cross (1993) distinguishes this kind of interventionist assessment from traditional assessment which seeks only to evaluate after the fact. To achieve that purpose, instructors should use the following Classroom Assessment guidelines: (a) Never assume that learning is taking place; (b) instead, ask the students for evidence of what, how, and how well they are learning; (c) give students feedback on the class's response and your plans for responding to it; (d) make appropriate adjustments to improve learning; and (e) after making adjustments, assess again to see how well the adjustments are working.

Four Classroom Assessment Techniques are particularly useful for the cost accounting course: Classroom Assessment Quality Circles, Self-Diagnostic Learning Logs, One-Minute Papers, and Directed Paraphrasing.

Quality Circles

The Classroom Assessment Quality Circle is a CAT originally adapted from industrial quality control circles where production-line employees work closely with managers to identify and solve production problems. To establish a Classroom Assessment Quality Circle, instructors conduct an election in each section of accounting they teach; students vote for one or two class representatives from a group of volunteers. Once the Classroom Assessment Quality Circle has been established, instructors encourage all students to take any course-related suggestions, complaints, or compliments they wish to express to their representative. To elicit as frank an assessment as possible, instructors must assure students that they will not request, and that the Classroom Assessment Quality Circle representatives will not reveal, any names of those providing feedback to the circle.

Instructors should meet frequently with the Classroom Assessment Quality Circle throughout the term. To communicate symbolically to the students the importance of the circle, meetings should be held, when possible, in a formal, high-prestige setting, such as a dean's conference room. Instructors can then arrange this room as it would be for a business meeting in a professional office.

Instructors will quickly gain the trust of their Classroom Assessment Quality Circle if they take care not to react negatively to comments or suggestions brought by representatives of the circle, no matter how trivial or immature these comments might initially seem. A working guideline for this and all other CATs is, "Never ask a student a question you don't want to hear the answer to." Instructors should also resist the temptation to probe for the source of student comments, no matter how their curiosity is piqued. Once trust is established, instructors will glean helpful information from the students in the circle. In particular, they will receive valuable feedback about student perceptions, both positive and negative, about cooperative learning structures and their effectiveness. Instructors will also learn about those rare instances when a group becomes dysfunctional because of personality conflicts, student apathy, conflicting demands on group members' time, or other reasons. With this information, instructors will be able to adjust their teaching to ensure that the class has a positive learning environment and that students are assimilating the course material. In the case of negative team-related experiences, they may want to work with the circle to seek a resolution. It is far better for the elected students to intervene in any class-related problems (either team or whole-class) than for the instructor to take unilateral draconian measures. Students are more likely to respect and to respond positively to changes suggested by their peers, particularly if they are aware of the serious deliberations behind them.

Self-Diagnostic Learning Logs

Instructors may view Self-Diagnostic Learning Logs as limited, tightly focused versions of academic journals. They are particularly useful in encouraging students to abandon the strategy of memorizing steps for working accounting problems. Instead, students resort to higher-order problem-solving skills.

Instructors should make a learning log assignment at the same time they assign a long problem or case from Hansen and Mowen's text. Instructors should explain to students that the purpose of their learning log is to enhance their ability to learn accounting concepts and principles. On the day the problems or cases are due, students will hand in a one-page learning log report that answers the following questions: (a) Which accounting concept or principle that you learned from lectures, from your work in your structured learning team, or from studying the current chapter did you find useful to you in working the current case or problem? (b) Which accounting concept or principle that you previously learned did this new concept or principle build upon? (c) If you experienced difficulty or were unable to work the problem or case, what information or knowledge would have enhanced your ability to work it?

Students writing learning logs are forced to identify and communicate the accounting concepts they are applying. They therefore learn these concepts and principles to a much fuller extent than by simply focusing on the end solution to an accounting problem or case. Their learning is further reinforced if the students spend a few minutes discussing their learning logs in their structured learning teams. This discussion aids in the group processing element of cooperative learning, and it helps students identify and—one hopes—support team members who are struggling. Because of the focus questions, teammates can more readily diagnose difficulties. Moreover, the learning logs cause students to practice and improve their writing skills, thus enhancing their marketability in a world which relies more and more heavily on rapid and effective communication.

Instructors also benefit from these added insights. They can identify specific accounting concepts which confuse many students and can then respond with carefully focused instruction.

One-Minute Paper

Instructors may use the One-Minute Paper as a technique for getting written feedback to one or two questions about a specific class session. For example, instructors might distribute index cards (or place them in the team folders) and ask the students the following question after a short lecture: "What was the most confusing point in the lecture you just heard?" Alternatively, instructors might ask variants to two questions: "What was the most important thing you learned today?" and "What questions still remain unanswered?" After conducting a cooperative learning activity, to focus on group effectiveness instructors might ask, "What did you learn from the members of your structured learning team?" or "What did you teach members of your structured learning team?"

Instructors should give students the option of responding anonymously on the One-Minute Papers. Responses are usually divided about evenly between those signed and those unsigned. As a result, instructors will want to use two methods of communicating back to students. For those students who are unclear about material and provide their names, instructors may write brief responses to their queries on the back of the cards. This response may consist of a reference to the appropriate textbook pages or it may be an invitation to come in and talk about the question. In other cases, instructors may write a complete explanation on the back of the card.

Instructors must respond indirectly to those students who choose not to divulge their names. Instructors can search for commonalities among the questions and concerns expressed on the cards, preparing a whole-class response when three or four cards raise essentially the same question.

As students grow accustomed to the idea that they must identify and express concepts and pinpoint things that remain unclear, they focus more upon their own learning processes. This metacognitive awareness helps them become better learners. Moreover, because they are constantly assessing their own progress, they are less likely to flounder unknowingly. Students who respond to questions about learning in structured learning teams acquire a greater appreciation for community and group learning.

Instructors will find that One-Minute Papers help them keep close to the pulse of the classroom. They can become aware of academic and group dynamic progress or problems. Their concern and their responsiveness helps build student rapport and trust.

Directed Paraphrasing

Instructors use this CAT to determine the degree to which students have understood and internalized the main point of a learning objective. From the students' attempts to concisely paraphrase a concept instructors learn how well they have understood it. Directed paraphrases are particularly useful for assessing students' understanding of important topics that they will later explain to others.

To initiate this assessment technique, instructors select a point in the course after the completion of a major reading assignment, a key lecture, or a complex cooperative learning activity. For example, instructors may choose a learning objective from Hansen and Mowen's text which they wish to emphasize. The directed paraphrase must have an imagined audience. Instructors must select a realistic yet challenging audience to whom students are to direct the paraphrase. Instructors identify the audience and also give students time and space limits for the paraphrase.

The Directed Paraphrase usually takes the form of a short written exercise that students turn in to the instructor. As an alternative, instructors may use this CAT to strengthen the important instructor observation and monitoring phase of cooperative learning. While visiting with a group, the instructor asks a student, perhaps one who has not been an obvious participant, to summarize learning points after a group activity such as Structured Problem Solving. Instructors who use this technique at once reinforce their concern for student learning and strengthen student perception of individual accountability.

After the paraphrases are complete, the instructors must provide feedback so that students will know how well they are mastering the material. Alternatively, instructors can combine this CAT with a cooperative learning structure such as Think-Pair-Share, enabling students to receive feedback from one another as well. Directed Paraphrasing allows instructors to find out quickly and in some detail how well students have understood a given learning objective. They force both instructors and students to consider the wider relevance of the accounting topic being studied and the necessity of weighing the needs and interests of the audience being addressed.

An Example

Learning Objective 2 of Chapter 4 in the Hansen and Mowen text suggests that students should be able to compute a predetermined overhead rate and use the rate to assign overhead to product. A Directed Paraphrasing could take this form: Ask students to imagine an owner of a small manufacturing firm who expresses confusion as to how the cost of the machinery in her factory can be included in the cost of the product produced by the factory. The owner does not have an accounting background and indicates she has little time to engage in technical jargon. As a hypothetical management accountant working for the company, the students should spend ten minutes preparing a two-page memo that would concisely and clearly explain the process of assignment of overhead to product.

SUMMARY

Like all professionals, college faculty want to continually grow in the application of the skills they use. Because of its adaptability, cooperative learning gives instructors the flexibility to use it in conjunction with other teaching methods. Instructors who use cooperative learning often will become comfortable about mixing different components of the structures to create applied activities. Furthermore, they will be able to use these structures with other sound pedagogical practices such as using graphic organizers for focused thinking and using case studies to prompt analysis, synthesis, and applications. Cooperative learning, which complements virtually every sound pedagogical approach, works particularly well with CATs. Instructors who adopt both the philosophy and techniques of cooperative learning will themselves enter into a lifelong learning process.

REFERENCES

Angelo, T. A. (1994, Spring). "Using assessment to improve cooperative learning." *Cooperative learning and college teaching,* 4 (3), 5-7.

Angelo, T. A., and K. P. Cross (1993). *Classroom assessment techniques: A handbook for college teachers,* 2nd Ed. San Francisco: Jossey-Bass.

Cooper, J. (1990, May). "Cooperative learning and college teaching: Tips from the trenches." *The Teaching Professor,* 4(5), 1-2.

Cross, K. P. (1993, March). "The student side of classroom research." Presentation, National Conference on Higher Education, American Association for Higher Education, Washington, D. C.

Johnson, D. W., R. T. Johnson, and K. A. Smith (1991). *Cooperative learning: Increasing college faculty instructional productivity.* ASHE-ERIC Higher Education Report No. 4. Washington, D. C.: The George Washington University, School of Educational and Human Development.

McTighe, J. (1992). "Graphic organizers: Collaborative links to better thinking." In N. Davidson and T. Worsham (Eds.), *Enhancing thinking through cooperative learning* (pp. 182-197). New York: Teachers College Press.

CHAPTER 8

SOME FINAL THOUGHTS

"Thinking means connecting things, and stops if they cannot be connected."

G. K. Chesterton

Cooperative learning is about making connections. Through structured learning teams and the bonds that develop between students and through the mutual responsibility that instructors and students alike assume for learning, instructors can help students connect their lives with the discipline of accounting.

Furthermore, Angelo (1993) reminds us that effective teachers must also forge their own connections between what we know about research on teaching and what we do in the classroom. Thanks to years of careful study by cognitive psychologists, ethnographers, and other researchers, we know a great deal about how people learn. The challenge is applying that knowledge to our own classrooms in order to encourage higher learning. Higher learning, according to Angelo, is 'an active, interactive process that results in meaningful, long-lasting changes in knowledge, understanding, behavior, dispositions, appreciation, belief, and the like" (p. 4). Every classroom activity or assignment should be measured against these implied standards.

These connections between theory and practice can be nurtured by the connections faculty make with one another. The Accounting Education Change Commission (1992, August) encourages accounting faculty to adapt alternative classroom processes. They recognize that for meaningful changes to occur in a teaching repertoire, accounting instructors are most likely to respond to teaching strategies that colleagues have tried and recommend; these colleagues are likely to be other accounting instructors, with ideas specific to the accounting and business disciplines. Thus, for creative ideas and mutual support, accounting instructors must actively seek out other instructors who are familiar with cooperative learning. Instructors must also be willing to take risks. The AECC also notes that, not surprisingly, initial attempts at teaching innovations are more likely to deal with the least threatening aspects of teaching, such as the syllabus or course objectives.

Cooperative learning is not a strategy that necessarily comes easily to instructors accustomed to lectures supported by overhead transparencies and whole-group discussions. We encourage instructors to begin with some of the simpler structures, such as Think-Pair-Share, before moving to the more complex structures such as Jigsaw, which rely on structured learning teams.

More importantly, they should review the underlying tenets of cooperative learning, particularly the assumptions of positive interdependence and individual accountability. Students learn through this mutual interdependence that the intellectual power of a group far outstrips that of individuals in addressing such complex tasks as a challenging research problem in mathematics, accounting, or science; the design of new technology for an accounting information system or stereo system; or social issues such as ethics in accounting. They also learn that they are individually responsible for their own learning.

The other components of cooperative learning are equally important for accounting students. By working in heterogeneous teams, they learn to value diversity and the contributions of students with differing learning styles. With the team orientation of the work place, this ability to work with a variety of people is an important job-related skill. Similarly, the social skills practiced in cooperative classrooms, such as paraphrasing and asking probing questions, are essential for the work place. Even the group processing activities offer valuable models for monitoring individual progress and team progress.

Thus, it is important that accountants take a serious look at the opportunities afforded by cooperative learning as an instructional method. Weimer (1990) has cautioned that teaching is such a complex, value-laden experience, that it should not be demeaned by over-emphasis on "quick fixes" or "instructional tips, tricks, and techniques." Fortunately, all faculty can rest assured that cooperative learning is far from a passing fad or a "quick fix." Advocates have behind them years of solid research and practice. Establishing a cooperative classroom requires hard work, careful planning, and commitment. But the payoffs are enormous if we truly care about student learning and the contributions we can make to the accounting profession.

Cooperative learning, as suggested earlier, complements virtually every known effective pedagogy. Specifically, it helps faculty operationalize "The Seven Principles of Good Practice in Undergraduate Education," which have been widely distributed on college and university campuses.*

Led by Arthur Chickering and Zelda Gamson, a task force composed of prominent higher education researchers, meeting initially at Wingspread in July 1986, produced a set of "Seven Principles of Good Practice in Undergraduate Education." Based on research but emphasizing practical examples, the "Seven Principles" and the accompanying faculty and institutional inventories have been widely distributed throughout American colleges and universities. Over 150,000 copies of a special June 1987 issue of *The Wingspread Journal,* a Johnson Foundation publication featuring the "Principles," have been mailed. Instructors wanting to incorporate these principles into their teaching have looked for "action plans" compatible with their other, often discipline-related, educational goals.

Cooperative learning, a structured form of collaborative learning, provides both the theoretical framework and the "action plan" to fulfill the promise of the "Seven Principles." Thus, instructors willing to investigate cooperative learning will discover creative ways to involve their students in the learning process. Specifically, they will be putting into practice all of the "Seven Principles for Good Practice in Undergraduate Education." This closer look at the relationship between the "Seven Principles" and cooperative learning also provides a cogent summary of the material discussed in this book.

1. Good Practice Encourages Student-Faculty Contact

In traditional classrooms, faculty frequently stand behind podiums, distanced from their students. Even when discussion occurs, it is frequently teacher directed and teacher focused. In classrooms using cooperative small group work, the emphasis changes, and the instructor becomes not the "sage on the stage" but the "guide on the side." Instructors constantly monitor groups' progress by sitting with the students. They overhear their struggles to grasp the material and their efforts to help one another. They can laugh with students at "in-team" jokes and get to know them in meaningful, academically related ways.

2. Good Practice Encourages Cooperation Among Students

Grounded in theory, research, and practice, cooperative learning is a highly structured, systematic instructional strategy usually using heterogeneous small groups working toward common goals. Structured learning teams composed of four students work effectively because they are small enough to promote interaction, large enough to tolerate an occasional absence, and balanced enough to permit focused activities in pairs. Two features, positive interdependence and individual accountability, distinguish cooperative learning from other collaborative group work. Positive interdependence means that students—often because of carefully structured mutual goals, division of tasks, role interdependence, or group rewards—have a vested interest in working cooperatively together. Additionally, students are individually accountable for their own academic achievements and are usually tested separately under a noncompetitive, criterion-referenced grading system. Cooperation is also enhanced through appropriate grouping, so that students can work in pairs (sometimes called "dyads") or in larger groups, depending on the academic task. Many instructors also focus on social skills, routinely modeling them, and at times discussing their value directly so that students know how to interact in a group, particularly as they give constructive feedback or ask probing questions. Cooperation also grows out of the active student-faculty contract. The instructor's feedback is enhanced by the group monitoring done by students themselves.

3. Good Practice Encourages Active Learning

By its very nature, cooperative learning engenders active learning. Students engage in animated discussions as they carry out various structured class assignments. Often students perform various roles such as leader, monitor, recorder, and reporter. Cooperative learning structures such as Think-Pair-Share can promote active learning even in large auditoriums. With this structure, instructors ask students to contemplate a problem or issue for about 30 seconds (think); students then turn to a partner and discuss their ideas (pair); students within a group or within a classroom then share the results of their consultation. If the sharing is done as a whole-class discussion, to avoid repetition, the instructor should limit the responses to six or less. In another structure, Send-a-Problem, each group of students analyzes a different problem related to a single topic. A recorder writes down the group's solution and places it in a file folder. The folders are rotated to the next group who, without looking inside, likewise brainstorm and record their solutions before forwarding the folder again. In the final round, the third group opens the folder, reads the contributions from the previous groups, and selects the top two solutions. Many other structures, such as Three-Step Interview and Jigsaw, encourage higher-order thinking skills. Some, such as Value Lines and Corners, where students indicate choices by moving to designated locations, even get students up on their feet, making them physically as well as mentally active.

4. Good Practice Gives Prompt Feedback

With structured small group work, students have ample opportunity to receive continuous and immediate feedback from their peers. The instructor also is accessible as he or she moves among the various groups. Many cooperative learning structures, such as Think-Pair-Share, allow "rehearsal" time before students respond in class. They are constantly bouncing ideas off one another. Because students are individually responsible for their own learning, most instruc-

tors return exams promptly, giving individual feedback to supplement the group learning. If op-
tically scanned answer sheets are used, students can take tests individually, scan them in the
classroom to determine the incorrect answers, and then work as a team to prepare a second
answer sheet based on group consensus. Both exams are scored, one counting as an individual grade (individual accountability) and one, almost invariably higher, counting as part of an
on-going cooperative learning grade (positive interdependence). Students benefit enormously
from the discussion surrounding the immediate feedback.

5. *Good Practice Emphasizes Time on Task*

Instructors unfamiliar with cooperative learning may mistakenly believe that small group work is
time-consuming. This is not necessarily true if the tasks are timed and structured and the desired outcome is student learning tied to the course objectives. A Think-Pair-Share exercise
takes as little as five minutes. Many cooperative learning practitioners use a timer or bell to
signal shifts in the task. In the Three-Step Interview, for example, the instructor can quickly
form groups of four while students are discussing a focus question. The instructor might ask
students to find a partner they don't know well and interview that person for two minutes, ascertaining his or her opinion on a class-related topic; at the sound the bell, the two switch roles
and the other person is interviewed for two minutes. The partners then join with another set of
partners to form a group of four. For the next four minutes, each group member succinctly
shares his or her partner's ideas. After this eight-minute exercise, the newly formed learning
teams can then engage in another efficient exercise such as Roundtable, a two-minute brainstorming technique where one sheet of paper is passed rapidly from student to student. To
eliminate a common off-task problem associated with group work, instructors can build into
every activity an extra topic, assignment, or step for groups that work more rapidly than others.
In Three-Step Interview, for instance, groups finishing early can discuss an extra interview
question.

6. *Good Practice Communicates High Expectations*

Because cooperative learning emphasizes peer tutoring, collaborative learning, and positive
social skills, it automatically signals to students that their abilities are valued and respected.
The structured tasks, resulting in positive interdependence, build self-esteem because the
contributions of all students are valuable. In Jigsaw, for example, students typically divide a
task into four parts, each student assuming responsibility for a quarter of the project or material
to be mastered. Students then leave their original home teams/groups to meet in newly formed
expert teams with members of other groups assigned the same task component. In expert
teams, students discuss not only the content of their portion of the task, but they also rehearse
teaching strategies they will use in the home team to make certain that fellow teammates
master the same material. Expectations, in fact, are consistently higher in this type of learning
environment than in the typical teacher-centered classroom where instructors may assume that
they are challenging students with the complexity of their lectures when, in fact, they are actually overwhelming them.

7. *Good Practice Respects Diverse Talents and Ways of Learning*

Cooperative learning supplements, but does not replace, other methods of classroom delivery
such as lecture and whole-class discussion, a practice resulting in a diverse array of teach-
ing/learning approaches. Students with different learning styles can, in structured small groups,
teach each other, as Redding (1990) notes, "from their special and particular perspectives" (p

47). Cooperative learning's positive effects on minority self-esteem and student retention have been well-documented. The work of Uri Treisman, for example, is widely known and respected. Heterogeneous grouping—with mixed teams of high and low achievers, males and females, and younger and older students from various ethnic and cultural backgrounds—helps education become a vital reality for all students, including those at risk. As Slavin (1989-1990) concludes: "When students of different racial or ethnic backgrounds work together on a common goal, they gain in liking and respect for one another." (p. 52)

With the current cries for educational reform, instructors have an urgent responsibility to explore innovative teaching methods. Cooperative learning is a valuable tool, one well-researched and well-documented, to enhance classroom interactions which promote learning. The "Seven Principles of Good Practice in Undergraduate Education" printed in *The Wingspread Journal* can now figuratively take wing through cooperative learning techniques.

The cries for educational reform and of the challenges facing higher education and society in general are well-known. "Today's professors are challenged to teach a student population increasingly diverse in age, levels of academic preparation, styles of learning, and cultural background. Professors are now expected not only to 'cover the material,' but also to help students to think critically, write skillfully, and speak competently." (Ekroth, 1990, p. 1) Instructors teaching accounting students must meet these challenges. They must learn to help build supportive and active learning environments. They must learn to celebrate student diversity—minorities, older students, part-time learners, underprepared underachievers—and to find ways to both motivate and educate adults for the 21st century.

REFERENCES

Accounting Education Change Commission. (1992, August). "Exposure Draft, Proposed Issues Statement, Defining, Evaluating, and Rewarding Effective Teaching." Torrance, CA: Accounting Education Change Commission.

Angelo, T. A. (1993). "A 'teacher's dozen': Fourteen general, research-based principles for improving higher learning in our classrooms. *AAHE Bulletin, 45*(8), 3-7;13.

Ekroth, L. (1990). "Why professors don't change." In L. Ekroth (Ed.), *Teaching Excellence: Toward the Best in the Academy,* (Winter-Spring). Stillwater, OK: Professional and Organizational Development Network in Higher Education.

Redding, N. (1990). "The empowering learners project." *Educational Leadership,* 47(5), 46-48.

Slavin, R. (1989-1990). "Research on cooperative learning: Consensus and controversy." *Educational Leadership,* 47(4), 52-55.

Weimer, M. E. (1990). *Improving college teaching.* San Francisco: Jossey-Bass.